A QUESTION OF QUALITY:
Popularity and Value in Modern Creative Writing

A QUESTION OF QUALITY:

Popularity and Value in Modern Creative Writing

Edited by Louis Filler

Bowling Green University Popular Press
Bowling Green, Ohio 43403

Copyright © 1976   Bowling Green University Popular Press

Library of Congress Catalog Card No. 76-20958

ISBN: 0-87972-077-8 Cloth edition
ISBN: 0-87972-078-6 Paper edition

CONTENTS

CONTRIBUTORS

JOSEPH BLOTNER is Professor of English at the University of Michigan. In 1974 Random House published his *Faulkner: a Biography*. His *Selected Letters of William Faulkner* has been announced for publication in 1976.

EDGAR M. BRANCH is Research Professor in the English Department at Miami University (Ohio). He has published a pamphlet, a study, and a bibliography of James T. Farrell, and is working on a full biography. He has also edited writings by Mark Twain, as well as articles, chapters, and introductions on these topics and on J. D. Salinger.

RAY B. BROWNE is Director of the Center for the Study of Popular Culture, Bowling Green State University, and Secretary-Treasurer of the Popular Culture Association. He is author and editor of twenty books and sixty articles on American literature and culture.

LAWRENCE JAY DESSNER teaches literature at the University of Toledo. His articles include "Woodstock, a Nation at War," *Journal of Popular Culture* (1971); "Thomas Wolfe's Mr. Katamoto," *Modern Fiction Studies* (1972), and "H. G. Wells, Mr. Polly, and the Uses of Art," *English Literature in Transition* (1973).

FREDERICK ECKMAN is Professor of English, Bowling Green State University, where he teaches modern poetry, American literature, and creative writing. He has written essays on poets, such as Lorine Niedecker. His own books of poems include *Sandusky and Back* (1970). A new volume, *Nightmare Township* will be published in 1976.

LOUIS FILLER is Professor of American Civilization, Antioch College, and author of numerous edited books and articles, as well as, in literature, *Randolph Bourne* (1943, 1965) and *The Unknown Edwin Markham* (1966). His *Crusaders for American Liberalism,* revised and augmented, *Progressivism and Muckraking,* a narrative bibliography, and *Appointment at Armageddon* (1976), all relate social politics to culture and literature. He is preparing a study of the novelist David Graham Phillips.

GEORGE GRELLA teaches in the English Department, the University of Rochester. He has written widely in detective fiction, as in "The Gangster Novel: the Urban Pastoral," in D. Madden, ed., *Tough Guy Writers of the Thirties* (1968).

WILLIAM J. HARRIS teaches American Literature and Creative Writing at Cornell University. He has published poetry and articles in *American Scholar, The Poetry of Black America,* and *Chicago Review,* among others. His *Hey Fella Would You Mind Holding This Piano a Moment* is a book of poems. He is preparing a critical study of Amiri Baraka's (LeRoi Jones) poetry.

CHARLES SHIVELEY HOLMES (1916-1976) was Professor of English at Pomona College, and author of a study of James Thurber, *The Clocks of Columbus* (1973). At the time of his death he was working on a study of twentieth century humorists, of which his essay on Ring Lardner was to have been one chapter.

RONALD LORA is Professor of History at the University of Toledo, and author of *Conservative Minds in America* (1972), as well as editor of *America in the 1960's: Cultural Authorities in Transition* (1974). He is completing a book on American intellectuals.

JAY H. MARTIN is Professor of English and Comparative Literature, University of California, Irvine, and author of *Conrad Aiken* (1962), *Nathanael West* (1970), and collections of writings on *The Waste Land* by T. S. Eliot and the work of Paul Lawrence Dunbar, among others.

ROBERT OLAFSON is Professor of English at Eastern Washington State College, and has published articles on B. Traven in *Mexican Life, Organon,* and *Rocky Mountain Review,* among other publications.

DIANNE FALLON SADOFF teaches literature at Antioch College, with emphases on eighteen and nineteenth century English literature. She has written for *Victorian Poetry* and *The Victorian Newsletter*. Her thesis (University of Rochester) was "Waste and Transformation: a Psychoanalytical Study of Charles Dickens' *Bleak House* and *Our Mutual Friend.*"

DAVID SANDERS is Professor of English at Harvey Mudd College and the Claremont Graduate School. A baseball advisory editor for the *Journal of Popular Culture*, he has written on that subject, on Dos Passos, and on other twentieth century writers.

ABE C. RAVITZ is Professor of English at California State College, Dominguez Hills, and author of *Clarence Darrow and the American Literary Tradition* (1962), *David Graham Phillips* (1965), and editor of *The American Disinherited: a Profile in Fiction* (1970), and *The Disinherited: Plays* (1974). He is completing a study of Alfred Henry Lewis for the Western Writers Series.

MARK SPILKA is Professor of English, Brown University, and author of *The Love Ethic of D. H. Lawrence* (1955) and *Dickens and Kafka: a Mutual Interpretation* (1963). He has written numerous essays on "literary quarrels with sex and sentiment," and is currently editing a tenth-anniversary volume of essays from *Novel: a Forum on Fiction*.

PETER VIERECK is a historian and poet, Professor of European and Russian History at Mt. Holyoke College, and recipient of numerous honors and awards. His first volume of poetry, *Terror and Decorum* (1948) received the Pulitzer Prize. *Shame and Glory of the Intellectuals* (1953) and *The Unadjusted Man* (1956) concerned American human and cultural values. *Metapolitics from the Romantics to Hitler* (1941) and *Conservatism Revisited: the Revolt against Revolt* (1949), among other volumes, probed social impulses at home and abroad. See also his *New and Selected Poems, 1932-1967* (1967).

JOSEPH J. WALDMEIR, Professor of English, Michigan State University, has published a book on the World War II novel and numerous essays on modern and contemporary American fiction.

INTRODUCTION: A QUESTION OF QUALITY

LOUIS FILLER

Edna Ferber once told a *New York Times* interviewer that she hated to be called a best-selling author, with all its implications of poor writing and shoddy readership. Several of her books, she pointed out, had been in print forty years or more. What, she asked, did one have to do to prove one's title to durability and respect?

A prompt reply could have been, of course, that many writings of limited esthetic value have endured for other than esthetic reasons. And if she had then asked for an assessment of her well-regarded autobiographical *A Peculiar Treasure* (1939), she could have been answered that it ranked as social history, rather than as literature. But what then of *The Education of Henry Adams*, she could have insisted, of Sherwood Anderson's autobiographical writings, of Gertrude Stein's memoirs? The firm retort could and probably would have been that the difference was the difference between high culture and low culture, and that all the world knew in which category Ferber belonged.

All such exchanges prove little beside the fact that there is an answer to everything. What is important is to understand what interests are being more or less directly served by particular preferences. Mobs are more capable of following points of view than reasoned evidence. But even the most confident mob needs from time to time to refresh itself with data, if it is not to find itself empty-handed in an intellectual crisis. There are patent differences between street fights in poor neighborhoods, using milk

1

bottles for weapons and the tops of garbage cans for shields, and the duels which take place in UNESCO and Nobel Prize committees, but there are also similarities. We all recall the sense of dismay which stirred Humanities Departments when, in 1962, John Steinbeck received the Nobel Prize. He was the author of only one good book, discontented academics stoutly affirmed, though some of them also later conceded—if conceded is the word—that this was also true of F. Scott Fitzgerald. Again, what seems involved in such differences are disparate interests and attitudes, which would involve social history, but also literary standards.

This can be judged more easily in the past than in the present, as in the case of Herman Melville. William P. Trent's *William Gilmore Simms* (1892), published when Trent was Professor of History in the University of the South, summed up the situation nicely (pp. 329-330):

> Any comparison with Hawthorne is of course out of the question. With regard to romancers like Dr. Bird, Kennedy, and Paulding, to say nothing of romancers like Miss Sedgwick or Dr. Mayo or Melville, Poe would appear to have stated Simms' position correctly [as ranking "above the herd of American romancers, just after Cooper and Brockden Brown"].[1]

It helps, perhaps. to understand that Trent was a southerner, and was able to pass on his preferences and prejudices to such other southerners as Ludwig Lewisohn. Such vital details help explain one or another contemporary critique, but not all. And the presence of a prejudice is not full evidence that the opinion is therefore untrue.

For example, one sentiment is relevant because it is random and concerns a little controverted author. Says an academic litterateur:

> *David Graham Phillips* [a book] . . . is written in a brisk, journalistic manner ideally suited to describing the activities of a frenetically busy man who produced an appalling amount of trash before writing the novel, *Susan Lenox: Her Fall and Rise,* posthumously published in 1917, which accounts for what enduring reputation he enjoys. [The

author] is more sharply aware of his subject's failings than many celebrators of minor figures, pointing out that Phillips went far enough to outrage conventional people without going far enough to win the support of advanced thinkers.[2]

Here we get the hint of a cultural criterion which would aid us not only with respect to the unknown Phillips, but with the, until the 1920's, unknown Melville. It seems fair to judge that the Phillips commentator could not pass an elementary quiz respecting his subject, but that this fact would not redound either to his benefit or discredit, any more than it would to ours. The key to his judgment is the concept of "advanced" critics who help guide us into the future. Thus, instructors who had difficulty in the 1930's in getting Ernest Hemingway on their reading lists could, by the 1950's, offer Ph.D. topics in the subject. But who, in the 1970's, can claim status as the advanced thinker, now that the Hemingway stock is falling, and becoming part of literary history, rather than "living literature"?

Involved in this dilemma, and in such odd facts as the high popularity of Ken Kesey's *One Flew Over the Cuckoo's Nest* (1961) in literature courses, is the responsiveness of academic work to popular demand, and the blunt fact that the newer generation of novices in the field respond with limited enthusiasm to the Hemingway charisma. If one is not therefore to join Kurt Vonnegut in despising Hemingway merely for his celebration of primitive virtues—once so central to his charisma—as in Vonnegut's play, *Happy Birthday, Wanda June* (1970), one will have to get beyond the event of popularity or non-popularity to literary qualities which can help us to understand our own predilections and the reasons for them.

Popularity is a category which, in so open a democracy as our own, presents more opportunities and dangers than many another. It takes no more than a passing thought to realize that popularity by itself neither demeans nor dignifies a particular work. There have been great popular authors—Dickens and Mark Twain come to mind—and numerous authors who sell decade after decade without stirring interest or curiosity among academics, or whose vogue has passed with a generation. Theoretically, time should take care of the viable among them. Actually, as the Melville instance shows, whole generations may be deprived of his cultural insight thanks to the dereliction of popular critics and academics.

It is odd that people who fear the free market in economics will trust its validity in literature. Esthetic judgments may be devastatingly wrong, and changing them cannot be the task of a day. It takes dialogue, experience, experiences to refine intelligible arguments respecting one life-work or another, especially since our felt needs keep changing. There are striking analogies with food intake. And, as we would not trust the fanatical devotee of starvation diets, or of the steak and whisky diets, or of other combinations which discount medical advice, so we may confidently turn to the wider assortment of available literature to determine special wants and offerings for more general circulation.

The subjects treated in this symposium have one major characteristic in common, that they have all recently, or relatively recently, enjoyed high popularity among readers. Also, with perhaps one exception, they have received from substantial to torrents of comment. (Ross Lockridge was notable as having written with dedication, but as having attracted close to no criticism.) The case of Steinbeck has already been noted: a Nobel Prize winner whose status seems in question. His following is more in the nature of a clique, rather than a critique. The major question—the substance of his achievement, if any—is yet to be spelled out. The case of Irving Wallace is outstanding also: it enters deeply into the meaning of "popularity" and of quality, suggesting that both elements need to be shaken free and examined critically.

The case of Erich Segal is peculiar. One is reminded how readily students will say that such and such was written "to make money." There is a curious naivete about this comment, since most students—and mentors—hunger for money, and yet somehow maintain a faith in the justice of their own cause. Some residue of childish worship causes them to think of "genius" as above ordinary human wants. It helps to remind them that trash can be written under philanthropic and fame-seeking impulses, and is regularly published by vanity presses. Money-making has little to do with quality production in the long run. And to drive that point into students frees their minds of much cant. The present essay pays no attention to Segal's financial compulsions. It does focus profitably on some of the author's other compulsions.

All of the essays do not so much seek final judgments on their subjects—though a few seem to try to present such—as a sense of the components which make up the authors' resources. The essays consider not so much quality as qualities. They make contributions to the lore of the writings they examine—contributions which promise dialogue where some dialogues do not presently exist. It is not illuminating for one "critic" to judge anything as "trash," any more than it helps us to know that something else "bored" Dwight Macdonald. Macdonald might have been right to be bored, he might have been wrong. His admirers may learn a species of shorthand from such comments, and know where not to give their attention. But what of those whose appetites are differently arranged from Macdonald's, but who are too diffident to admit it? A cultural education which is not dictatorial properly respects their difference in temperament, and ministers to it.

In a time like ours which has seen the crumbling of standards, it seems wise to deal modestly with what are often doubtful and delicate matters of reputation and style, substance and interpretation. Generally, our contributors have looked for key issues, significant claims. They have worked to focus upon them as facts of life, whether true or false. The reader can turn back to the fiction or poem examined and know that there is a difference of opinion involved, and judge for himself which way his own feelings are inclined.

In general, our critics have preferred one of two approaches: the appeal to sentiment, and the appeal to reason. The critic who says "Blah!" takes a chance that all readers will not respond sympathetically. But he may hope that enough of them may for him to have established his point. But even the most careful analyst stands or falls by the examples he offers. If he judges a passage of narrative or verse as revealing the writer's confusion or lack of creativity, and says so, he may find that other grounds can be adduced for admiring the passage. After all, fictional logic is not legal logic, and when the case has been proved, it is still unproved. But, if there has been an honest day's work done, the argument is on higher ground than it was before.

The important thing in a democratic esthetics is to have the argument available. When it is not, the neophyte wanders among authoritarian statements which quell him, so that when their reality patently diminishes, he turns away from them with innocent cruelty, unaware that he has impugned a life, a career, a point of view. It is the major business of an academic criticism to make the transitions from old popularity to new popularity more understandable, and to provide continuity: to give the immediatist some reasonable relationship to past enthusiasms. All this helps qualify the excesses of publishers' hacks. It makes the gestures and configurations of writings more meaningful, and an adventure, rather than an academic chore.

I well recall the little man at my own undergraduate college who asked us in a then-modern literature course whether we thought there was "beauty" in Hemingway, while at the same time vigorously shaking his head from side to side. Someone asked whether there weren't different definitions of beauty, whereupon he raised his voice to say that he wasn't going to "accept" that line of argument.

Those days have passed, of course; the problem now is to rouse interest in the student, rather than to cow him. But, as the Hemingway mystique goes the way of earlier academic enthusiasm, it becomes a challenge not only to attract students, as with Kesey, but to clarify standards of quality for a puzzled generation. Who says that Hemingway's "stock" *has* fallen, or that Cozzens's has not risen? Are moral standards involved in such judgments, or are they functions of a changing esthetics? As an ideal, we might well look back to the 1920's, when the market places and campuses raged with the study of creative writing of every sort, from politically radical to conservative, from *avant garde* to traditional.

In a time which sees university presses closing down and Harvard University Press "remaindering" its inventory, possibly to the chagrin of Marboro Books, there seems a need for rebuilding the reputations of *books,* rather than this book or that book, and especially the reputation of creative writing. There was a time when novels were an instrument of social concern as well as a diversion from serious matters. No doubt fiction was especially abused; Steinbeck's art may have suffered to a degree from artistic misrepresentation. Whether John Dos Passos, B. Traven, and others have suffered similarly, the reader may judge after reading some of the following essays.

It appears that one of the tasks of present literary practitioners is to rebuild a sense of the esthetic gains implicit in unexamined popular writings. This need not make them fearful of their mentors' opinions; if anything, mentors, these days, are themselves seeking purposes and directions which will give new vitality to departments and recreate projects which patently serve society, and which can be justified in institutional budgets.

Every reader will think of another author who could have gained from such an examination as these we have offered. He may believe that someone not treated here, someone he favors, far exceeds in interest several authors in our own table of contents. It merits underscoring therefore that, first, there might well be another volume to supplement the present one with further assessments. Secondly, what has here been sought has been *approaches* to reading, rather than definitive statements: approaches which could service the reader in pursuit of his own preferred author. Most of our essayists have not tried to "cover" their authors. They have looked for essences of style or treatment which help explain the author as a changing human: Dos Passos as a conservative as well as a "radical"; the case for James T. Farrell; Stephen Vincent Benét's due place between academe and the general public. The admirer of Donn Byrne, or of Pearl Buck, or of John O'Hara might well wonder how his favorite would fare in a new, disinterested analysis, or, indeed, how he or she fared in earlier ones. Such thoughts can be stimulating. They will not crowd an over-crowded canvas; it is all too notorious how fiction has declined as a serious field, except, sadly, as in the case of a Solzhenitzen, and in nations other than the U.S.S.R. There are things to do in the literary arts, and our authors try to help.

ERICH SEGAL AS LITTLE NELL, OR THE REAL MEANING OF
LOVE STORY

MARK SPILKA

What can you say about a young author who identifies with his dying heroine and her hockey jock so as to wind up crying in paternal arms? That he gets to indulge his feminine impulses, and then be forgiven for them, in one of the most profitable and widely-shared acts of public wish-fulfillment in recent entertainment history? Or more fairly, that he gets to play the tender person he surely is against the tough one he would like to be, until the latter has been tenderized by love and grief? Either way the story reads more interestingly, and makes more sense, as the author's fantasy than as his sentimental art.

It makes more sense because the answer to the narrator's opening question, "What can you say about a twenty-five-year-old girl who died?" is not the one which the book's title and much of its plot proposes: *That she taught her Harvard athlete how to love;* but rather *That she taught him how to love his father.* And it reads more interestingly because the homoerotic threat to that love, which the author's sentimental art disguises, is now exposed as the prominent clue to the story's resolution it really is. *Love Story* is the working out, through fantasy, of one man's role-confusions which, through sentimental art, has released the generation-bridging tears of modern millions. It is *The Old Curiosity Shop* of our time and Erich Segal is its Little Nell.

Consider how resonant words and acts become once the heroine is seen as Erich Segal in drag and the hero as his would-be

Reprinted by permission from the *Journal of Popular Culture,* Bowling Green State University, Volume V:4, pp. 782-798.

out. There is the opening description of her as "a bespectacled mouse type" which is later echoed when the hero's father says: "Stay here and talk like a man," and the hero thinks: "As opposed to what? A boy? A girl? A mouse? Anyway I stayed." There is the opening connection of the hero's name, Oliver Barrett, with the poet Elizabeth Barrett who had such troubles with her father on Wimpole Street; and there is the accompanying connection of the heroine's uncapitalized handwriting with a fellow poet's: "who did she think she was, e. e. cummings?"; and the later confusion of her name, Cavilleri, with *Cavalleria Rusticana* by Barrett's mother. A chivalric city mouse himself (see his cover photo), Segal may or may not wear spectacles, have brown eyes or A minus legs like his heroine, but this is literally all the description he ever gives us—via narrator Barrett—of Jennifer in the flesh. She is not physically imagined, though she herself frankly imagines the narrator physically, as when she responds to his opening question, "Why did you bulldoze me into buying you coffee?" with "I like your body"; or when she responds to his vengeful promise from the penalty box, "Oh how I'm gonna total that bastard Al Redding," with "Are you a dirty player? . . . Would you ever 'total' me?" Her healthy delight in hockey-rink violence may be common among Radcliffe intellectuals, and not a sign of the author's sporting predilections as an ex-Harvard runner; but compare the narrator's descriptions of athletic life with his blankness on her physical existence. Here is his locker-room rhapsody after the first hockey game:

> Every afternoon of my college life I walked into that place, greeted my buddies with friendly obscenities, shed the trappings of civilization and turned into a jock. How great to put on the pads and . . . take the skates and walk out toward the Watson Rink.
> The return to Dillon would be even better. Peeling off the sweaty gear, strutting naked to the supply desk to get a towel.
> "*How'd it go today, Ollie?*
> "*Good, Richie. Good, Jimmy.*"
> Then into the showers to listen to who did what to whom how many times last Saturday night. "*We got these pigs from Mount Ida, see . . . ?*" . . .Being blessed with a bad knee . . . , I had to give it some whirlpool after

10

> playing. . . . I let my whole pleasantly aching body slide into the whirlpool, closed my eyes and just sat there, up to my neck in warmth. Ahhhhhhh.
>
> Jesus! Jenny would be waiting outside. . . . How long had I lingered in that comfort while she was out there in the Cambridge cold?

This loving evocation of the whole experience of turning into a jock, of male nudeness, vicarious virility, and narcissistic self-absorption tells us where the author lives; he is by contrast scarcely alive in the love scene which follows, in which Oliver rushes out into the cold, kisses Jennifer lightly on the forehead, then kisses her "not on the forehead, and not lightly." "It lasted a long nice time," is his only reaction to the experience, while she merely doesn't like the fact that she likes it.

The narrator's reticence about sex is of course thematic. When his roommate asks for details of his love-life with Jenny, he refuses to give them. Like Salinger (without whose diction he virtually could not speak), he doesn't want to discuss sex when love is his real concern. Jenny has been schooling him in that subject, and in the fifth chapter he gets his crucial lesson. "I would like to say a word about our physical relationship," he begins in his best Salinger manner; then he speaks of their only contact, "those kisses already mentioned (all of which I still remember in greatest detail)"—though in fact he remembers only a few details. Next he cites his standard of fast action, and how a dozen girls at a Wellesley dorm would "have laughed and severely questioned the femininity of the girl involved," if told "that Oliver Barrett IV had been dating a young lady *daily* for three weeks and had not slept with her." Well, yes, femininity *is* in question, and masculinity too, but not for the points we are being hit with, that they are not defined by availability or conquest. We see how they are defined when Oliver finally admits he is dying to make love to Jenny and "It all happened at once":

> Our first physical encounter was the polar opposite of our first verbal one. It was all so unhurried, so soft, so gentle. I had never realized that this was the real Jenny— the soft one, whose touch was so light and loving. And yet what truly shocked me was my own response. *I* was gentle. *I* was tender. Was this the real Oliver Barrett IV?

Well he might ask in a scene where there are no bodies to "encounter," only affects.   But there is one object Oliver can grasp: the golden cross which "had been her mother's" which Jenny wears "for sentimental reasons" on an unlockable chain around her neck—"Meaning that when we made love, she still wore the cross"—meaning that sex has been sanctioned, possibly purified, certainly spiritualized, through sentiment.   And of course he can also grasp those obvious spiritual lessons: that a really feminine woman wants gentle sex, that a really masculine man may give it without losing virility, and finally, that affection can move gently, unhurriedly into sex, and perhaps right through it, without ever changing into passion.

This passionless sex seems to move a step beyond the sexless loves of J. D. Salinger; it is not where contemporary youth are at, but it leans in that direction by stressing the affections and by dissolving the urgencies of sex and self which characterize much romantic love.   Thus Oliver explains that he was afraid to rush Jenny into bed because "she might laugh at what I had traditionally considered the suave romantic (and unstoppable) style of Oliver Barrett IV."   We never see that style in the story, no more than we "see" what happens here.   But we are told what happens, in the same way that the book's title tells us—or a Beatles' song tells us—that affection, fondness, relaxed play, have replaced the intensities and passions we generally associate with romantic songs and tales.   New attitudes have been announced—new cliches really—which contemporary readers plainly recognize. Segal, who helped to write the script for the Beatles' cartoon movie, *Yellow Submarine,* knows that "love" means something other than "romance" in songs like "All You Need is Love"— means indiscriminate affection, really, as stylized and hence qualified by insouciance, spoofing, spontaneity, in the best Beatles' manner.   To his credit Segal tries to build such attitudes into his own literary manner and to some extent succeeds.   My reservation here is that he also builds into his work his sexual fears, and that his reticence hides the sources of those fears, though they keep coming back like a song.

Or fail to come back at all.   Mothers, for instance, are so strangely absent from this tale as to seem unthinkable.   Jenny's mother is dead and is directly mentioned only twice; Oliver's appears *only* in chapter 7 where she functions as a half-educated adjunct to his father when he brings Jenny to meet his parents. He literally never thinks of her before this occasion, and only twice after, when he notes her handwriting on an envelope and when he sees her picture on his father's desk. Such unthinkability is, to say the least, peculiar for a narrator who hates his father and who either cannot or will not imagine women physically or describe sexual love. Happily it enhances the thinkability of fathers and so clears the ground for a rich return of repressed material.

Sometimes the repressed returns in the form of double-takes which allow both author and reader to experience slight neurotic alarms without looking too closely into them. Two such moments occur in the fourth chapter when Oliver learns that Jenny is making a phone call in her dormitory lounge. Approaching the phone booth, he hears her tell a man named Phil that she loves him and sees her blow kisses into the phone. He has been thinking about his apparent rival, a music student named Martin Davidson, and now he hastily concludes that "some bastard named Phil" has beaten out both suitors, has crawled into bed with Jenny while he was off playing hockey at Cornell. The man turns out to be her father, and the type of love, affection; but Oliver's mistake allows us to think for a moment of Jenny in bed with her father, and he will himself speak of incest as Jenny's family problem as the same dialogue continues. Meanwhile we learn that Jenny has been raised by her father, a Cranston, R. I., baker; that he refuses to let her drive because of her mother's death in a car crash; and that this was "a real drag" when Jenny took piano lessons in Providence in her high school days, though "she got to read all of Proust on those long bus rides." Such resonant compensations remind us that our well-read author originally conceived his Italian girl from Cranston as a Jewish girl from New York—that is to say, as someone like himself—until Hollywood made him change her background and her buses.

Whether Jewish or Italian, Jenny's first-name basis with her father indicates that she comes from one of those warm "foreign" families we have all met in Steinbeck and Saroyan. Oliver comes from one of those cold New England families in Marquand where the fathers always forbid their sons to marry common girls. When Jenny asks him what he calls his father, Oliver's reply is "Sonovabitch," and he goes on to mention his intimidating attributes—his stony face, the "gray stone edifice in Harvard Yard" named Barrett Hall which it recalls, and the "muscular intimidation" of his athletic status as an Olympic sculler. When Jenny remains skeptical we get our second double-take:

> "But what does he do to qualify as a sonovabitch?" Jenny asked.
> "Make me," I replied.
> "Beg pardon?"
> "*Make* me," I repeated.
> Her eyes widened like suacers. "You mean like incest?" Jenny asked.
> "Don't give me your family problems, Jen. I've got enough of my own."
> "Like what, Oliver?" she asked, "like just what is it he makes you do?"
> "The 'right things,' " I said.

By the "right things" Oliver means being "programmed for the Barrett Tradition" and "having to deliver x amount of achievement every single term" which is then taken for granted. Jenny continues to find such explanations unconvincing and exclaims "Thank God you're hung up about your father" as the chapter ends. For a moment she has defined that hangup for us as incest, or fear of homoerotic love with his father, which does seem like a better explanation for hostility than those he cites; but when he jokingly passes the problem off as Jenny's the explanation is abruptly dropped. Still, if Jenny chiefly represents a feminine attachment to fathers which is both tender *and* erotic, then she is herself what Oliver fears in his own suppressed attachment: which is why he has to leave his father to marry her and be widowed to return.

Oliver's marriage to Jenny is in fact briefly viewed as psychological rebellion. "You bug him and bug him and bug him," says Jenny in her resonant way. "I don't think you'd stop at anything, just to get to your old man." He might even marry her for this reason, since "in a crazy way" he loves her "negative social status" just as she loves his name and numeral as parts of himself. Oliver feels humbled by her perception and her courage in facing up to dubious motives. But when his father shows the same perception about his motives and calls for the same courage from him, then asks him to finish law school before marrying, Oliver gets angry. He sees his father's time-test as arbitrary, sees himself as "standing up to" his "arbitrariness," his "compulsion to dominate and control my life"; and when his father apparently yields to that compulsion and says "Marry her now, and I will not give you the time of day," Oliver rebels. "Father, you don't *know* the time of day," he declares and walks "out of his life" to begin his own.

Yet Oliver III does know the time of day. As a former member of the Roosevelt administration and as present head of the Peace Corps, he must at least be credited with more social awareness than his son ever shows; and as a concerned father he must at least be judged as more sensitive and perceptive than his son at these early interviews. Segal has worked hard thus far to telegraph these points (who could miss them?) through Oliver's misjudging eyes. Yet now he would have us believe that Oliver III reverts to stereotype, becomes Old Stonyface, and gives his son an ultimatum straight from Wimpole Street. All signals are reversed, Oliver is right about his father's villainy, and we have an act of social rebellion which must comfort millions by its reassuring familiarity, but which otherwise makes little sense. Whether the father's action is "impulsive" as "you bug him" implies, or "compulsive" as Oliver asserts, we have not been given sufficient evidence to judge its credibility. All we have seen so far is the perceptive loving man Segal telegraphs and the villain Oliver creates to protect himself from engulfment and from his own tender feelings. Missing from this picture is the overwhelming conviction of the father's power which would drive those tender feelings into hiding and turn Oliver into an unfeeling rival. As Jenny confirms, Oliver himself presents that power as an unconvincing set of intimidations, social, athletic and paternal. We never see it as an aspect of character strong enough to create this kind of cold hostility and suppressed affection. What we do see is a melodramatic action which chiefly serves to unite a divided personality in unholy matrimony.

Unholy because these two young atheists perform their own ceremony and again betray themselves through poetry. Jennifer reads a sonnet by (who else?) Elizabeth Barrett which begins with the marvelously phallic lines, "When our two souls stand up erect and strong, / Face to face, silent, drawing nigh and nigher, / Until the lengthening wings break into fire . . ." and which ends by predicting (what else?) early death. Oliver chooses lines from Walt Whitman, that indiscriminate lover, inviting some camerado to take his hand and travel with him on the open road for life. So blessed by nineteenth-century poets, our young moderns of the '60s begin the life of an establishment couple of the '50s. Jennifer works to put Oliver through law school; both work in the summer; they scrounge for money but not for love; he "achieves" honors and gets the highest bid from the best law firm in New York; and they continue to use profanity as Salinger used it in the '50s, to guarantee their own authenticity and lack of phoniness and to control their own excessive sentiment.

Meanwhile there is another phone scene, probably the most vital scene in the book since it sets the novel's theme, provides its punchline, and exposes its suppressed assumptions. An invitation arrives from Mr. and Mrs. Oliver Barrett III requesting our young marrieds to attend a dinner celebrating Mr. Barrett's sixtieth birthday. Jennifer says "Ollie—he's reaching out to you," cites his advanced age as a basis for reconciliation, invokes the future resentment of their son (nicknamed Bozo) at his own intimidating ways. When Oliver resists each argument she sets the book's theme with what he calls "an absolute non sequitur":

> "Your father loves you too, Oliver. He loves you just the way you'll love Bozo. But you Barretts are so damn proud and competitive, you'll go through life thinking you hate each other."
> "If it weren't for you," I said facetiously.
> "Yes," she said.

Here is the real "love story." Jenny's role is to bring the Barretts together, to make them realize their true affection. All her schooling of Oliver—her systematic deflation of his self-importance, her correction of his views on sexual love—is designed to make him less adamant in his pride, less resentful in his rivalry, and less afraid of his own tender feelings. If he has "grown up with the notion that he always had to be number one," as he tells us in the novel's second paragraph, Jenny has placed him more equably among the things she loves—Bach, Barrett, the Beatles, Mozart—

in merely alphabetical order. In this chapter she speaks virtually as that part of himself he has suppressed.

Deciding to call the older Barretts instead of sending a negative RSVP, she gets Oliver's father on the phone. As the conversation proceeds she keeps putting her hand over the mouthpiece to plead with Oliver not to say no, not to let his wounded father bleed, just to say hello, if only for her sake: all of which Oliver rejects yet at the same time visualizes as a psychic parable with the three of them "just standing (I somehow imagined my father being there as well)," waiting for him to act. When he does nothing Jenny calls him a heartless bastard in "whispered fury," proceeds to speak to his father for him, and provokes an "insane" reaction from him which reveals the book's suppressed assumptions:

> "Mr. Barrett, Oliver does want you to know that in his own special way . . ." She paused for breath. She had been sobbing, so it wasn't easy. I was much too astonished to do anything but await the end of my alleged "message."
> "Oliver loves you very much," she said, and hung up very quickly.
> There is no rational explanation for my actions in the next split second. I plead temporary insanity. Correction: I plead nothing. I must never be forgiven for what I did.
> I ripped the phone from her hand, then from the socket—and hurled it across the room.
> "God damn you, Jenny! Why don't you get the hell out of my life!"
> I stood still, panting like the animal I had suddenly become. Jesus Christ! What the hell had happened to me? I turned to look at Jen.
> But she was gone.

Lacking, as Oliver says, a "rational explanation" for his actions, let us try an irrational one. To tell your father you love him "very much" is to become a sobbing woman. Having brought into the open what Oliver fears about himself, having the means of conveying that feared love ripped out of her hand, "then from the socket," Jenny of course disappears. Oliver has told her to get out of his life and she does, and not merely for the evening, but from this point onward as the living agent of his homoerotic fears and revulsions. There is something more than a touch of comedy when Oliver, searching for the woman he has "scared to death," opens the door of one of the piano practice rooms at Radcliffe and sees at the piano not Jenny but "An ugly, big-shouldered hippie Radcliffe girl" annoyed at his invasion. Repellent femininity lives, whereas from now on—the chapter is 13—the "real Jenny," the "soft one," will be dying. Yet she is there on the steps when he returns home late that night, and though vengefully deprived of love's vocal instrument, she is still good for a dying aphorism. And so, when Oliver tries to tell her he is sorry, she stops him with the quiet but now famous line, "Love means not ever having to say you're sorry."

Let us be generous and put this a cut above the "Love is a warm blanket" series from which it derives its currency for modern millions. Segal means to convey a guilt-free relation which, if it is good, contains angry outbursts without any need for fixing blame. But this kind of homely psychology for young marrieds doesn't begin to contain the meaning of Oliver's violence, which reaches back to his "animalistic" hockey fights whenever his father watches him and forward to Jenny's death, and for which he cannot forgive himself. It is as wise as saying "never go to sleep on a quarrel" as these lovers proceed to do; and perhaps less wise than another implicit counter-aphorism from Lawrence's *Sons and Lovers,* that love means being responsible enough to say you're sorry when you've mucked things up this badly, as Walter Morel cannot do. Apologies can be abject or courageous, depending on circumstances, and it is the measure of this tale's essential shallowness that it sets up this aphorism as its pathetic trigger for the closing scene without looking closely at these or any other circumstances. Its method is the snapshot sequence, as in its own film trailer or in Oliver's locker-room album, and for this new kind of slick sentimentality snappy sayings are just right.

Fortunately there is much to learn from sentimental art even when, or especially when, it runs to shallowness. We still ponder the thumping morbidities of Edgar Allen Poe, who believed that the death of a beautiful young girl like Annabel Lee was the only theme for poetry; and we cope willingly enough with Dickens, who moved an international audience to tears with the death of Little Nell. We may want to give Segal at least passing consideration for choosing his theme with Poe's deliberation and pursuing it with

Dickens' zeal for popular success. He has done his predecessors one better, moreover, by making his young girl's death the occasion for reuniting a prejudiced father and his prideful son. This new twist could be important if it means that modern readers are responding sentimentally to a new kind of family romance, one in which the role-confusions of childhood may be "resolved" by a young girl's gallant sacrifice to the cause of male identity. So on to that gallant sacrifice.

Jenny's blood disorder is not apparent until Oliver graduates from law school, gets his first job, and the young marrieds try unsuccessfully to have a baby. When they go to a doctor to discover where the "insufficiency" lies, Oliver is told that it lies with Jenny. She is unable to have a baby because she is dying of a rare form of leukemia. Or perhaps she is dying because she can't have a baby. The causal sequence is blurred by questions of sterility vs. virility, of insufficiency vs. fertility, of programmed vs. spontaneous sex, and of the conception of a superjock named Bozo, an incredible 240-pound diapered infant who will chase Oliver through Central Park shouting "You be nicer to my mother, Preppie." Oliver hopes Jenny will keep Bozo from destroying him for mistreating her; but as we have seen he has already destroyed her by tearing out her telephone. Perhaps she is dying from that curious "insufficiency."

Let me speak more plainly about the sex-myths working through this incident. Women bleed every month, as if periodically wounded, presumably by the brutes who sleep with them; and so, to the unconscious minds of men afraid of hurting women, sex may seem like the cause of blood disorders. As may pregnancy, the inflation of wombs to the point where deflation or birth must seem like the bloody and deathly ordeal it sometimes is. Yet pregnancy may also seem enviable to men whose love for each other is limited by lack of issue; and the realization that they cannot have children, or be complete women, may have some bearing on decisions to give up one sexual role and try another. In *Sexual Politics* Kate Millett talks about "womb envy" in Lawrence but seems disappointed that he gave it up for penis-worship; presumably she would approve of trading it in for some form of penis-retaining tenderness, which seems to me what Segal has done in killing Jenny off (Kate wouldn't like that) so that

Oliver may embrace his father and still be manly. When we ask such questions as, "Who else can't have a baby?" and "Who else might like to be a superjock?" among collegians of "foreign" extraction connected with this novel, we see how this equation after all makes a hell of a lot more sense than the apparent story. The union of father and son is not an incidental consequence of this remarkable young lady's life and death: it is the whole point of the novel, a deliberate and significant revision—as we shall see later on—of the filmscript on which it is based. But back to the long death.

Even after its discovery Jenny's dying continues to be couched in sexual terms. When she goes to the hospital the cab driver mistakes the trip for an approaching birth and the young marrieds play out the illusion with him. When Oliver speeds to Boston to ask his father for $5,000 for an unexplained purpose, his father asks if he has "gotten some girl in trouble" and Oliver says "yes." When Jenny's father arrives to live with Oliver while Jenny is dying, he copes with grief by cleaning their apartment, washing, polishing, scrubbing—activities which she describes as "not being man's work" when Oliver tries them. In her last moments she kicks Oliver out of the room so she can speak to her father "man to man"; then she calls Oliver back and asks him to climb into bed with her and hold her and dies when he does. Segal means this to be a supremely tender moment, the epitome of pure creaturely love; but it is not unlike the similarly asexual embrace in death of the drowning brother and sister in George Eliot's *The Mill on the Floss,* or the burial of Grandfather Trent in the same grave with Little Nell, or Dickens' dream of being buried in the same grave with the prototype of Nell, his wife's sister, Mary Hogarth. The embrace in death which allows forbidden love to happen while at the same time expunging and denying its occurrence is a familiar sex-myth, one which helps to explain why we never "see" these lovers go to bed together in this novel except at this point. This is the impossible homoerotic embrace, the laying of his own feminine ghost, which Oliver must undergo if he is to embrace his father without fear. If there is a birth in question in this death, it is surely his birth as a man capable of tenderness without loss of manliness.

This is of course what Segal means us to feel without looking closely at the forbidden aspects of the experience. He shows Oliver fighting his need to cry in these last moments, calling himself a "tough bastard" who never weeps. He even has Jenny tell him "to stop being sick," to stop blaming himself for her death and feeling guilty about it; but this is only more homely psychology from the wise young lady who knows that Oliver blames himself for depriving her of a musical career in Paris, and the point of this guilt is surely that Oliver wants her to die, to get out of his life as the agent of homoerotic fears he is now expunging, and that Segal too wants her to die. "In death they were not divided," says George Eliot of her loving pair; but the nice thing about this death is that they *are* divided.

The chapter which follows is not anti-climactic, then; it is the real revised, restored, redemptive climax. Inexplicably Oliver's father arrives at the hospital for the necessary confrontation. When Oliver pushes past him into the open air outside the hospital, he follows and says "I'm sorry" at the news of Jenny's death, meaning that he regrets it and wants to offer sympathy. But Oliver brushes past that meaning to his own need for forgiveness for hating the man who made him fear the erotic impulses behind affection. "Love means not ever having to say you're sorry," he says, "Not knowing why" he says it. Then he does "what I had never done in his presence, much less in his arms. I cried." Which seems to me a happy enough ending, if a slightly dishonest one, since it covers up the frightening but very human sources of his need for forgiveness along with the very great difficulties of asking for it in this way, of reaching this point of emotional development, most of which Segal passes off as the sensitizing effect of prolonged and bravely shouldered grief. The terrible cost of role-confusion in modern culture is being expressed here without really being paid. The resolution is too easy, which may be one reason why it appeals to so many people. But then not everyone has a dying girl handy for the payoff.

Leslie Fiedler tells us that an Age of Sentimentality is at hand. The popular success of *Love Story* seems to support him, though there is some question as to whether he would return the compliment. *Love Story* is too safe, too conventional in its expert blend of old and new cliches to suit Fiedler's taste for wild, marvellous and grotesque as well as sentimental effects. To meet his exuberant demands the tale would have to show Oliver growing shoulder-length hair and keeping house for Jenny's father after Jenny dies in his own father's arms; or the director of the inevitable Broadway musical would have to cast a transvestite in the role of Jenny, to give further piquancy and point to the father's objections to his son's marriage. But then I have already shown that such extravagant devices are in fact appropriate to the whole psychodrama as it stands and may even explain the novel's unforeseen success. If the author's fantasies are somehow shared by his readers, if there is something in their own experience to which these fantasies appeal, then we may be present at the birth of a sentimental sex-myth as potent for this century as the Nell-myth was for the last.

The myth is that our children know what love means, and that they will use this knowledge to embrace and save us all. Generations will be joined, role-confusions will be resolved, starved affections will at last be fed. It is of course a family myth, one which derives its potency from the fact that modern millions are indeed starved for affection, confused about sexual roles, and frightened by new parent-child polarities. *Love Story* eases all these conditions with its facile wisdom and its sacrificial sop—the death of Jenny—to the real difficulties of family relations. It builds toward and delivers its one-two punch of pathetic effects with admirable tact and economy.

Back in the 1920s, I. A. Richards defined a sentimental response as one which was in excess of what a given situation warranted or inappropriate to it. The response was crude rather than discriminating, and it generally disguised an inhibition of unsafe feelings through an effusion of safe ones. It seems only fair to say at this point that the affections have been as repressed and inhibited in modern times as sex was in Victorian times. In its attempt to release the affections *Love Story* is as modern as Salinger, the Beatles, and *The Strawberry Statement* can possibly make it. The new easygoing love, the diction and profanity which protect it, the converted athlete who learns what it means— such borrowings account for whatever liberation the tale affords. And yet it applies these borrowings in such narrow, poorly defined, safely old-fashioned contexts as to nullify their freshness. The rebelling athlete in *Strawberry* responds to contemporary political forces which disrupt a campus and threaten his militant beloved; the rebelling athlete in *Love Story* responds to a situation from *The Late George Apley* and *The Barretts of Wimpole Street* which affects a music student. The Beatles respond sympathetically to urban loneliness, the drug experience, and the new sexual freedom as well as the new affection; Segal responds to hockey, music, and filial piety. Salinger deals directly with sexual squalor and depicts contemporary middle class mores with satiric sharpness; Segal fakes sexuality and handles race, class, and religion as so many props and slogans. Within such vacuous and innocuous contexts the new affection threatens to become as safe and stale as its surroundings; working chiefly as a set of new cliches, it tends to trigger rather than convey the "feel" of new relations; and finally, like old-fashioned sentimentality, it invites effusions which seem far in excess of what this modest story warrants.

What seems particularly old-fashioned about *Love Story* is the idealization of its heroine. A wonder-girl like Little Nell, she is always right, always penetratingly wise, always courageous in the face of adversity, always loving and self-sacrificing. These ideal qualities are tempered by her systematic profanity by which we know she is authentic, and by her smartass putdowns of the hero by which we know she loves him. But otherwise she is the most nobly perfect young lady in popular fiction since Nell. We have only to remember that domestic saint writ small, that intrepid heroine who led Grandfather Trent across industrial England, saving him from wicked pursuers and bad habits, seeking refuge finally in a ruined Gothic Church in the country, then dying from the strain of self-sacrifice—to see that Jenny also lives and dies in accord with nineteenth-century myths of women as moral and spiritual guides for unworthy men and of young girls as the best and purest of those guides. As bumbling Oliver acknowledges: "What I had loved so much about Jenny was her ability to see inside me, to understand things I never needed to carve out in words. . . . Christ, how unworthy I felt!"

Unworthy Oliver continues nonetheless to tell us "nothing but good" about Jenny, after the old Roman maxim for the dead. Seen always from his admiring point of view, she even looks good while dominating his life exactly as his father was supposed not to do. Probably her dominance insures her appeal for many women and for men who identify with strong women and perhaps even for bumbling men; but it scarcely furthers selfless, guiltless love. Jennifer's last name, Cavilleri, was shaped by Segal from the Latin verb, *cavillor,* meaning to scoff, to jeer, to satirize. This is how Jenny treats Oliver from her opening jeer ("I'm not talking legality, Preppie, I'm talking ethics") to her final instructions on how he must behave during and after her death. By this time even Oliver may feel that the net effect of her method is to emphasize her own importance by diminishing his. This is of course the flaw in the book's attack on self-importance in men or women. Together with the flaw in its repression of sexuality (which won't stay repressed), it indicates the serious limits of the new knowledge about love. However liberating and refreshing the new affection may be, it doesn't begin to meet human needs in any full or complex way.

The secret of its popular reception may be found in the spareness of Segal's style. Following McLuhan's advice, he has left interstices in text and film for his audience to fill, asking them in effect to supply what they already know, to leave out what they fear, and to enjoy what they have always wanted. His reviewers have proven more than ready to comply. Though the tale is old-fashioned they have praised its contemporaneity; though the characters are mere sketches they have found them "memorable" and haunting; though neurotic sexuality is rampant they have cheered its healthy absence; and they have taken the book's pathos at face value. They have also called for vicarious involvement of the crudest kind. Thus, for one reviewer who feels "less like a reader than an unwritten Segal character, living it all out from the inside," it is not so much what Segal says "as what he leaves to the reader to grasp—between the words. In this 'Love Story' you are not just an observer." As indeed you are not, if to become an unwritten Segal character is to live out your fantasies inside the book as its signal system allows.

That a sophisticated classics professor can create an audience of such unwritten characters is interesting; but more interesting still is the fact that so many people are so willing to return with him to that stage in youthful development when they first needed a father's love and either failed to get it like Oliver, or like Jenny got more than they could handle. If this is the common denominator for the tale's appeal, then its bourgeois audience merely seeks release from fantasies indulged more directly by our far-out unisex cults, and role-confusion is more widespread among us than even these blenders have imagined.

The film version of the tale argues against this interpretation. It works in several ways to shape Oliver in a more confidently masculine mold. First, it scraps the explicit theme of gentleness and shows him pushing for sexual love with Jenny against *her* fears, not his own; and simply by making Jenny visible and showing the lovers nude in bed it avoids his visual lapses in the novel. Second, it scraps the final embrace with his father and the whole issue of masculine tears; he simply delivers the punchline about love and walks on past his father to a rink where Jenny had last watched him skate and where the film had retrospectively begun. Though there is a hint of reconciliation, the chief effect is of a sad but firm putdown of the father (cast grossly as a heavy and denied even his Peace Corps post!); *he* is the "sorry" or guilty person here and is surpassed now by his son in stoic wisdom and restraint. What we get, then, is the story of Oliver moving from strength to strength with a few timely assists from Jenny. Her death leaves him alone but intact, and its sentimental appeal rests entirely with her nobilities as his girl guide during their shortlived bliss.

This ending is at least more consistent with the title theme; it also seems less sentimental than the book's conclusion since it punishes one father—his—for not knowing what love means, after first rewarding the other—hers—with a final tearless squeeze. The theme of parental reconciliation is thus muted and the homoerotic threat which runs through the novel is largely subdued. But the novel's one-two punch is also lost along with most of its case for filial piety and the viability of tears. Segal seems to have got his own back by writing the book: he presents Oliver as a tough inflated bumbler who needs softening and deflation, casts Jenny as his all-wise sacrificial softener and deflater, gives the father finer qualities, and restores or reshapes the mutually redeeming climax which these changes invite. These restorations get him into trouble, as we have seen, but they also make the book more interesting than the film. At least it attempts a larger dream of reconciliation and a gentler form of manhood at the risk of fantasies which, for all their extravagance, bring us closer to our hidden selves.

*   *   *

It has occurred to me since writing this essay that Samuel Richardson's *Pamela* provides another literary model for Segal's Jennifer Cavilleri: the girl from the lower classes who converts and marries a rich aristocrat and becomes the moral paragon of her day. If Segal has combined Pamela with Little Nell to create his modern heroine, he has successfully exploited the most popular novels of the eighteenth and nineteenth centuries in England while creating his own international bestseller for our century. His genius for pop-culture combinations would in this light seem extraordinary.

RING LARDNER: RELUCTANT ARTIST

CHARLES S. HOLMES

Lardner is a striking example of the writer as both popular entertainer and genuine artist. He was first, last, and always a journalist. He started out as a sportswriter and columnist in Chicago, and after the success of "A Busher's Letters Home" in *The Saturday Evening Post,* in 1914, the bulk of his writing appeared in the big slick mass-circulation magazines—the *Post, Collier's, The American Magazine, Cosmopolitan, Redbook.* His syndicated newspaper column brought his iconoclastic wit and comically low-brow idiom to an even larger national audience. At the peak of his fame, in the middle 1920's, his writing earned him between $50,000 and $60,000 a year, and he was almost as well known to the average American as Babe Ruth.

At the same time he was recognized by writers and critics as a craftsman and satirist of rare talent. H. L. Mencken and Carl Van Doren first called attention to his superb imitation of common American speech ("a comic philologist," Van Doren called him),[1] and with the publication of the collection *How to Write Short Stories,* in 1924, his reputation as a figure of literary importance was established. His stories of illiterate ballplayers, vanity-ridden song writers, bickering old folks, foolish social climbers and other small-minded and self-deluded lower-middle-class types struck exactly the right note for a generation enthusiastically engaged in debunking old idols and rejecting traditional pieties. Sherwood Anderson and Edmund Wilson asserted that he was far superior to Sinclair Lewis,[2] a judgment reaffirmed by

26

Virginia Woolf a year or two later. Lewis dealt in caricatures only, she said, whereas Lardner created authentic American types.[3] His reputation and influence grew steadily throughout his life. None of our writers has been so widely imitated. Writers as diverse as Hemingway, James T. Farrell and Arthur Kober have spoken of their indebtedness, and James Thurber did two stories in direct imitation of him—"The Greatest Man in the World" (after "Champion") and "You Could Look It Up" (a baseball story in the Lardner idiom). However, the example of his brilliant characterizations through language has been so thoroughly assimilated that it would be pointless to try to identify a specific Lardner line of influence. To be sure, there are certain obvious derivations, like the baseball novels of Mark Harris (or in the world of journalism, the column of Jim Murray), but the fact is that the Lardner presence is inescapable in American literature.

Although he enjoyed the praise of intellectual opinion-makers like Mencken and Van Doren, Lardner was uneasy about being labeled an artist. Like Mark Twain, he saw himself as a journalist and entertainer, and he went out of his way to dissociate himself from art and the intellectuals. "I ain't no satirist. I just listen,"[4] he said in an interview, hiding behind the mask of one of his own character creations, the Wise Boob. He seems to have felt no connection with the literary movements of the day. The Chicago Renaissance was at its height when he was writing about the Cubs and the White Sox, but he had nothing to say about the figures who were transforming American literature under his very nose, or about the realist movement, which, however indirectly, shaped his own development as a writer. In New York, he was close to F. Scott Fitzgerald personally, and he established a friendly working relationship with Maxwell Perkins, the great editor of Scribner's, but he never considered himself a part of the world inhabited by Hemingway, Fitzgerald, Wolfe, Dos Passos, and Faulkner. Most of his friends were journalists, sportswriters, and members of the Broadway theatrical crowd—Franklin P. Adams, Grantland Rice, George S. Kaufman. Literary status and reputation meant little to him. The popular audience and the popular forms suited him best and rewarded him handsomely. His great ambition was to be a writer of Broadway musical shows. (Ironically, he had only one success in this genre, *June Moon,* on which he collaborated with

Kaufman, in 1929.) Unlike Fitzgerald, he had no misgivings about courting the popular taste; on the contrary, it was the threat of being kidnapped by the highbrows that disturbed him. When Maxwell Perkins, at the urging of Fitzgerald, suggested that *Scribner's* would like to publish a collection of his short stories, Lardner was unenthusiastic. He had not bothered to save any of them, and Perkins had to search out back copies of the magazines in which the stories had appeared before he could put the collection together.[5]

When *How to Write Short Stories* did appear, he felt obliged to preface the book with a clowning introduction mocking not only the "How To" books but his own stories and the career of authorship as well. He introduced his second collection, *The Love Nest* (1926), and his mock-autobiography, *The Story of a Wonder Man* (1927) in the same way. The preface to the latter offers this advice to the reader:

> Another request which I know the Master would have wished me to make is that neither reader nor critic read the book through at one sitting (Cries of "Fat chance!" and "Hold 'em, Stanford!"). It was written a chapter at a time and should be perused the same way with say, a rest from seven weeks to two months between chapters. It might even be advisable to read one chapter and then take the book back to the exchange desk, saying you had made a mistake.

He doubtless wished to reassure his readers that here was the same old Ring Lardner, in spite of the fact that he was being published by Scribner's, but he was also trying to reassure himself. The short story, "Rhythm" (1926), quite untypically autobiographical, supports the view that Lardner was concerned over his professional identity. It tells of a song writer who is successful as long as he turns out popular tunes, mostly plagiarized from the classics, but whose professional career and personal life are ruined when he is discovered by the critics and begins to take himself seriously. Only after he gives up his false image of himself as serious artist and returns to his popular line does he win back his audience and his girl. In its cautionary theme, the story resembles those parables on art and the artist which Henry James wrote in the late 1880's and 1890's, when he was brooding over his failure to sustain his popularity. As more and more critics hailed him as a significant American artist, Lardner undoubtedly felt some anxiety about the possibly damaging effects on his talent of thinking too much about this new highbrow audience.

Many of those who admired him as an artist in spite of himself worried over his refusal to take his talent seriously enough. Maxwell Perkins, whose high opinion of Lardner increased over the years, constantly prodded him to write a sustained piece of fiction, something bigger and more demanding than the magazine-length short story. Edmund Wilson, reviewing *How to Write Short Stories* questioned whether Lardner could ever break from the mold of popular journalism, acknowledge to himself that he was a serious artist, and "go on to his *Huckleberry Finn.*"[6] Fitzgerald wanted him to write the kind of fiction that would reveal more of himself. He saw Lardner as a great talent frustrated by having to expend it on limited and trivial areas of human experience, like baseball. As a result, Fitzgerald theorized, Lardner developed "the habit of silence" both as a man and as a writer. "Ring got less percentage of himself on paper than any other American author of the first flight," he complained.[7] Fitzgerald obviously saw Lardner in terms of his own problems—as he did when he made him into Abe North, in *Tender Is the Night*—and it is doubtful that writing about baseball frustrated Lardner in any way, but his obituary essay, "Ring," is convincing in its suggestion that there were layers of self-protective irony and emotional and imaginative inhibition within Lardner which may have made it impossible for him to think of himself as an artist—or at least to admit to it in public.

Such well-intentioned expressions of hope and disappointment really miss the point. It is probably true that Lardner was such a complex and private man that *all* comments about him miss the point, but it takes only a brief dip into his better work to see that he was not a frustrated genius who turned out his journalistic pieces with cynical indifference, but a scrupulous craftsman, a writer who was a master of his medium and who treated it with respect. Take this passage from Chas. F. Lewis' first letter to Miss Gillespie, in "Some Like Them Cold" (1922).

> Still "Better late than never" you know and maybe
> we can make up for lost time though it looks like we

> would have to do our makeing up at long distants unless
> you make good on your threat and come to N. Y. I wish
> you would do that little thing girlie as it looks like that
> was the only way we would get a chance to play round
> together as it looks like they was little or no chance of me
> comeing back to Chi as my whole future is in the big town.
> N. Y. is the onely spot and specially for a man that expects
> to make my liveing in the song writeing game as here is the
> Mecca for that line of work and no matter how good a man
> may be thay don't get no recognition unless they live in
> N. Y.

Lardner's ability to represent a character's social class, mind, and
values through speech alone is not lowbrow clowning, but art of a
high order. The run-on sentences, misspellings, barbarisms, and
clichés of Lewis' prose style reveal the emptiness and banality of
his spirit with devastating clarity.

The center of Lardner's genius was his sensitivity to the
rhythms and diction of the common man's speech (Midwestern
variety), and he took great pains to recreate it into an expressive
instrument of comic characterization. He was impatient with
writers who pretended to speak in the vernacular but got it wrong.
His 1921 review of J. V. A. Weaver's *In American,* an effort to
write a folksy colloquial verse, shows how demanding his standards
were. Weaver's ear often betrays him, Lardner says.

> It has told him, for example, that we say *everythin'* and
> *anythin'.* We don't. We say *somethin'* and *nothin',* but
> we say *anything* and *everything.* There appears to be some-
> thin' about the *y* near the middle of these words that impels
> us to acknowledge the *g* on the end of them. Mr. Weaver's
> ear has also give or gave (not g'in) him a bum hunch on
> *thing* itself. It has told him to make it *thin'.* But it's a real
> effort to drop the *g* off this little word and, as a rule, our
> language is not looking for trouble. His ear has gone wrong
> on the American *fellow, kind of,* and *sort of.* Only on the
> stage or in "comic strips" do we use *feller, kinder,* and
> *sorter. Kinda* and *sorta* are what us common fellas say.

Worse yet, Weaver neglects "the favorite American adjective—
lousy."[8]

Lardner developed his command of the vernacular early, and
he was at his best when he stayed within its limits. Even before

his days as a sportswriter he was playing with the humor of
incorrect English in letters to his friends. But it was during the
years when he covered the White Sox and the Cubs (1908-1913)
that he became seriously interested in the artistic possibilities of
what Mencken called "common American." He traveled with the
players, sat with them in Pullman cars and hotel lobbies, played
cards with them, drank with them, and listened to them talk.
They were, he recalled later, a loud, salty, opinionated lot, many
of them without much education or training in manners. They
spoke a coarse, lively, and ungrammatical language. He first began
to experiment with this lowbrow idiom as a storytelling medium
when he took over the "In the Wake of the News" column on the
Chicago *Tribune,* in 1913.[9] Less than a year later "A Busher's
Letters Home" appeared in *The Saturday Evening Post.*

The vernacular mode suited him so well that he retained it as
his own public voice, most notably in his widely read column for
the Bell Syndicate, which he wrote in the character of the Wise
Boob, the usually shrewd, uncouth, semi-literate, wise-cracking
lower-middle-class Midwesterner who appears so often in his
stories. In the great tradition of American humorists, he felt
easiest when he spoke through a mask or persona. George Ade and
Finley Peter Dunne, both of whom created vernacular characters
for themselves, were his favorites.[10] He was curiously lukewarm
about Twain, saying that he simply didn't know Twain's people.
Although he told an interviewer in 1917 that he was sick of doing
dialect stories, all his best fiction is told "in character"—the Busher
tales, *The Big Town* series, "The Golden Honeymoon," "Some
Like Them Cold," "Haircut"—or, like "Zone of Quiet" and "The
Love Nest," is essentially monologue or dialogue framed by a little
conventional narration. When he moves into Standard English,
his limitations as a writer are much more obvious. The overrated "Champion" and "A Day with Conrad Green," for example,
are effective as satire but thin in fictional interest. They lack the
subtlety, richness, and life which the speaker's voice gives to the
vernacular narratives.

The first series of Busher stories, which appeared in *The
Saturday Evening Post* between March 7 and November 7, 1914
(published as *You Know Me Al,* in 1916), are the quintessential
Lardner. The comic fool of a protagonist, the vernacular style,

and the ironic view of life which are the heart of his work are all here. As time went on, his subject matter was to become more varied, his method more versatile, and his tone more harshly satirical, but the basic Lardner (and in the opinion of some readers, the best Lardner) is to be found in these stories of 1914.

The Busher stories tap two great reservoirs of popular interest —baseball and the tradition of vernacular humor. Baseball has always occupied a special place in the national imagination. In Lardner's day, and indeed, up until World War II, it was a living part of American folklore and mythology. It had its heroes, legends, drama, and comedy. Then as now, newspapers and magazines fed the public appetite for inside stories about the game and its players. Charles van Loan, writing in 1910, called baseball "the great outdoor melodrama of the country."[11] When Virginia Woolf said that Lardner had opened up a wholly fresh and indigenous literary subject in writing about Americans in terms of their national sport, she was exactly right. There had been baseball stories before Lardner, of course, but they were either in the Frank Merriwell tradition of gentleman-amateur heroics, or in the O. Henry tradition of slickly plotted entertainments touched up with a little local color. Lardner's stories, with their focus on character and authentic speech, evoked the world of professional baseball with such accuracy and such humor that Americans saw themselves and their annual pageant in a wholly new light.

But it is Lardner's adaptation of the long tradition of vernacular humor to his own subversive purposes which gives the Busher stories their distinction. The vernacular in America has always carried with it special historical and cultural overtones. It calls up echoes of our frontier history and our equalitarian ideals. One of our most enduring stereotypes is that of the superiority of the natural man, the rough child of the people, to the man of formal education and social training. The enjoyment of the incongruity between the illiterate or "low" speech of a character and his practical talents and native wit has always been a special source of American humor.

Lardner treats this tradition with considerable irreverence. The uncouth manners and semi-literate speech of his ballplayers show not their honesty and simplicity of heart but their ignorance and oafishness.   There is more than a touch of irony in the possibility that readers accustomed to the reassuring conventions of plain-folks talk and the solidly conservative fare of *The Saturday Evening Post* may not have fully realized the iconoclasm of his picture of the baseball world. As Gilbert Seldes observed long ago, Lardner "pricked the bubble of sports worship."[12] If the cult still flourishes, at least its devotees view its rituals more skeptically and critically than they used to. And part of the reason is Lardner.

Jack Keefe, the protagonist of the Busher letters, belongs to a well-established convention in sports writing, that of the initiation of the small-town or farm-boy rookie into the big leagues and into big-city ways. (See, for example, Charles van Loan's "Making Good in the Big Leagues," in *Outing,* June, 1910.) Out of this stock figure, Lardner creates a comic character in the classical mold. Jack Keefe is vain, boastful, ignorant, insensitive, stingy, over-reaching, foolish and vulnerable. He is obnoxious in his crudity and pathetic in his naivete and ineptness. Above all, he is monumentally self-deceived. The essential comedy of the series lies in the gap between his childishly high opinion of himself and the truth he unconsciously reveals as he writes his letters to "friend Al" back home.   During the exhibition season, Callahan, the manager, tries to give him some advice:

> We road back to Oakland on the ferry after yesterday's game and he says Don't you never throw a slow ball? I says I don't need no slow ball with my spitter and my fast one. He says No of course you don't need it but if I was you I would get one of the boys to learn it to me. He says And you better watch the way the boys fields their positions and holds up the runners. He says To see you work a man might think they had a rule in the Central League forbidding a pitcher from leaving the box or looking toward first base.
>
> I told him the Central didn't have no rule like that. He says And I noticed you taking your wind up when What's His Name was on second base there today. I says Yes I got more stuff when I wind up. He says Of course you have but if you wind up like that with Cobb on base he will steal your watch and chain. I says Maybe Cobb can't get on base when I work against him. He says That's right and maybe San Francisco Bay is made of grapejuice.

34

> Then he walks away from me.
> He give one of the youngsters a awful bawling out
> for something he done in the game at supper last night. If
> he ever talks to me like he done to him I will take a punch
> at him. You know me, Al.

Keefe obviously thinks that he has come off well in this exchange, but in fact he shows himself to be so locked into what Maxwell Geismar has called his Bush-League Ego[13] that he is incapable of learning or, as the last paragraph makes clear, of understanding what is really being said to him. The measure of his complacent self-deception is his often-repeated refrain, "You know me, Al."

Although this passage contains relatively few of the misspellings, malapropisms, and grammatical outrages which characterize many of the Busher's letters, it is perfectly tuned to the rhythms and phrasing of colloquial speech ("he says Don't you never throw a slow ball? I says I don't need no slow ball. . . ."), and particularly to the heavy-handed kidding which is such a distinguishing feature of the language used by American men to one another. Here it is relatively good-natured, but essentially it is a hostile and competitive form of humor in which the aim is not so much communication as one-upsmanship.[14] No writer, not even Hemingway or Sinclair Lewis, has done so much with this special feature of American speech; and as his misanthropy deepened, the kidding in Lardner became more hostile, until in "Haircut" the big kidder and practical joker appears as a sadistic scoundrel.

The conflict between a character's deluded image of himself and the reality apparent to the reader (or sometimes to other characters in the story) appealed to Lardner's profoundly ironic view of life. It is his basic plot, and he rang the changes on it throughout his career. Unlike Cervantes or Molière, however, he did not see this collision as bringing about any changes, either in the deluded character or in the social reality outside. His people are impervious to advice or experience, and the world is not changed by their presence. The implicit pessimism of Lardner's version of this classic incongruity is one measure of the essentially satiric cast of his imagination. Inability to communicate or to respond is a permanent condition in Lardner's world. His people talk but they do not listen to one another. Here, from one of his columns, is a bit of dialogue overheard on the train:

> "How long since you been back in Lansing?"
> "Me?" replied Butler. "I ain't been back there for 12 years."
> "I ain't been back there either myself for ten years. Where are you headed for?"
> "New York," replied Butler. "I have got to get there about once a year. Where are you going?"
> "Me?" asked Hawkes. "I am going to New York too. I have got to go down there every little wile for the firm."
> "Do you have to go there very often?"
> "Me? Every little wile. How often do you have to go there?"
> "About once a year. How often do you get back to Lansing?"[15]

The significance of his nonsense plays is precisely this despairing sense that nothing connects up with anything else.

This is not to say, however, that the main line of Lardner's work is black humor or comedy of the absurd. There is blackness and absurdity in Lardner, to be sure, but for the most part, his conception of comedy is in the classic tradition. People are ludicrous when they are vain, self-deluded, obsessive, irrational—in short, when they violate the canons of common sense and decency. Lardner was an old-fashioned moralist from a stable, small-town Midwestern home, and the positive standard against which he measures the vanity and folly of his characters is a traditional mixture of reason, social convention, and accepted moral values. In the Busher letters, the long-suffering friend Al, and the managers, Callahan and Gleason, represent the norm of common-sense humanity in contrast to which Jack Keefe looks so grotesque; in *Gullible's Travels* and *The Big Town* the norm is established by the ironic, wise-cracking narrator, who mockingly reports on the social ambitions of his women-folk (although as Wise Boob, the narrator himself is at times the object of ridicule); and in "Love Nest" and "Zone of Quiet," the presence of an intelligent interlocutor makes an implied critical judgment on the comic protagonists. As he grew more and more disenchanted with American life, however, Lardner tended to omit these touchstone characters, as in "Some Like Them Cold" (his masterpiece), and "Haircut." The result is a devastating picture of vanity, stupidity, and sadism unrelieved by ordinary human decency. In "Haircut" there are decent people, to be sure, but they are hapless victims, not potential antagonists.

Lardner's mode might best be described as satiric comedy.[16] His early work has the tolerance and good humor of comedy; his later work is increasingly marked by the hostility and bitter tone of satire. The difference between the Busher letters of 1914 and *How to Write Short Stories* (1924) is striking. During this ten-year period Lardner broadened out his subject matter from the iconoclastic picture of the world of sports to an anatomy of American lower-middle-class life etched in pure acid. He presents Jack Keefe with a certain amount of sympathy: for all the big busher's primitive crudity, his provincial innocence is so total that we cannot help feeling some pity for him when he writes—as he so often does—"Al, I am up against it again."[17] Besides, Lardner really liked his ballplayers, filled his stories with references to real-life baseball personalities, and wrote about them admiringly and affectionately in a series in *The American Magazine,* in 1915, and again, in his reminiscence-pieces in *The Saturday Evening Post,* in 1931-1932.

In contrast, the pen pals of "Some Like Them Cold" are so false and self-serving that all we can feel for them (through our laughter at their absurd affectations) is a painful and embarrassed dislike. Even "The Golden Honeymoon," which, like "My Roomy," shows a more sympathetic understanding and a desire to go a little deeper into character than Lardner usually does, is essentially satiric. The real burden of the story is to break down our sentimental stereotypes about old age and to show the old couple not as wise, benevolent and philosophical, but as boring, mean-spirited, and given to petty bickering.

Lardner's fiction touched on a wide variety of segments of American life, and in every case, the people and their values are shown to be foolish, empty, and hypocritical. It is as though he set about systematically to destroy the reigning myths which sustain popular culture. For the world of sports, there is "Champion" (which so effectively destroyed the stereotype of the sports hero that it has become a stereotype itself); for the glamor

of show business, there is "A Day with Conrad Green"; for courtship and romance, there is "Some Like Them Cold"; for marriage
there is "The Love Nest"; for youth there is "I Can't Breathe";
for old age, there is "The Golden Honeymoon"; for the pleasures
of city life, there is *The Big Town;* for the values of suburbia,
there is "A Caddy's Diary"; and for the virtues of small-town
life, there is "Haircut."

What caused Lardner's progressive disenchantment with
American life? On the surface, he would seem to have had everything needed for happiness—a secure childhood, a good marriage,
professional success. Yet, deep down, he could not believe in any
of it. A constitutional melancholy and pessimism prevented him
from assenting to the things other people put their trust in.
Donald Elder, his biographer, suggests a more immediate reason—
the Black Sox scandal of 1919.[18] This cynical betrayal of the
great national game shook the country profoundly. Teapot Dome
and the Stock Exchange scandal were bad enough, but if baseball,
the shrine of popular hero-worship, was also fixed, where could a
man put his trust? Elder may well be right in thinking that the
Black Sox sell-out (which involved a number of men Lardner knew
and liked) permanently shattered his faith in the values of American society, and beyond that, his faith in man. Certainly it is true
that after 1920 his work was more consistently and harshly
satirical than it was before.

Yet, strangely enough, although Lardner cast a vote of No
Confidence, his audience continued to have faith in him as a comic
interpreter of American life. It is not hard to understand the
popularity of the early Busher stories: readers of the *Post* could
enjoy them for the inside look at baseball and the comedy of the
language; more sophisticated readers could enjoy these values as
well as the way in which Lardner inverted popular conventions
while seeming to stay within them. But it is harder to account
for the fact that his bitter satires appealed to the general public
as well as to the critics. Ray Long, of *Cosmopolitan,* paid him
more money for his "serious" satires than George Horace Lorimer
of *The Saturday Evening Post* ever did for the Busher stories.

Part of the reason is that this was the age of Mencken and
Lewis; iconoclasm, satire, and the castigation of American culture
were in fashion. At certain moments in the history of any society,

there is a public masochism which positively delights in being artistically scourged. Then, too, such stories as "Golden Honeymoon" and "Zone of Quiet" are funny and entertaining at the same time that they undercut our comfortable stereotypes. Critics who follow Clifton Fadiman's influential view that Lardner's work is primarily an expression of cold hatred overlook the *humor* which Lardner derives from the speech and behavior of his people. And part of the reason is that Lardner's reputation as a funnyman (earned with the Busher letters and sustained through his syndicated column) may have shielded his popular audience from what he was really saying. Twain and Thurber resented the public's refusal to take them seriously; Lardner was apparently satisfied with the role of popular entertainer, although Fitzgerald thought otherwise.[20] In any case, Lardner is yet another reminder that it is often the fate of the humorist to succeed by being partially misunderstood.

Was there, as Fitzgerald thought, a real split in him between journalist and artist? It is doubtful. As a writer, he was a realist, an ironist, and a satirist. The sharpness of observation and the iconoclastic view of life which served him as a newspaperman were also the basis for his fiction. The journalistic nature of his talent, however, points up some of his limitations as an artist. The depth and range of his response to life was limited. As a reporter and satirist, he was content to deal with surfaces and with types rather than with highly individualized characters, and this is the reason that his fiction looks thin in comparison with that of Anderson, Hemingway, and Fitzgerald, although it has more life and originality than that of Lewis, with whom he is more properly compared. He was essentially a comedian of language. His great artistic accomplishment was the transformation of the speech of the American common man into a wonderfully expressive satiric medium. His best stories are those which exploit the vernacular and the irony of the self-deluded narrator. The closer he gets to Standard English and conventional story-form, the less interesting he is.

Most readers would agree on the Lardner canon: *You Know Me, Al* (the Busher's letters), *Gullible's Travels, The Big Town,* "The Golden Honeymoon" (Lardner's own favorite), "Some Like Them Cold," "My Roomy" (a remarkable study of the dark side of the Busher character-type), "Alibi Ike" (a much underrated story of compulsive behavior and the comedy of talking at cross-purposes), "A Caddy's Diary," "The Love Nest," "Zone of Quiet," "Haircut," and the nonsense-plays (perhaps overrated at the moment, but still important). "Champion" and "A Day with Conrad Green" are much admired but artistically inferior to the others. While his newspaper columns reveal no important new dimensions of his talent, there are flights of comic characterization in them equal to all but the very best of his fiction. Here he is, for example, in the role of the Wise Boob, his favorite persona, explaining to his readers that although he has promised his wife a fur coat if the Cincinnati Reds beat the Yankees in the 1922 World Series, he would be foolish to make good on it:

> Further and more I met a man at supper last night that has been in the fur business all his life and ain't did nothing you might say only deal in furs and this man says that they are a great many furs in this world which is reasonable priced that has got as much warmth in them as high price furs and looks a great deal better. For inst. he says that a man is a sucker to invest thousands and thousands of dollars in expensive furs like Erminie, Mule-skin, squirrel skin, and kerensky when for a hundred dollars or not even that much, why a man can buy a owl skin or horse skin or weasel skin garment that looks like big dough and practically prostrates people with the heat when they wear them.[21]

This is what Lardner did best—to create out of living speech a comic and distressing image of the American common man.

ERSKINE CALDWELL'S SINGULAR DEVOTIONS

JAY MARTIN

> What I endeavor to be, day by day and year by year, is a storyteller in the written word. And if there is such a thing as the art of storytelling I must admit a devotion to it. It is with this singular devotion that here I strive, with the use of words and the meanings of words and the ideas of the mind, to communicate with the reader by way of the shortest possible distance and the most meaningful implications that fiction has the ability to convey.
>
> —*Writing in America* (1967)

1925. At the beginning of the year one of the last of the great nineteenth-century writers, George Washington Cable, died. Very few of the new writers felt any debt to what they called the "Brown Decades" of the previous century or to the writers who had flourished in them; Cable they classed with other antiques. The writers who published books that year had names that would have been unfamiliar to him: Sherwood Anderson, John Dos Passos, F. Scott Fitzgerald, H. D., e. e. cummings, T. S. Eliot, Alfred Kreymborg, Ezra Pound. The titles of the books of 1925 were equally strange: *In Our Time, An American Tragedy, The Making of Americans, Roan Stallion, In the American Grain.* If a connection between the dying Cable and the new writers existed, it was only, as a writer for the *Nation* remarked, that in *The Grandissimes* and *The Negro Question,* Cable had "anticipated the critical spirit . . . in the present generation. . . ."[1]

Perhaps still another connection existed—between Cable and a young Georgian named Erskine Caldwell, who decided in 1925 to give up his scholarship at the University of Virginia and take a post writing obituaries for *The Atlanta Journal.* In many ways Caldwell would be clearly in the tradition of Cable: both Southerners are concerned with the impact of the old South on the new, as well as, contrariwise, the pressures of modernity to break down what was best of the old South. Both find their main theme in racial conflict and focus their most stringent criticisms against racial injustice. Both are writers for whom the imagination is central—for Cable, imagination took form in a visitable past, the strange, the mysterious, the romantic; for Caldwell, imagination derived from the wonder over the commonplace consisting in a visitable present. Both, finally, are distinctly (and in the best sense) regional writers. Yet both were driven out of their regions by a sense of external and internal antagonism. Cable lived in Northhampton, Massachusetts, for forty years; and Caldwell's first book was not written until after he moved to Maine.

Caldwell has very clearly stated his preference for regional fiction, which he says has been "the lever-and-wedge of American literature. More than any other kind of writing, it keeps the records for, and makes the interpretation of, the social and racial structure of the nation."[2] He himself edited the American Folkways series in twenty-five volumes.[3] And in his best novels, stories, pictorials, travel books, and autobiographies—*Tobacco Road, God's Little Acre, You Have Seen Their Faces, Georgia Boy, Around About America, In Search of Bisco,* and *Deep South*—he has sought to participate in the various folkways of the country, to write not only his own tale, but also to set down an imaginary diary of the ordinary person. Furthermore, Caldwell recognized, as Cable had, that American regions were defined not alone by their topography but also on the basis of race relations. Racial antagonism and racial integrity kept the American peoples from being composites, amalgams; race, then, not only made regions, it made them "distinctive and fertile with the rich materials of fiction."[4] Whether he is writing of the lynching of a black in the South or a country full of Swedes in Maine, Caldwell characteristically focusses his analysis upon region and race.

But Caldwell was born in 1903, fifty-nine years after Cable. Inevitably, these years made a difference, and the later writer's talent reflected some of the special preoccupations of the twentieth century. While we must acknowledge the nineteenth-century tradition from which he springs, we must also understand his relation to his contemporaries.

Generally speaking, Caldwell has not been sympathetically treated or intelligently understood by his critics. Usually placed by them in the naturalistic tradition, he is not really a naturalist, unless naturalism is defined, as it probably should be, to include the naturalism practiced by such Trancendentalists as Emerson and Thoreau. Certainly, in *Nature* and in *A Week on the Concord and Merrimack Rivers* these two writers spelled out the terms, on a naturalistic level, of the quest for a life in nature. Caldwell's naturalism is a modern, imaginative version—not a scientific materialism—of the doctrines of the great American Transcendentalists.

Persuasive evidence points toward Caldwell's immersion in other modern literary movements. From 1926 through 1928, Caldwell was an unpaid book reviewer for several Southern papers; during these three years he read or at least scanned twenty-five to thirty books a week, some 2,500 volumes in all.[5] Many of these were popular romances; but this was the very period when experimental writers such as Hemingway were beginning to appear under the imprint of commercial publishers, and a number of the best writers of the period came under Caldwell's scrutiny—Cabell, Faulkner, Fitzgerald, Ellen Glasgow, Anderson, Frances Newman, Elizabeth Madox Roberts, Conrad Aiken, and others. Caldwell followed in the tracks of these writers; and before he achieved publication in mass circulation magazines, he saw his first stories published in the experimental or *avant-garde* little magazines which he read avidly. His first published story was accepted by *The American Caravan*, edited by Alfred Kreymborg, Lewis Mumford and Paul Rosenfeld.[6] Within six months other tales were accepted by *Transition, Hound and Horn, Pagany,* and *Blues;* later, *This Quarter, Clay, Story, Contact* and *Contempo* published his stories. *The Yale Review* awarded him its prize for the best story in 1933. His first book, *The Bastard* (1929), was published by an experimental publisher of New York City, The Heron Press, and was illustrated with etchings by Ty Mahon.

Through his intensive scrutiny of the new writing appearing in the mid to late twenties as well as through his intimate knowledge of the experimental writing appearing in the little magazines, Caldwell absorbed several currents of the new writing. The modern movements which most influenced him were clearly *perspectivism* (as a technique of characterization); *imagism* (as a device for the realization of scene); and *impressionism* (as a guide to the conception and construction of a tale).

First of all, like most of his contemporaries, Caldwell followed the principles of fiction discussed by Henry James in the prefaces to the New York edition of his novels and subsequently elaborated by Joseph Conrad, Ford Madox Ford, and E. M. Forster. Of these, the most important principle for Caldwell was that of perspective; for him, characters are not complete human beings, but humans seen from a certain point of view. Accordingly, he makes no claim in his fiction that his characters are "true to life." Indeed, he emphasizes that they are creations—constructions through the perspective from which a story is told; his characters are as simple or as complex as his story requires. Only that which is significant in the telling is revealed of the characters. Steadfastly held to by Caldwell, this principle results in a great variety of characters, but often characters possessing in themselves little variety. Still, the various perspectives he takes give his fiction great liveliness: the variety of his perspectivism is one of the central facts of his work and is probably fed by the compulsion, evident in his life, to remove himself from the scenes about which he was writing. He could, for instance, only begin to write *Tobacco Road* after he had left Georgia and settled down in New York City. "The perspective I gained by going there was what I had been seeking," he says in discussing this book's genesis.[7] Perhaps Caldwell's perspectivism can be seen in its most direct form in the texts which he wrote for Margaret Bourke-White's photographs in the series of remarkable books on which they collaborated: *You Have Seen Their Faces* (1937), *North of the Danube* (1939), *Say, Is This the U.S.A.* (1941), and *Russia at War* (1942). After Bourke-White's camera has "created" a character from the perspective of a lens, a certain angle, and a particular lighting, Caldwell goes one step further to characterize the human subject verbally. Above the photo of a grimacing woman ignoring the outstretched hands of an infant, he writes: " 'Snuff is an almighty help when your teeth ache' "; below the photo of an aging woman whose lips are drawn together tightly is inscribed: " 'I've done the best I knew how all my life, but it didn't amount to much in the end.' "[8] Perspectivism can be more complicated, of course, even in the one-line caption. For instance, the photograph of a forlorn looking black child standing beside his dog is accompanied by the ambiguous, ironical line: " 'Blackie ain't good for nothing, he's just an old hound dog.' "[9] Clearly, by having practiced perspectivist techniques in his earlier fiction, Caldwell discovered how to turn the conception of illustration around and make words illustrate photographs.[10]

The verbal equivalent to the photograph, of course, is the image. Both imprison the fluidity of life in a flash of perception;[11] *nature mort,* both insist, is nature alive—made alive with meaning. One of the most important movements in modern poetry was imagism. Ezra Pound, Amy Lowell, H. D., and others—Pound made his selection of them in his anthology of 1914, *Des Imagistes* —all proposed to concentrate on the concrete image as the most adequate symbol and to practice image-making as the heart of poetry. By the twenties, Pound and Lowell had quarreled; and he had rejected "Amygism" and gone on to Vorticism and pointillism. Completed as a poetic movement, Imagism, then, began to influence prose writers. For Caldwell, as for the Imagists, the image, the object seen in an incandescent flash, is of central importance. His first book, *The Bastard,* exhibits his reliance upon the sharp image on its first page. Searching for his mother, the main character, Gene Morgan, is shown a crude postal card photo of her: "Licking his teeth with his tongue, the stranger recounted some of the things that had occurred when they were together in New Orleans, Havana, and Tia Juana. But Gene was not listening—he was looking. . . . There were the red and blue scars sinking into her hips, the long knife-slash furrowing her belly like a drain ditch cut through a Louisiana swamp, and there too was her left breast nippleless where some drunken horseman had severed it with his teeth. It was she all right. . . ."[12] In all Caldwell's novels his characters look instead of listen; and they usually see, as accurately as Gene does, the ragged outlines of reality. Like the works of Beckett or Robbe-Grillet, Caldwell's work is tense with silences filled to the brim with unspoken visions.

Accuracy must not be confused with simplicity or the image with a surface. A novel written two years after *The Bastard,* titled

The Sacrilege of Alan Kent (1936), is a book of images and a book of mysteries at one and the same time. Consisting of forty-nine very short one- or two-sentence observations, or deep dream images, this book is a "sport"—Kenneth Burke's term[13]—only in form, not really in manner. A few examples will illustrate the imagistic method pursued to the exclusion of narrative by Caldwell:

XVIII

On my birthday my father gave me a large new pocket-knife. That afternoon I stole into the depot and slashed open two or three hundred bags of shelled red corn.

XXI

In a store at the crossroad I saw a man hang a dozen or more dead rabbits on a wire and sell them for fifteen cents apiece. The rabbits' eyes were always looking at something that nobody else could see.

XXIII

There was an old negro who was almost a hundred years old. When he worked in his cottonpatch, the buzzards walked behind him all day and clawed the red earth with their feet and pecked at it with their beaks, and at night they roosted on the top of his house and flapped their wings until the sun rose.

XXVI

One day I was walking through the swamp and I found the skeleton of a man leaning against a tree. When I tapped the skull with a stick, some lizards came out and forked their scarlet tongues at me and ran back inside. When I tapped the ribs, a chipmunk heard the vibrations and began to sing overhead.

XXXVI

Once at midnight the sun suddenly burst through the darkness overhead, but there was nobody awake to see it.

XXXIX

There was a man who caught blue-racer snakes in a basket and built a fire under them. He held them in the flame

until their feet burst through their bodies and then they
rolled out of the fire and walked away as quickly as they
could.[14]

Put into the context of narrative, polemic, or recollection,
such images are fundamental in Caldwell's work after 1931.
Farm tenancy, he writes in *You Have Seen Their Faces,* for
example, "is not self-perpetuating. It can survive only by feeding
on itself, like an animal in a trap eating its own flesh and bone."[15]
Writing in a very different spirit, but employing the same technique, in *North of the Danube* he sees in the gutters of the roads
"the unmelted fringes of snow glistened white and unsoiled,"[16] an
image resembling Pound's "In a Station of the Metro." A late
book, *In Search of Bisco* (1965), consists almost entirely of fragmentary images existing as intimations of the continuing life, at
least as a symbol, of Caldwell's black childhood friend Bisco.
The first chapter of the book consists of three imagistic scenes,
when Caldwell's youthful association with blacks was intimate and
significant—scenes that "continued to remain clear and meaningful and unchanging."[17]

Caldwell's perspectivism and his imagism are connected
through the general impressionism of his work. He constructs
his tales, this is to say, not in an attempt to convey characters,
objects or scenes as they must be, but only as they are perceived. He intended in *Say, Is This the U.S.A.,* to "give the impression and feel of America,"[18] and by no means a statistical
report. The publication of Wilson Follett's edition of Stephen
Crane's *Works* in 1925 stirred renewed interest in this impressionist writer, and Caldwell's own impressionism was very likely
influenced by Crane's. In the construction of narrative both rely
on a sequence not of things, but of the perception of things.
Crane put his doctrine this way: "An artist . . . is nothing but a
powerful memory that can move itself at will through certain
experiences sideways."[19] His and Caldwell's best work cut
obliquely across American society, in the channel of the artist's
understanding, as the writers offer to the reader a succession of
sharply outlined pictures, each of which leaves a definite impression.[20] The fiction thus produced is impressionist in that its basic
narrative is the connected chain of the imaginative residue of these
perceptions.

Again, *The Bastard* offers evidence of Caldwell's use of this method from the very beginning of his career. Consisting of Gene Morgan's perceptions of experience, the book drives more and more away from the pretense of coherence sustained by narration. At the end Gene is whirled in a disconnected, fitful sequence of impressions:

> It was dark and desolate along the waterfront. Lights from the Jersey side sparkled indifferently on the crests of sluggish waves. Distantly came the rumbling sounds of automobiles on bumpy streets. Overhead a string of clanging cars sped on the elevated, rocking the earth till the world chattered its teeth. . . . .
>
> . . . .
>   Below in the wet darkness the water lapped endlessly. A chunk of water-logged driftwood bobbed nervously at Gene's feet. In the river, masts and lights were nailed against the sky, and somewhere somebody laughed foolishly from the base of his throat . . . .
>
> . . . . . .
>   Gene hurried up the steeply inclined cobblestreet until he came to a lighted restaurant. It was nine-thirty by the fly-specked clock on the wall. Two sailors had a couple of women at a table. One of the seamen was snoring. His feet were on the table, and from his breast pocket a green railway ticket was falling. The girls were tickling the other man under his arms, trying to make him say something. He got mad, hitting one of the women with his fist. She didn't care. She hit him with her fist. He knocked her hat off her head. She hit him between the legs with her fist. The other sailor woke up, spitting on the floor.
>   It was ten by the fly-specked clock on the wall.
>   Gene paid his sixty cents and the girl smiled at him from behind her mountainous breasts.[21]

Crane's work had already illustrated how great is the impressionist writer's risk. His impressions determine the character of his perspective and the images he will employ. Once the impression falters, is imprecise or dull or careless, the whole edifice of fiction, characters and plot and narrative, comes tumbling down. In Crane, as later in Caldwell, the distance between the accomplished and the banal is almost imperceptible, the flicker of an eyelid, a moment's wavering of perception.

To characterize the driving motives of Caldwell's fiction in terms of perspectivism, imagism and impressionism must engender questions about the reasons for his popularity, since on first inspection (waving aside the fact that impressionism was the first popular modern movement in painting) such an experimental background as I have outlined offers no way to understand the source of Caldwell's widespread appeal. In order to chart the route by which Caldwell crossed the bridge from experimental to popular fiction (without, at his best, destroying the bridge behind him), I must mention one more esoteric doctrine of modernist aesthetics that, surprisingly, moved Caldwell toward an aesthetics for fiction that might be popular.

Like such writers as Wilde, Pater, Stevens or Borges, Caldwell rejected the notion that literature represented actuality in any direct way: *writing*, all argue, *is writing*—it constitutes its own reality and is supremely "about" its own fictiveness. This principle is always central in Caldwell's descriptions of the nature of his fiction. "When asked why I wrote fiction," he comments, "I could only say that I liked to write. . . ."[22] A variant question, "Do the characters in your stories and novels really exist?—Are they real people?" was invariably answered, "No. They are fictional characters. I strive to make imaginary people true to life."[23] In 1943, when Caldwell made a selection of his best short stories in *Jackpot* and wrote a preface for each of them, he stressed the principle of the fictiveness of fiction. Four of these prefatory remarks are of special interest:

> Almost every short story writer and novelist who creates the characters that people his fiction is beset by readers demanding affidavits that such characters "actually exist." No writer worth his salt is ever guilty of such gross adynamia as the demand implies. All fictional characters are created from the materials of human experience, but rarely are they replicas of living persons. It is to the credit of fiction as a form of art that readers are moved to ask for proof, but it also shows a lack of discrimination on the part of readers when they are unable to distinguish between fantasy and reality.

> ---

> After having experienced both, with a small measure of

success in each, I think I can safely say that there is nothing so dispiriting as adventure, nothing so exciting as imagination.

The lives of fictional characters are sometimes almost as painful as the lives of living persons.

Once, many years ago, there was a critic who did not begin every review he wrote by saying that the author exaggerated his material and that his characters were not true to life. However, this method of criticism was so unconventional that readers believed the critic was pulling their legs, and his boss had to let him go. The damage had already been done, though, and readers quickly got into the habit of going out and having fun, instead of reading about it in books. MORAL: Literature would be exceedingly dull Stuff if Authors did not try to Improve upon Nature.[24]

The conclusion which Caldwell reached is easy to understand: he began writing and thinking about fiction while fully committed to perspective and to producing the image created in the mind by the act of perceiving: guided both by post-Kantian aesthetics and by the assumptions and conventions of the Southern oral tale, he arrived at the conviction that the artistic faculty was the imagination and that art-expression was therefore in the image, "projected upon the mind and perceived by the emotions."[25] Many prose writers of the nineteen-sixties would make one of the main themes of their work its fictive quality; John Barth, Peter S. Beagle, Stanley Elkin, and Ronald Sukenick all inherited this aesthetic from the modernist poets of the nineteen-twenties. Less obviously, Caldwell had arrived at the same position, deriving it from the same source, thirty years before they did; what was more, he had joined this modernist position with the aesthetic of popular novels.

Had either group ever paid attention to the other, experimental modernist writers and mass circulation, popular authors would have been mutually surprised (and doubtless irritated) to recognize that they had reached precisely the same conclusion. Indeed, several decades before the contextualist poets and critics, popular writers had understood that fiction compelled the attention of an audience in ways that life could not do, and that its power to hold lay in the nature of its own fictiveness—in formulas, stereotypes, and basic plots—in short, in the illusions it could oblige the reader to entertain and be entertained by.

The writer who held firmly enough to this position—from E. P. Roe and Elizabeth Stuart Phelps to Harold Bell Wright and Gene Stratton Porter—inevitably would take the next step: art was artifice; fiction, fictive. Fiction should be vivid and lively and convincing enough to persuade a reader to be more concerned about this artificial something that did not happen than with something that did. To feel pity, envy, revulsion or excitement for an illusion while having only mild interest in the actual—*that* would constitute successful fiction. If fiction was fictive, Caldwell also came to believe, then it should be as fictive as possible: its illusions should be thoroughly convincing, its "lies" more true than truth, the pleasure or instruction it confers as intense as possible. Thus, Caldwell joined the *avant-garde* position that literature was a supreme fiction with the view of popular writers that fiction was the art of dissembling. This proposition was the pivot on which Caldwell turned from (but not *away* from) the experimental tradition which was at the base of his writing to the popular tradition which seemed to give literary experimentalism pragmatic validity.

On the question of who is to judge the success or failure of a work of fiction, the modernist and the popular writers diverge sharply. The *avant-garde* poet or critic tends to make the elitist assumption that the masses are too locked in commonplace and naive materiality and propositional language to comprehend or appreciate fictions. The writer himself and, secondarily, the modernist critic, are held to be the proper source of judgment. In contrast, the writer in the popular tradition holds that the public—with its deeply human craving for, and instinctive appreciation of, persuasive fiction—offers the only adequate and certainly the decisive judgment. Fiction can be judged by its power to persuade readers to accept it and be moved by it. The opinions of authors, philosophers, critics, or reviewers concerning a book's merit thus, in the popular aesthetic, become irrelevant. Caldwell has placed himself—as Whitman did—on the side of the popular tradition in this matter. "In my credo," he writes, "reviewers could look elsewhere for bootlicking; readers were to be the ones to pass final judgment on my books."[26]   Again attacking the critic in *Jackpot,* he asserted: "final acceptance or rejection is in the hands of readers, and readers alone."[27]

One more thrust of Caldwell's sensibility and temperament is important in this connection. Years before American Marxist critics called for the creation of a proletarian novel, Caldwell was writing naturally the indigenous version of Socialist Realism, the novel concerning what Edward Dahlberg called the "bottom dogs" of society. Unlike Dahlberg, however, he did not so much write out of a rage of deprivation as out of a direct and deep sympathy for the buried lives of underdogs. Regional writing, which is predominantly concerned with the folkways of the common man, and the writings of Walt Whitman and Jack London gave Caldwell literary modes and models for writing about the lower classes in society. But, clearly, his personal inclinations led him in that direction on his own. Caldwell's best explanation of the drives lying behind his kind of bottom dog literature occurred when he attempted to defend himself against charges of writing "obscene, lewd and immoral" material in *The Bastard.* This was in November of 1929, while Caldwell was living in Maine. The book was confiscated from the Portland bookshop operated by his wife Helen and banned in Cumberland County. Immediately, Caldwell issued a now rare one-page printed sheet titled "In Defense of Myself." After explaining the background circumstances of the seizure, he went on to his *apologia:*

> *The Bastard* was conceived and written as an important and untouched phase of American mores. That this custom of life in the nation had previously been unknown outside its own sphere was its own necessity for expression and valuation. It so happens that this sphere is at times realistically uninhibited. Among those who live there and die we find a man who, when his belly is content, and when he feels no immediate fear of violent death, takes a female of his own stratum for relaxation, beauty and contentment. He plays no golf, he has no club; the churches were not built for him. He cannot read. . . . Here is a woman, a girl in years, who has no friends with whom she can play bridge. She works in a cotton mill. She is a lint-head. She earns eleven dollars and fifteen cents from one Saturday to the next. The mill lays her off six weeks. Neither her

mother, nor her father, if either she has, can afford to give
her money to buy a pair of stockings and a hat. Somebody
else can. A man. She goes with him and he buys her the
clothes she wants so much. A week later he is in New
Orleans, in Chicago, in Detroit. She gets along the best
way she can. We all do. I did not write this novel with
obscenity, lewdness and immorality in mind. I wrote it,
the book it is, because I have a deep sympathy for the
people in it. I hoped it would be a good novel. I know it
is not perfect. It has faults, grave faults. For ten years I
have tried to overcome them. Ten, twenty, thirty years
from now I hope to be still trying to overcome faults. But
I have not finished what I have to say about the people in
this novel that has been suppressed; I have an intense
sympathy for these people. I know them and I like them.
I have slept with them in jails, I have eaten with them in
freight cars. I have sung with them in convict camps, I
have helped the women give birth to the living. I have
helped the men cover up the dead—but I have said enough.
I have said that I know these people, that I love them.
That is why I could not stand silent while the story of their
lives was branded obscene, lewd and immoral; because this
story belongs to them even more than it does to me. It is
of no concern to me that I, too, have had this same brand
placed upon me by Cumberland County. But these friends
of mine—I shall defend them until the last word is choked
from me. I cannot disown them.[28]

These contentions echo "The Sleepers" or *The People of the
Abyss.* But the tone of conviction is genuinely Caldwell's.

Clearly, his interest in the lives of the bottom dogs and his
sympathetic identification with them influenced Caldwell's style.
To be sure, like Faulkner, he learned elements of his style from
Southern speech, rural lingo, political harangues, urban slang, and
sermons. But Caldwell tends far less than Faulkner to emphasize
the Southern modes of ornate public oratory, the tall tale, or the
elaborate styles of preaching and exhortation practiced in the
white or black evangelical churches. He writes in the Southern
rural understated plain style, and in the discursive mode of preaching taught in Erskine Theological Seminary, where his father, an
ordained minister in the Reformed Presbyterian Church, was
trained. He is more interested in the emotional content of a tale
than in calling attention through style to its artificer. Faulkner

himself once pointed to Caldwell's talent:

For plain, simple style, it's first rate.[29]

In Caldwell's work, I have been trying to say, two impulses have equal primacy. One is the experimental, modernist impulse. And the other is the influence of journalism and popular writing. He contrives a style to achieve the stimulation of the senses and intellect through impressionism and image making. But he is also interested in the arousal of emotions through a concentration on emotion-rich content. He is the conscious author of the printed, obviously artificial tale; but he also feigns with great success the oral, less apparently artificial tale. As a writer he relies upon the well-defined image or impression as perceived by the author or his surrogate, the narrator; but he is also interested in and manages to convey the archetypal or even the typical (and perhaps the stereotypical) character, custom, or event in his stories. On the one hand, Caldwell gives primacy in style to the illuminated flash; on the other, in story he seeks to set forth intelligible but complex mores and customs. One impulse leads him to concentrate on the discrete image; another, to write what he had termed "a cyclorama of Southern life";[30] one to emphasize the singular; the other, the anonymous and quotidian. Like Dos Passos, he balances the individual "Camera Eye" with the mass "Newsreel," accompanying the unique perception with the twice and thrice told tale. The one impulse is derived from the *avant-garde* tradition, the other from the habits of popular writing.

Caldwell has written several books largely in the experimental mode—*The Bastard, Poor Fool, The Sacrilege of Alan Kent, In Search of Bisco* and *Deep South,* as well as the text-photo books (such modernist writers as Archibald MacLeish and James Agee also worked in this last mode). And he had written a number of books in the popular tradition—including *The Courting of Susie Brown, Jenny By Nature, The Last Night of Summer, Summertime Island,* and *The Earnshaw Neighborhood.* The distinction, of course, is arbitrary and never entire. But in at least two novels the distinction is impossible to maintain: in *Tobacco Road* and *God's Little Acre* Caldwell brings the two impulses together in a remarkable way.

Dramatized, *Tobacco Road* played for seven and a half years on Broadway, while second and third companies toured the country; for years it held the record for the longest dramatic run on Broadway. The novel itself has sold over 3,000,000 copies in paperback and is now in its forty-first printing. *God's Little Acre* has been an even more spectacular popular success, selling over 8,000,000 copies in sixty-one printings.[31]   Both are distinctly regional books.   In each, Caldwell based his narrative upon a variety of relations: between the sexes, the old and young, the town and country, landowners and tenants, machine civilization and rural life, black and white.   A few characters in each are sharply enough delineated to stand out against a background of anonymous, mass life on the farm or, sometimes, in the factory. Yet, the fact that both books were written in places far removed from their East Georgia scenes—*Tobacco Road* in New York City and *God's Little Acre* in Maine—suggests that distance and perspective are as important in these novels as urgency and involvement.

In *Tobacco Road* Caldwell orchestrates his narrative and the character-development from which the narrative derives around the images of the road and of the automobile purchased by Sister Bessie.   This machine causes more excitement than any other thing, man or nature, in the book.   Through the promise of purchasing a "brand new" auto, Bessie persuades the sixteen-year-old Dude to marry her.   After the purchase, Bessie's evangelism is mocked when she forces Dude to kneel down beside the Ford: " 'Dear God,' she prays, 'we poor sinners kneel down in this garage to pray for a blessing on this new automobile trade, so You will like what me and Dude is doing.' "[32]   From the first, when Dude realizes his dreams in sounding the horn over and over, to the end of the novel, the automobile is a kind of measure of the human decline occurring in *Tobacco Road*.   Within a matter of days this triumph of civilization has been broken and torn and bent, its bearings burned out, its headlight and fender smashed, its radiator destroyed.   It has carried Jeeter to the city where he tries in vain to sell a load of wood at any price; it has transported Bessie to a brothel where she is shifted from one room to another all night long; it has run over and killed the old, inarticulate, neglected grandmother.   By the end, hardly anything but its horn operates, and that horn sounds now like a comic Gabriel's horn blowing forlornly for the promised end. Marriage, religion, fuel gathering, economic exchange, family relations, machine society, sex and food—all the concerns of the book—are gathered around this central image. Once, when agricultural production provided a center for a humanly satisfying way of life, the heavy hogsheads of tobacco that were rolled along the high ridges from East Georgia farms to the Savannah River made thoroughfares of active commerce—"tobacco roads" these were called. Then, the roads were signs of fertility in nature and satisfaction in man. Now, only shattered machines rattle down the tobacco roads.

The central symbol in *God's Little Acre* is, of course, the enormous holes which Ty Walden and his sons dig in search of gold. Driven for years by gold fever, he has neglected the productive possibilities of the land; only on the Negro section of the property is any food or crop produced. Moreover, Walden digs closer and closer to the house until the last great hole threatens to undermine the house's foundations, as the endless digging has undermined and destroyed the domestic life of his family. Unlike Thoreau, this Walden will not simplify and be content: rather, he is driven by visions of pure gold to complex plots for impossible success. Ultimately, of course, like his sons and son-in-law, he is digging his own grave. Very nearly his last words are: " 'I feel like the end of the world has struck me,' . . . 'It feels like the bottom has dropped completely out from under me. I feel like I'm sinking and can't help myself.' "[33] Father, children, house and human hope all sink in the pits he digs, until he and his family disappear from sight.

The triumph of both these novels—and to a lesser extent that of *Georgia Boy* and *In Search of Bisco*—lies in Caldwell's ability to convey the quality and condition of archetypal, mass life through the perspectives of sharply differentiating images, and to concentrate and convey emotion in them. He is in love with language. His dictionary, he remarks in *Call It Experience,* is his most valued possession: "I read the dictionary instead of reading novels and magazines, in my estimation, nothing had been written that was as fascinating, provocative, instructive and fully satisfying as a book of words and their alluring meanings."[34]

But he also loved people, even in their silences. Style and characters each pull him toward them. Each of his books is his temporary working out of the claims upon his imagination of style or character. When that dialectic is unsuccessfully articulated, a Caldwell book may appear wooden in plot, lacking in style, overwritten, characterless or too crowded by characters. But when he holds the two together, style is character and character makes style. He has not always succeeded, but his career as a writer has been singularly devoted to the possibilities of that special achievement.

BY LOVE POSSESSED: THE COZZENS-MACDONALD AFFAIR

RONALD LORA

"My social preference is to be left alone," James Gould Cozzens once wrote in a rare personal statement, "and people have always seemed willing, even eager, to gratify my inclination." Except for the controversy that attended the appearance of *By Love Possessed* in 1957, this mutual indifference has characterized his literary career also, something many have noted but done little about. *BLP*, Cozzens' twelfth novel, was a provocative rendering of controversial themes that had concerned him for nearly three decades.

The majority of reviewers were ecstatic. Brendon Gill, writing in the *New Yorker*, called it "Tolstoyen in size and seriousness." No other American novelist had "the resources of intelligence, literary technique, and knowledge of the intricate . . . ways of the world" to equal those of Cozzens. Such was the power of this masterpiece, Gill concluded, that "life may never be the same for us." For readers of *Saturday Review*, Whitney Balliett declared that *BLP* "is brilliant, if rather staggering proof . . . that its author has become the most mature, honest, painstaking, and technically accomplished American novelist alive." From "the editor's Easy Chair" of *Harper's*, John Fischer nominated Cozzens for the Nobel Prize in literature. So successfully did Cozzens write about American society (these people "*are* society") that the result "comes close to being the truth, the whole truth, and nothing but the truth, so help me God." After taking this oath, Fischer ventured a prediction especially dear to realistic social novelists: "If your great-grandchild should ever want to find out how Americans behaved and thought and felt in the mid-years of this century, Cozzens' major novels probably would be his most revealing source." Granville Hicks added his praise, writing that "talk of greatness is not irrelevant."

Lesser known reviewers responded at least as favorably. In six weeks *BLP* sold more copies (170,000) than had Cozzens' eleven earlier novels combined (140,000). Both Book-of-the-Month Club and Reader's Digest Condensed Books selected it for their readers. *Time* placed Cozzens on its cover and Hollywood paid $100,000 for film rights.

Although several reviewers commented negatively on Cozzens' popular novel, it was the veteran social critic Dwight Macdonald who blew the whistle on the Cozzens boom and created "l'affaire Cozzens." In a review of reviews titled "By Cozzens Possessed," Macdonald in the January 1958 number of *Commentary* penned a strident, eclectic attack on *BLP* which then ranked first on the best seller lists. It was written in prose, he argued, of "an artificiality and complexity that approaches the impenetrable—indeed often achieves it." The humpbacked syntax, Faulknerian meandering and Latin-root polysyllables were pretentious elements of a palpable bid for immortality. Cozzens' depiction of women, love, and sex bothered him, as did the character of Arthur Winner. Cozzens' mind lacked "clarity, control, and form." Moreover, he committed the "unforgivable novelistic sin: he is unaware of the real nature of his characters, that is, the words and actions he gives them lead the reader 'to other conclusions than those intended by the author." Near the end of his *Commentary* piece Macdonald explicitly acknowledged his opposition to the moral and philosophical views expressed in the novel: Cozzens wrote the "Novel of Resignation" in which "the highest reach of enlightenment is to realize how awful the System is and yet to accept it *on its own terms.*"

Finally, Macdonald took the reviewers to task for responding so enthusiastically to "a very defective novel." The "sincere enthusiasm for a mediocre work," he argued, "is more damaging to literary standards than any amount of cynical ballyhoo." Its enormous success, he wrote characteristically, signified "the latest episode in the Middlebrow Counter-Revolution."

What is one to make of this broad assault on Cozzens? Surely Macdonald was justified in reminding book reviewers of their duties. Their analyses were cliche-ridden, generally innocent of serious thought, and far below the level at which the novel itself operated. Nor, for the most part, did they give critical attention to the moral vision of the book. That failure obscures some of the reasons for the relative unpopularity of this "popular" novelist.

One question that unavoidably intrudes when considering Cozzens is the vision inherent in the totality of his work. Henry James, in his brilliant essay "Ivan Turgénieff" (1874) put it this way:

> The great question as to a poet or novelist is, How does he feel about life? What, in the last analysis is his philosophy? When vigorous writers have reached maturity we are at liberty to look in their works for some expression of a total view of the world they have been so actively observing. This is the most interesting thing their works offer us. Details are interesting in proportion as they contribute to make it clear.[1]

It was his concern for the totality of meaning that led Macdonald to characterize *BLP* as a "Novel of Resignation." Although this designation is not quite accurate, there are enough suggestions of determinism in *BLP* to raise the possibility. Early on in the novel, Judge Fred Dealey, a minor cynical realist, asks Arthur Winner, "Could you ever have changed what's going to happen?" And answering himself, "You know this much: Whatever happens, happens because a lot of other things have happened already. When it gets to where you come in—well, it's bound to be pretty late in the day. . . . Freedom, I read at college, is the knowledge of necessity." While listening in on a trial, Winner meditates on his son Warren who had died in a military service accident caused by his disobedience of orders. He recalls Warren's endless series of rash, foolish acts, and concludes that "except in some short-term view, limited and, so, ignorant, *accident here this date* was just what Warren's death hadn't been." Again, when Winner fears that his withholding of information from Helen Detweiler possibly contributed to her suicide, Julius Penrose eases the strain by arguing that "what happens to people is simply what was always going to happen to them. To think otherwise is vain visioning." This reasoning holds for the idiot Caroline Dummer. There *was* no point at which one could intervene to change what nature had destined for her.

But the overall picture of Cozzens' novels does not suggest complete resignation—at least not for his heroes. In every novel since *The Last Adam* Cozzens' protagonists are brought to accept life's dreadful circumstances but recognize their responsibility to make the best of things as they are. They act as if they had free will. The pragmatic heroes seek not to rebuild society, however, or even to reform it. It is sufficient to keep it functioning. Their chief method of control is the capacity for reasoned analysis which at times can limit the damage caused by outpourings of passion, that is, feeling and irrational desires.

There are moments in the works of Cozzens when the solid courage of the major characters and their quiet efforts to operate society evoke sympathy. At the end of the third day in *Guard of Honor,* when the ugly racial situation at the Ocanara air base had been contained, General Beal tells Colonel Ross:

> "Judge, I have some little weaknesses, like having to do things my own way; and Jo-Jo thinks I'm just a fly boy, and I am. No, I'm no master mind; but spell it out for me, and I'll pretty often get it. You tell me what you think I don't know, and I'll tell you what I think you don't know and we'll get there." . . . .
>
> "I'll try," Colonel Ross said. "An old man like me, a man I knew once—he was a judge, too—used to say: *sed quis costodiet ipsos custodes.* Know what that means?"
>
> "Hell, no," General Beal said. "There are quite a few things I don't know."
>
> "Well, in this case it might mean, who's going to pick up after me."
>
> General Beal slapped his shoulder lightly. "I could take care of that when it happens," he said. "I'll do the best I can, Judge; and you do the best you can; and who's going to do it better?"

It is not an exciting venture that Cozzens offers us, but rather the matter-of-fact activities that constitute the dailiness of life. James Gould Cozzens is superb in portraying what men can do within the limits he imposes, but there are for this Realist, oh, so many limits to human possibility.

The character of Arthur Winner, which troubled Macdonald, raises questions about the limitations of Cozzens' philosophy and, ultimately his art. Reviewers were not always sensitive to this. One wrote that "Winner is the grandest moral vision in all Cozzens's work," and another that Winner is "the quintessence of our best qualities." The fifty-four-year-old lawyer is shown to be a decent and conscientious father, son, husband, lawyer and friend. In the course of two days he faces an astonishing number of problems including rape, suicide, infanticide, alcoholism, and embezzlement, as well as several troubling recollections that echo out of his past. At first he seems to be in command of events, and is complacent because of it. It is this man that Macdonald saw as priggish, that is, "one who delights in demonstrating his superiority on small occasions." When his daughter asks whether she and a friend might have a car, Winner replies: "At the moment, I think I must answer the telephone. . . . I'll take the matter under advisement." To his daughter's further importunities, he closes the discussion thus: "I've engaged to look into the question further; and to find out how Priscilla's father feels. Nothing more is implied, nothing else is to be inferred." In the example that Macdonald cited, Winner, emerging from the garden after his embarrassing conversation with Mrs. Pratt, was met at gunpoint by a seduced girl's angry father. "Be very careful! Return the gun [said Winner]; and meanwhile, show it to no one else. Don't take it out of your pocket; and don't consider pointing it. Pointing a deadly weapon is a separate indictable offense, and would get you an additional fine, and an additional jail term." It may be questioned whether this qualifies as a "small occasion," but the overwhelming superciliousness is there.

Of greater importance is the contention that Arthur Winner is a grand moral vision. He is educated, successful, a busy man about town, and the sort of person one with problems likes to see. He is, alas, human and as he moves from crisis to crisis and his secure world in Brocton (population 15,000) begins to come apart, we see him trading on his integrity. Flashbacks reveal to us that years earlier he had cuckolded his best friend and partner, and had failed in the education of his son. Now, he agrees to support an incompetent ward healer for appointment as district judge in exchange for the dismissal of charges against a client.

Because Winner decides not to inform Helen Detweiler, she commits suicide. In looking through her affairs at the office, he makes the crucial discovery of the novel, i.e., that his senior partner has embezzled a large sum of money.

What is a man of reason to do? Julius Penrose enters the office at this point and becomes momentarily the central consciousness. Having known of the embezzlement for years, he counsels the expedient course, the basic ethic of which is the advice an old wise man once gave him: "Boy, never try to piss up the wind. Principle must sometimes be shelved." After all the apologies and explanations are offered, the bare fact is that Arthur Winner has committed a criminal offense by covering up other criminal acts. One may admire the wish to avoid sending the elderly Tuttle to jail (if indeed that would have been necessary) but something remains not quite right. We are asked to accept as a "grand moral vision" a person whose field of choice is severely constricted. There are possibilities, artistic and moral, which remain unexplored. It is in such situations that Cozzens' well-known conservative philosophy inhibits the creative imagination and contributes to an aesthetic deficiency.

The limitations we see in Cozzens may be due in part to the genre of the social novel in which he works. Cozzens tries to portray the interrelationships of men and women belonging to the white Protestant upper-middle class of medium-sized towns in America. Although as individuals they are responsible for their actions, their membership in a distinctive social group implies allegiance to the manners and morals of that group; their behavior is importantly conditioned by the opportunities and limitations inherent in that membership. In identifying with a particular social class in time, and in wishing not to falsify its life, Cozzens at once imposes limits on himself and becomes vulnerable to the whims of fashion.

The novel of "resignation" (as Macdonald saw it) and the details of the class that interest Cozzens pose a special problem for intellectuals like Dwight Macdonald. The intellectual has a distinctive role to play—given by tradition, his conscience, and his cultural peers. He is concerned with the moral code that governs society and serves as the articulate custodian of abstract ideas like justice and truth and reason. When André Gide wrote,

"To be at odds with his times" is the *raison d'etre* of the intellectual, he described accurately the career of Macdonald. For nearly four decades, Macdonald has played an important part in the cultural and political wars that mark the existence of intellectuals in Western societies. During the intellectually exciting thirties, Macdonald helped to revive the revolutionary socialist, but anti-Stalinist *Partisan Review,* resigned from it because of his condemnation of World War II, and joined the Trotskyist party (1939-1941). After World War II he edited *Politics,* during which time he took up the causes of anarchism and pacifism. Having become pessimistic about political solutions by 1950, Macdonald evolved into one of the chief theorists of mass culture, his central interest when BLP appeared. His intellectual evolution provided him with an important vantage point from which to investigate and criticize American society, but it did not endear him to the artistic efforts of so conservative a writer as James Gould Cozzens.

Thus one of the realities of the Cozzens-Macdonald affair was the conflict between the artist and the intellectual. These categories are not mutually exclusive and the distinction is not invidious. But Cozzens emphasized the functions of one, and Macdonald, the other. As an intellectual, Macdonald was especially sensitive to the moral-philosophical shortcomings of *BLP* even if he planned his attack on too wide a front.

He immediately perceived, as many had not, Cozzens' inadequate treatment of love and sex. *BLP* is a splendidly organized story of people possessed by all manner of love. Love is examined at several levels—primitive lust, self-sacrifice, friendship, familial love—and in a variety of sexual modes including youthful courtship, prostitution, onanism, lesbianism, rape, marital and extramarital relationships. Unfortunately, this particular literary work is a vulgar treatment of love. Love is passion; it overrides reason, disrupts order, and ultimately destroys. Hope Winner dies in childbirth, a victim of sex. Helen Detweiler, fearing and hating sex, commits suicide because of her overwhelming love for her hopeless brother. Dr. Reggie Shaw becomes an alcoholic and faces possible mental collapse because feeling prevents his manly acceptance of suffering. Ralph Detweiler, brother of Helen, allegedly rapes a girl with a scandalous reputation, and later runs away from home upon learning that a second lower-class girl, "possessed" by a need for affection, carries his child. Finally, in a somewhat contrived situation, the aging Noah Tuttle is shown to have resorted to embezzlement because of his feeling for townspeople whom he could not bear to see lose on an investment.

The sexual episodes are clothed in an atmosphere of mockery. The setting for sex is at times natural enough, as with Ralph and Veronica's clumsy performance in the back seat of a parked car. But elsewhere, Cozzens' disgust with youthful sex becomes merely melodramatic, as in the case of Caroline Dummer who works in a laundry and acquires a community-wide reputation for her sweaty efforts in the sorting room, which take place, of course, on the dirty clothes. In still other instances it is presented in tedious detail devoid of trust and beauty. During his conversation with the lickerish Mrs. Pratt, Arthur Winner thinks of himself and Marjorie Penrose as having been nothing more than "slippery lovers," "cheap sneaks" misguided by passion.

> Deaf as yesterday to all representations of right, he [Arthur Winner] purposed further perfidy, once more pawning his honor to obtain his lust. Deaf as yesterday to all remonstrances of reason, he purposed to sell himself over again to buy venery's disappearing dross—some moments of transient dallying with eye or hand, to which untied impatience quickly set a term; some impassioned moments of the now engendered beast of two backs, of that acting androgyne whose he-half was excitedly prodding and probing, whose she-half was excitedly prodded and probed. The little life span of the beast soon sped, its death was died. At the she-half's flings-about in her extremity, the he-half's spoonful of phrenetic sensation was tweaked to spend itself—and, there! There was the buy, the bargain, the prize, the pearl of price!

For Winner it is hardly different with his wives. What should be a positive sexual relationship with Hope, his first wife, soon becomes a minor comedy with references to "piacular pollution" and to their "joint obscenity." Clarissa, wife number two, experiences sex with Winner as a kind of technological achievement: "thrilling thuds of his heart . . . moist manipulative reception . . . the mutual heat of pumped bloods . . . the thoroughgoing, deepening, widening work of their connection; and his then no less than hers, the tempo slowed in concert to engineer a tremulous joint containment and continuance . . . the deep muscle groups, come to their vertex were in a flash convulsed." To Macdonald it sounded "like a *Fortune* description of an industrial process." Little wonder that he was perplexed by the reviewer who wrote that "the passages having to do with physical love have a surprising lyric power."

Perhaps the single really fine evidence of love in the novel emerges in the friendship of Arthur Winner and Julius Penrose. Winner is shocked to discover that his adultery with Penrose's wife was known all the while. Yet Julius has secretly forgiven him and even thanked him for trying to conceal something which in other circumstances might have destroyed a solid friendship:

> Unsmiling, compassionate still, still steady, Julius's gaze, the speaking clear dark eyes, rested on him, as though without use of words to say: Yes, I know that you have been afraid I would find out. But you had nothing to fear. Don't you see, I've known all along. Our pact is: As I am, you accept me; as you are, I accept you.

With an exception made for the friendship of Winner and Penrose, Malcolm Cowley's observation that Cozzens' novel was "not so much about love as against it," is perceptive.[2] Selfishness, impulsiveness, mechanical efficiency, yes—but not intimate love. Aesthetically, Cozzens' rendering of the love motif is deficient in that human beings, when they love, are at once selfish and altruistic. One looks for a subtle intimacy somewhere in *BLP* but seldom finds it. Thus Cozzens' heroes exemplify what E. M. Forster once called the "underdeveloped heart"—not frigid, but short on growth and sympathy.

Something of Cozzens' spirit, temper, and presence emerges through several illiberal themes that together produce a somewhat contemptuous atmosphere in *BLP.* Recurrent scenes indicate a bias that is anti-woman, anti-Negro, anti-Catholic, anti-Semitic, anti-liberal, as well as anti-love. I trust it is clear that Cozzens has a right to these views. Our interest is to inquire whether they cut him off from things and limit the creative possibilities in the novelistic art. In the best aesthetic experiences, feeling is deepened, accorded new power and meaning. We are forced to confront our hidden selves and to appreciate the moments of doubt that trouble even the settled people of the world. Does Cozzens afford us this experience?

A complaint of Julius Penrose, set in the context of love and prejudice, suggests at once the illiberal themes that are ubiquitous in the novels of James Gould Cozzens and the one-dimensional political morality that frequently appears. Penrose wonders why "the only people who may be openly criticized, found fault with, and spoken ill of, are those of white, Protestant, and more or less Nordic extraction." Catholics may freely abuse him, he grumbles, and "each self-pitying Jew, each sulking Negro, need only holler that he's caught me not loving him as much as he loves himself, and a rabble of professional friends of man, social-worker liberals, and practitioners of universal brotherhood—the whole national horde of nuts and queers—will come at a run to hang me by the neck until I learn to love." This gratuitous attack on liberals, Catholics, Jews, Negroes, social workers—the "nuts and queers"—has many precedents in Cozzens' works and can be found in *The Last Adam, Men and Brethren, The Just and the Unjust, Guard of Honor,* and *Ask Me Tomorrow,* the most autobiographical of his novels. And it is the protagonists who offer them. Characters who challenge the conventional moralities are caricatured into disgruntled liberals such as Lieutenant Edsell, a leftist writer from the North who argues the case for integration in *Guard of Honor.* He is portrayed as dogmatic and willing to work hard for what he "passionately" believes in, something Cozzens makes clear is destructive. The basic cause for liberal reformism is resentment, or so it would appear from Cozzens' analysis of Edsell's face in repose.

> Left to itself, it still expressed those mixed, some-times antagonistic sentiments which it was most often called on to express—suspicion mingled with contempt; derision never wholly free of resentment; impulsiveness hampered by calculation; vanity unsettled by doubt.
>
> Left to itself, not roused to fight, not exercised with scheming, Lieutenant Edsell's face expressed also despond-ency and defeat. While he brooded, faraway, he acknowl-edged some considerable reverse he must have suffered in his long standing quarrel with the state of things, some new disappointment added to that sum of disappointments whose galling recurrence were no doubt his real casus belli.

> It was the face of the unresigned man of sorrows, angrily
> acquainted with grief—the well-known sorehead.

Reform, then, is simply the means by which the Edsell's of the world escape feelings of anomie.

The hostility shown toward liberals extends also to minority Americans who get little sympathy from Cozzens. It leads to serious weaknesses in characterization. Take, for example, *S. S. San Pedro* (1931), which is based on the actual sinking of the ocean liner *Vestris* in 1928. It is a terrifying story of the human chaos that results when crew members and passengers become aware that the ship is doomed. The Negro firemen mutiny and in a blind, drunken attempt to escape force passengers out of the lifeboats. Unfortunately, this was a distortion of the testimony before the London Board of Trade which investigated the case. Negroes had not acted unreasonably in leaving their stations, the Board concluded, and it "could find no evidence of confusion during the launching of the steamship's lifeboats."[3] True, Cozzens was writing fiction, not history. But there was no literary necessity for his distortion; and to distort so important an issue as racial relations and conduct to the further degradation of minority peoples suggests enormous insensitivity and hints at a limited artistic imagination.

Racial problems are handled with greater sophistication in *Guard of Honor.* Yet the officers express the most biased notions of black men. This includes, significantly, Colonel Ross, the protagonist who argues that social relationships should not be changed since the white man is "to a black man's sorrow and his shame, a little too much for most black men." Ross may or may not have been speaking in an auctorial capacity, but suspicions on that score were not lessened when Cozzens stated in an interview, "I like anybody if he's a nice guy, but I've never met many Negroes who were nice guys." The literary consequences are unmistakable, however. The insistence that segregation is inevitable simplifies his handling of black officers and produces contempt for the white officer who disagrees with them. Thus, Edsell, who represents the typical liberal, must be reduced in complexity to a sorehead seeking social reform to conceal personal disappointments.

For a final and eloquent example of Cozzens' sentiments

68

towards minorities listen as the "old Yankee" Dr. Bull, one of the most famous characters in Cozzens' gallery of heroes, expatiates on the decline of Connecticut as ethnic and religious strangers move in.

> New Winton was a place to live, then; not something a road
> went through. You didn't have a bunch of bums rushing
> by all the time. . . . Look at the mills down at Sansbury
> and the Polacks! Time was when Sansbury was a white
> man's town. Look at the Roman Catholic convent there,
> or whatever they made of the Jenny place! What the hell
> are these monks and priors and novenas of the Little
> Flower doing in New England? Same with a lot of these
> Jew artists, like Lincoln over in the Cobb place. Jumping
> Jesus, what's he mean by calling himself Lincoln? Early
> American house! Why doesn't he go restore himself a
> synagogue in Jerusalem?

Twenty-five years later, as we have seen, we hear Julius Penrose saying much the same thing.

Suspicions of auctorial intrusion here are based on several factors, all suggested by the foregoing material. First, the same attitudes appear repeatedly in the novels, and they are voiced by the protagonists, not merely by minor characters. Second, Cozzens' characters are most rhetorically eloquent when giving voice to their prejudices; and third, Cozzens' personal statements sound as though his characters were speaking through *him*. He has said, "I am more or less illiberal, and strongly antipathetic to all political and artistic movements. I was brought up an Episcopalian, and where I live the landed gentry are Republican." In an interview during the celebration of *BLP* he declared, characteristically, that his Tory ancestors felt themselves high quality because they opposed the American Revolution: "They inculcated this feeling in me, so, to tell the truth, I still feel I'm better than other people." To criticism that his life is dangerously isolated for one who needs people for subject matter, Cozzens replied: "The thing you need to know is yourself; you are people." Thus, if we can assume that Stephen Dedalus is James Joyce, then Arthur Winner, Colonel Ross, and Dr. Bull are James Gould Cozzens.

The atmosphere of the underdeveloped heart continues in *BLP,* especially in reference to women, youth, and Catholics.

One is continuously forced to ask, why the cruelty here, why the hostility there, or why the unending depiction of women as sentimental, weak-willed, half-wits unable to deal with abstract concepts? Perhaps readers should have been prepared for this. In *Guard of Honor* Lieutenant Turck, as able as she is, concludes that a woman must have a man or suffer through life half a person. Mrs. Ross, recognizing the folly and hypocrisy, the callousness and conceit of men, nevertheless believes that men should retain an "ascendency of strength, courage, and intelligence." Women need to be dominated.

Whatever their beliefs, Lieutenant Turck and Mrs. Ross possessed some capacity for analysis and getting on in life. This changes in *BLP*. The sex hostility is now open and is strongly flavored with the condescension of the superior white male. It is a depressing collection of women we encounter. After first meeting Arthur Winner's mother, well on the road to senility, the reader is introduced to the unsubtly named Caroline Dummer, a "low-grade moron" who killed her bastard child, tried to conceal the deed, and eventually found happiness in the secure confinement of jail. There is Veronica Kovacs, also not very bright ("I gather the girl comes from down the county; Pole; Hungarian; or something."), a prostitute who, with an equally dumb-brute mother (she scowls and growls like simpletons do) attempts to fix a rape charge on Ralph Detweiler. Meanwhile, Ralph has engaged in amorous relationship yet another low-class, unattractive girl who insists that she carries Ralph's child. She appears to represent for Cozzens how the passion for recognition and affection produces silly behavior.

His parents dead, Ralph has been cared for by an older sister, Helen, who is also the chief secretary in the law firm of Tuttle, Winner, and Penrose. She is a hard-working and responsible woman who frequently loses her composure and who knows love only as self-sacrifice. Unable to help herself as crisis hits, she unwisely wishes to bribe Miss Kovacs into dropping charges against her son. This dismays Arthur Winner, her lawyer, but he persuades himself that he must recognize the strange "quirk" that is "integral to most female minds—seeing a so-much-wanted end, no means could ever be unjustified." He must accept, as other Cozzens' males do, that the motives and feelings of women have deep psychoneurotic origins which make them surrender to vain wishings. As an office secretary Helen is excellent in handling reams of complicated figures, but since she is unable to grasp their significance she never suspects that her boss is an embezzler.

The sickest woman is Marjorie Penrose who is nearing forty, is married to a cripple, and is genuinely confused about life, in part due to a background devoid of love but filled with abnormal sex experiences. "Preordained to fumble," according to her husband, and filled with an "oestrual rage," she has slept with her husband's law partner, become an alcoholic, and is about to "confound confusion" by joining the Catholic Church. Mrs. Pratt, a friend with whom one guesses Marjorie had a low-keyed lesbian relationship years earlier, is already a Catholic and intent on Marjorie's conversion. This most obnoxious woman, as one critic has written, "easily wins the blue ribbon in Cozzens's populous and impressive gallery of unpleasant people."[4] Considering herself a sage counselor, she engages Winner in a lengthy conversation ostensibly to discuss Marjorie Penrose but in reality wishes to masturbate her own sexual fantasies. She is treated with a contempt that may be unequalled in recent serious fiction. After thirty pages of conversation she spies a snake, becomes thoroughly addled, and must ask directions to the bathroom.

Finally, there are the two wives of Arthur Winner. Hope, the first, is weak physically and dependent on her husband, though she has courage to face unpleasantness. Wanting children meant doing "acts of darkness," and she did them. Clarissa, Winner's second wife, is the strongest woman in *BLP* and enjoys what appears to be a satisfactory marriage. Yet like the other few healthy women in the Cozzens collection, she is manlike, athletic, and as a child had very much wanted to be a man. One suspects that this longing occasionally pressed upon her as she matured. Even with her masculine qualities she senses an inferiority to males. It is expressed in several ways. On hearing of Ralph and "Joanie's" predicament, she allows as how she cannot help feeling that the girls are mostly at fault—they are such "fools." Or, when conversing with Arthur, she can only echo what her weaker sisters say: "I never expect to be able to tell you anything—I mean, I'm flabbergasted all the time, in my limited dumb way, to find you really know almost everything about almost everything." She

admits, moreover, to having what Francis Ellery said characterizes women who act as women—"a sort of vital, sustaining,
bitchiness."

The men in *BLP* agree. Arthur Winner, Noah Tuttle, Julius
Penrose, Reggie Shaw, and Fred Dealey are unanimous in the
opinion that women are fools most of the time. Moreover, there
is a continuing cruelty in their relation to women, as Dwight
Macdonald noted. An elderly and unobtrusive client of Noah
Tuttle, wishing to change her trust fund slightly, is told: "You're
getting senile, Maud. Try not to be more of a fool than you can
help." Dr. Shaw, upon meeting a friend's wife at a party,
immediately puts her down: "What's your trouble, baby? Or
can I guess? . . . Tell Pappy how many periods you've missed.
. . . You know as well as I do you're one of those girls who only
has to look at him to get herself knocked up." After she leaves
the room indignantly, and Clarissa gently reproves Shaw—"Reg,
you're not being very funny"—he continues his tirade: "That's
right, I don't feel very funny. Sometimes you get your bellyfull
of women—their goddamn notions; their goddamn talk-talk-talk;
their goddamn sacks of tripes!" This savage intrusion into the
novel ends as quickly as it began. No reason is offered for it. It is
gratuitous, tactless, too palpable a straining for an unearned
response.

Youth is also portrayed unsympathetically and usually
through the consciousness of Winner. He sees youth as "a kind of
infirmity" which recalls Lancy Micks of *Cock Pit* saying youth's a
"disabling disease." Ralph's trouble, thinks Winner, is the "fault
of youth, the ordinary far-reaching flaws in judgment, the usual
failures in discrimination." In this sense, Ralph Detweiler is merely
a more pathetic version of hot-headed Benny Carricker and the
professional reformer Lieutenant Edsell. Specifically, Cozzens
has always despised the "irresponsible" criticism that at times
emanates from the young who experience life without power.
This theme finds its most effective expression in *The Just and the
Unjust* when district attorney Martin Bunting lectures his assistant
who had complained of having to accept office from a political
boss:

"What right has Jesse to decide who's going to be

what?   Does he own the county?"

Bunting said, "Standing off and saying you don't like the way things are run is kid stuff—any kid can work out a program of more ice cream and less school and free movies and him telling other people what to do instead of people always telling him. . . . If things were run according to your ideas instead of the way they are run, it would be much better. Who says so? Why you say so! That's what the dopes, the Communists and so on, all the boys who never grew up, say."

No doubt youth is often brash, just as responsibility sobers and age often brings wisdom. But it is a half-truth; and one of the literary possibilities Cozzens fails to exploit involves the merits of youth— their idealism, happiness, energy, faith. He stacks the cards against them, as he does against women. It is a case of pleading too hard, akin less to the novel than to the tract.

The atmosphere of contemptuous disapproval deepens during the course of the novel with Cozzens' treatment of Catholicism, a factor Macdonald does not discuss. In several preceding novels Cozzens dealt with the topic but never extensively. There was little that was remarkable about his coverage except that beginning with *Men and Brethren* we notice a deep distrust of the Catholic Church. In *BLP* that distrust is a major theme as Winner, Mrs. Pratt, Julius and Marjorie Penrose are deeply involved in the matter. Should Marjorie, who is suffering and unable to cope with life, become a communicant as she seems ready to do? Her husband suggests grossly, without irony, that men and women who join the Catholic Church with its "preposterous theology" are "ill-balanced." "Not a few of the male converts, for instance, have to me the look of former homosexuals; not a few of the females, the look of former alcoholics." Because he has no sympathy for mystery and religious aspiration, Marjorie's turn to Rome seems to him "a futile little ignominy" that has "the sheer vulgarity of all frightened acts."

Judge Lowe thinks of Catholics only as "the base and obscure vulgar" who are a politically troublesome mass vote, and in religion are "willing dupes of their priests." Winner, who had reproved Penrose for prejudice, nevertheless agrees that Catholics are a "loud" and "dangerous" minority. Later, after Mrs. Pratt had invoked the scriptural injunction "Do not judge, that you may not be judged," Winner, the man of reason, displays that he has internalized nearly every prejudice against Catholics:

> The wording, so flatly wrong-sounding, the jar on the ear as of misquotation, meant, Arthur Winner recognized, that this was (which of course it would be) the Douay, or whatever the present Catholic, version's version. A prejudicing trifle; yet ample, Arthur Winner, half-amused, must admit, for a hostile mind's purposes of distrust. What impertinence! Testy, the mind, the jarred ear, made correction: *Judge not, that ye be not judged!* What else? What else? What was this presuming, obtuse and alien, that mouthed the word-established over, that defiled a well of English? . . . Yes; Julius was right! Regard that overweening hierarchy; above those mostly poorboy bishops, elated by their local power, those impudent princes of the church— this plump canting judge of an eminence here; this malapert, threatening ignoramus of an eminence there! Regard that state within a state which, flown with insolence, could arrogate to itself (if covertly; still daring hardly more than whisper of blackmail to nervous newspapers, to nervous advertisers, to nervous politicians) a privilege of foreigners to tamper with laws of the land, to abrogate an act of assembly duly made and provided, to exempt itself and its property from regulations all good citizens saw as reasonable, to refuse those rights of the governed in their government on which our free society rested.

Finally, the Catholic woman Polly Pratt, who speaks for her church is made to appear silly and hypocritical to the point of caricature. By the end of her conversation with Winner we know that this pompous windbag is equated with Caroline Dummer in that both have withdrawn from the world: Caroline to the "lovely jail," and Polly Pratt to Catholicism. Surely it is the novelist's prerogative to hold up behavior, institutions, and ideas for examination. Cozzens has the intellectual power to do so. But sensitivity and balance are needed to keep art from descending into malicious caricature and propaganda. We can readily believe that people are prejudiced, bitter, indelicate in manners and taste. That is but one side of them, however. We need to see the other side also. For literary purposes, and most certainly for anyone who covets a designation as "realist," it is necessary to invent other characters to express divergent views.

This Cozzens fails to do—or when he does, creates Lieutenant Edsells and Polly Pratts.

On the topic of atmosphere, which is intertwined with Cozzens' view of the world, let it be briefly noted that the themes discussed above crop up repeatedly in matters of smaller importance in *BLP*. They are unconnected except in their contribution to a climate that carries a heavy cloud of disgust. Driving home late one night Arthur Winner passes the decaying old houses of Brocton and feels melancholy: "Ye shall know the truth; and the truth shall make you sick!" an uncomfortable message of "true experience's malaise." Noah Tuttle cannot think of childbirth except as an "ugly," "revolting," and "cruel" experience. Judge Dealey allows as how he'd "really like to be nicer to people—the stupid bastards!" And Arthur Winner can hardly control his disgust over the alleged homosexuality of Elmer Abbott who is, predictably, a choirmaster. Although Abbott had suffered grievously from the prejudice of those around him, his behavior upon being acquitted of charges of indecent advances toward choirboys brings only contempt from Winner:

> Here was Elmer Abbott, an Orcutt, a well-off man (with all that meant in the way of perfect freedom to quit himself like a man) so tame, so pridelessly relieved at the withdrawal of a fake charge, at the permission to continue his namby-pamby round, keep his piffling post, his unpaid job's clung-to-prerogative of inflicting on a captive audience his mediocre music, that he cried!

It is because of this and other examples adduced above that we find in Cozzens a lack of compassion and understanding for people who daily must face the suffering situations of life. I believe it goes far to explain why sensitive readers such as Dwight Macdonald find Cozzens so difficult to read.

Macdonald devoted considerable attention to Cozzens' idiosyncratic style. He found it artificial, impenetrable, full of pointless inversions and inexpressive words, a transparent attempt to write the Big Book. Fearing that his damnation of Cozzens' style might reflect on that of Henry James and William Faulkner, he added that "James's involutions are (a) necessary to precisely discriminate his meaning; (b) solid parts of the architecture of the sentence; and (c) controlled by a fine ear for euphony.

Faulkner does meander, but there is emotional force, descriptive richness, behind his wanderings. . . . Their style is complex because they are saying something complicated, not, as with Cozzens, because they cannot make words do what they want them to."

Macdonald did find examples of poor writing but the grating selections were not "typical, run-of-the-mill" sentences, "chosen at random." They were highly selective ones, wrenched out of context. Note the following, which surely is one of the worst.

> The succussive, earthquake-like throwing-over of a counted-on years-old stable state of things had opened fissures. Through one of them, Arthur Winner stared a giddying, horrifying moment down unplumbed, nameless abysses in himself. He might later deny the cognition, put thoughts of the undiscovered country away, seek to lose the memory; yet the heart's mute halt at every occasional, accidental recollection of those gulfs, admitted their existence, confessed his fearful close shave.

No one would wish to defend this *in toto.* But only the first sentence is beyond redemption with "succussive" followed by "earthquake-like," and three additional awkward hyphenated expressions. "Close shave" may be stylistically anticlimatic, but Macdonald's complaint about "mute halt" is nit-picking at best. The context of the passage is important. Winner has been caught off guard by the questions of Mrs. Pratt and is meditating under pressure. Remembrances of the unanticipated death of Hope (the arrangements that had to be made, the errands to be done), memories of his dead father, his delinquent, dead son, and his first sexual encounter with Marjorie Penrose—all this flashed through his mind. The writing is unstable as Winner himself is unstable. And if Cozzens also faltered in rendering Winner's reeling mind, he at least did not fail to communicate clearly.

More typical of Cozzens' style than the passages Macdonald selected are ones such as the following.

> *How dies the wise man?* said the far-from-jesting preacher—and stayed him for his answer. *As the fool!* Like Alfred Revere's, Howard Minton's other helpers failed, his comforts fled. Swift to its close ebbs out life's little day! Colonel Minton was well along in his particular form of

> that ruination to which, for which, men were born. . . .
> With order (those pressed old trousers; those polished old
> shoes!) with control (from the body of the morning's death,
> delivery waited on high noon), Howard Minton had devised
> himself a way of life. The careful budgeting of his pension
> money, never a penny wasted on nonessentials; the studied
> arranging of his affairs (his simple prescription was to
> eliminate in the interests of drinking all other business or
> activities) made possible the spending of most of Colonel
> Minton's waking hours in *I am's* grateful numb bemuse-
> ment. . . .

The sentence structure is sometimes more dense than this but the
meaning is fully clear on a careful reading. Allusions from the
important English poets, numerous quotations from Shakespeare
and the Bible are frequently worked into the text, at times with,
at times without, acknowledgment. Cozzens is among the best
read of novelists and compliments the reader by assuming an equal
erudition on his part.

On balance, Macdonald's criticism of Cozzens' writing is
much too harsh, even ill-tempered. Cozzens has always paid the
closest attention to style, by which I mean the use of language to
objectify a vision. Precision of meaning, and, until *Guard of
Honor,* economy of style, have been the trademarks of this literary
craftsman. In *BLP* he experimented with a richer, more ornate
prose, partly because of his love of language, but also because
the world he loved was in dissolution and as such resisted the
usual precise characterization. In this sense, at least, his style is
related to meaning—of which, more later. The parenthetical
expressions and qualifying subordinate clauses occur generally in
the meditative passages and purposely reflect the often disorderly
patterns of the mind. Awarenesses constantly intrude that
influence conversation but which are not directly expressed.
Finally, it should be noted on behalf of this self-confessed aristocrat that style enables him to keep readers at a comfortable,
respectful distance.

The major difficulty with the Corinthian elaborations of *BLP*
is not their intrinsic quality but their jarring inconsistency with
the novelist's insistence that the dry light of reason should pre-
dominate in human affairs: passion should remain under control,
or better, out of sight. An embroidered romanticism of style

scarcely befits so unromantic a man as James Gould Cozzens. This, together with his weakness for uncommon words—like "presbyopic," "vellications," and "hypnagogic"—makes Cozzens' style resemble at times what Henry James said of Swinburne's: "It is always listening to itself—always turning its head over its shoulders to see its train following behind it."[5]

Thus, Macdonald's criticism of Cozzens' style is understandable even if, as I believe, he let polemics run riot in his attack. His assertion that Cozzens' mind "lacks clarity, control, and form" is more curious, however. Technical competence, the precise ordering of events and characters have distinguished the author of BLP as one of the most accomplished architects in recent literature. His novels are coherent, their parts internally consistent, with plot, style, and characters contributing to the central purpose of the book. Orchestration nears perfection in the compact, dense, and extremely complex Guard of Honor. BLP is excellently organized also, but perhaps suffers from excessive control; the form seems not so much "found" as "imposed." We sense in the slightly mechanical quality of the characters, in their tendency to make speeches rather than to converse, an attention to craftsmanship at the expense of spontaneity.

The foregoing considerations permit us to ask whether BLP, a popular novel, was bad, mediocre, good, or great. Distinctions are necessary. Bad novels take us into the world of make-believe, always distort the truth of life, and often are technically inept. Or, if technically competent, their values are perverted: brutality is called manliness; sexual possession is called love; crime is called the search for meaning. Good novels reveal half-truths. They do depict living people and accept unhappy endings as individuals in life frequently must. Brutality, ugliness, and selfishness are exposed. But the merely good novelist tells us little that is new. His insights seldom transcend those of the readers. The good novelist can interest us but is unable to change our feelings, and, by extension, our behavioral patterns.

The great novel, on the contrary, creates in us an awareness of truths not hitherto imagined. Our conception of ourselves is deepened and extended to a new range of possibility. The uniquely satisfying artistic work also permits us to transcend the stifling pieties and rigidities of the conventional moralities.

In a word, their field of force points us toward freedom. Thus, there is in great art a discovery and not merely a reaffirmation. Tolstoy makes us touch base with the deeper meanings of love in. *Anna Karenina.* Herman Melville is revealing on the nature of man and his place in the universe as his Captain Ahab chases the white whale.

As a technical achievement, *BLP* is a superior novel, but it does not approach greatness because the values upheld are the well-worn customs of the expedient way. Arthur Winner and Julius Penrose never surprise us, and as rounded in characterization as the former is said to be, he is, in a significant sense, flat. Winner's acquiescence in criminal behavior is without the surprise that attends the incalculability of life. He had struck a deal with an ambitious district attorney and deceived his closest friend. We can fairly guess the result of the novel's ultimate test of his moral character. Instead of fresh vision and imagination—the stuff of a genuine aesthetic response—we see a reaction similar to others he has already made—and we are not moved.

In his recent study of literature, *Bright Book of Life,* Alfred Kazin offers an interpretation which leads to a fuller understanding of *BLP*.[6] He suggests that Cozzens is sick at heart with the knowledge that his WASP world is in disarray, is breaking up from the strains imposed by socio-economic developments. The complicated style is explained by "Cozzens' loss of respect for his own class." Kazin's observation is much to the point. Like other novelists, Cozzens had to face the continuing confusion of values in America, a confusion made worse after World War II by the spread of mass society and the collapse of assured distinctions in culture as in society. The upper-middle class was not exempt from this development; consequently, Arthur Winner is seen to have shortcomings.

Perhaps this helps to explain Cozzens' continued snapping at his pragmatic hero. On several occasions Winner is deflated, sometimes by ridicule. Walking the streets of Brocton after being surprised and humbled by his crippled friend, he is forced to remember:

> To Helen Detweiler he had said: *Everything you do must be straight. No other way works, and there aren't any*

exceptions. . . . Oh, indeed? To Helen, he said: *I can
tell you something else; these things pass. . . .* Oh, they
do, do they? *None of this will be easy. . . .* (Friend, you
can say that again!) He would patch grief with proverbs?

He had tried but discovered that in life we cannot have everything
we want. "Victory is not in reaching certainties or solving
mysteries; victory is making do with uncertainties, in supporting
mysteries." Be reasonable. Forget your dreams and work with
what you have. Do not risk upsetting stability by creating
possibilities. This suggests the central deficiency of *BLP.* The
attitude of accommodation, in an age obsessed with conformity
though in need of social and political imagination, prevented truly
creative art, even in so talented a novelist as James Gould Cozzens.

JAMES T. FARRELL: FOUR DECADES AFTER *STUDS LONIGAN*

EDGAR M. BRANCH

I

Recently I came across an early version in manuscript of James Farrell's poem "Breathless" entitled "What Makes Jimmy Run?" This is it:

> Why am I as I am?
> Because when young,
> I learned
> That the eternity of time
> Is the thief of youth,
> So then, I began
> To run the seconds of my life,
> Breathless,
> And I shall run
> As I am running
> Racing Time, the thief,
> And racing Death,
> The master of the thief,
> Until I have no breath,
> Nor any second
> Left to me.
> Then, I shall not be
> As I am.
> I shall simply
> Not be anymore.

What makes Jimmy run and how *far* has he run?—forty years after *Studs Lonigan*. The above poem suggests some reflections on time, naturalism, and the self in Farrell's fiction.

II

James Farrell's first published fiction was a little story called "Danny's Uncle" which appeared in 1921, fifty-four years ago, in his high school magazine. But not until 1927 did Farrell make writing his real life work. In that year he committed himself to literature, and probably about then he began seriously thinking of his life as a race with "Time, the thief" and with "Death, the master of the thief." Since then, he has been unremittingly conscious of time's passage. Time beats slowly through the *Studs Lonigan* trilogy and leads inexorably to Studs' death. In the O'Neill-O'Flaherty books time is measured by the hundreds of occurrences that help shape the lives of Danny and his family by eliciting their choices and forming their habits. Farrell's character Bernard Carr sees life as a race with time, a race whose real victor is death. That awareness deepens Bernard's compassion and his understanding of his past, and Bernard, the successful writer, temporarily comes to terms with his life. This pervasive sense of time in Farrell's three completed cycles of novels reflects the author's intensely personal feelings about man's brief existence on earth.

Having completed his series on Studs, Danny, and Bernard, in 1958 Farrell began to write an ambitious new cycle of fiction that he called *A Universe of Time.* He planned the cycle to include approximately thirty related volumes, seven of which have been published, and he has said it will provide "a relativistic panorama of our times."[1] Presumably, from the vantage of his maturity, Farrell wants to reinterpret American experience as he has known it. And he wants to demonstrate that just as the past lives in the present, so the past grows and changes as the present becomes the future. The very magnitude of this project has intensified Farrell's sense of his life as a race against time—it has made Jimmy want to run even faster. Eddie Ryan, the autobiographical character of *A Universe of Time,* reflects this desire in the novel *The Silence of History.* Eddie learns—or wants to learn—to treasure every moment. Walter Pater's "Conclusion" to *Studies in the History of the Renaissance* speaks powerfully to Eddie. It tells him that each moment should have value and quality and should be lived to the full. For Eddie, this means in practice to be aware, to study and to write. The novel focuses on the inner springs of Eddie's courage, will, determination, and defiance— the subjective weapons which Eddie will use to gain whatever advantage he can in his race with time. According to Farrell, the entire cycle of *A Universe of Time* is predicated on the idea of man's creativity and his courageous acceptance of impermanence —in time.

As recently as September 1973, Farrell reaffirmed his belief in the gospel of artistic creation as a means of combating the ravages of time. In a ringing short article he endorsed H. L. Mencken's view that work is the only cure for living. He wrote: "I am harrier in the race which I have been running for more than forty-six years—on the thought that the race would be irrevocably ended. And I do not want that race to end. I do not want it to end until I have completed my life work of writing. . . . The work of an artist, or a thinker, is an answer to death. . . . One of the personal motivations of an artist, perhaps the supreme vanity, is to speak beyond the grave. It is not simply the wish but the determination to express thoughts that death cannot encompass or obliterate. . . . Work does make one free, free for a while. . . . We might ask for more, and we might expect more, but we will not get more.[2] Like a Walt Whitman stripped of his idealistic pantheism but containing multitudes pressing from within for release, for five decades Farrell has been keenly aware of the intimate relation between creative expression and man's companions, death and the thought of death. Ironically, this consciousness has nourished a youthful greediness for life apparent in his fiction.

Farrell's reference to the artist's supreme vanity is of interest. It points up his potent ego, his abiding assertion of self as an independent creative force to be sustained at all cost. The poem "What Makes Jimmy Run?" reminds me of Stephen Crane's poem that goes:

> A man said to the universe:
> "Sir, I exist!"
> "However," replied the universe,
> "The fact has not created in me
> A sense of obligation."

Both poems present a lone, striving man confronting an invincible antagonist. Crane's cocky speaker is static, or, as in another poem, earnestly tries to reach an illusory horizon. Farrell's man, knowing full well the outcome of his race, still runs doggedly. The ego that supports Farrell's runner in such a losing contest is indeed formidable. It gave Farrell his staying-power as an artist, and it lies behind his activism. With reference to a line from Yeats, Farrell has written: "I, too, spit into the face of time even though I am aware that . . . time slowly transfigures me just as it transfigures all of us."[3]

If you leafed through the University of Chicago student newspaper, the *Maroon,* for the summer of 1929, you would find a brash, humorous piece by Farrell called "Me Incorporated." There he offered to sell stock in himself to make "Me Incorporated" a truly solvent concern, its purpose being to create art. Undergraduate Farrell wrote: "At present [Me Incorporated] is badly saddled with debt, and handicapped from the production of superior products by a shortage of its gin supply. Similarly, it finds it essential to move to New York temporarily, where it is to confer with a prospective publisher on its first book; and it is without resources. Then too, it needs some clothes in order that it can present an appearance attractive enough to get women, who will furnish it with enough sex to further its artistic production."[4] Farrell's article spoofs Bohemianism at the University of Chicago in the 1920s, but also it was written about the time its author began to pile up the manuscript that became *Studs Lonigan.* That sustained effort was an astonishing assertion of self-faith made before he had proved himself. It was the expression of an ego, we may feel, whose intangible assets were indeed great and rapidly becoming mature enough to be figuratively incorporated as early as 1929. The fiction which that ego was to create would painstakingly chronicle the growth of the successful self, counterpointed against Studs Lonigan's self-destruction.

III

Farrell's poem "What Makes Jimmy Run?" is a kind of shorthand for the author's naturalistic view of existence, a view implying his compassionate and purposeful humanism. Time transfigures all of us and leads to death. Therefore, Farrell has written, "There is no security in an insecure world. There is no final home on a planet where we are homeless children. In different ways, we find a sense of security, of permanence, or of home—for a while. To me, impermanence renders everything good and beautiful all the more rare. It stimulates my ambition and it strengthens the stoicism which is at the root of my outlook about experience."[5]

In a more technically philosophic sense, Farrell has defined his naturalism as the doctrine that "whatever happens in this world must ultimately be explainable in terms of events in this world. I assume or believe," he continues, "that all events are explainable in terms of natural origins rather than of extranatural or supernatural origins."[6] But some occurrences are the consequences of man's will, as real a force to Farrell as events which, willy-nilly, simply happen to us. However, he wrote, "I do not . . . look on free will as an inherent attribute of man; rather, I believe that free will is an achievement of men, gained individually and collectively, through knowledge and the acquisition of control, both over nature and over self."[7]

This view of existence and of the degree of man's control over his destiny is articulated in Farrell's 1961 novel *Boarding House Blues*. There the autobiographical character Danny O'Neill, keenly aware of death's inevitability, is shown on Chicago's north side early in 1930. He looks at people walking by on Michigan Avenue and reflects: "They were all men and women and kids, going somewhere, going many places, full of dreams as important to them as his own dreams were to him. Each one was a bundle, a nexus, a collection, an inner organization of pain and sorrow and hopes and dreams; each one of them carried a world of memories; each one was living out" a life, just as he was. And every man's "life is blown by a wind called destiny, and that wind is controlled by the mind as much as by circumstances."[8]

IV

In that last sentence lies the essence of Farrell's tough-minded realistic view of how the self is formed. Any man's destiny is a wind controlled by the mind as much as by circumstances. When

Farrell began to write *Studs Lonigan* he had read widely in the American pragmatists, especially in John Dewey's works. Dewey, George Herbert Mead, William James, and C. Judson Herrick helped Farrell arrive at his dynamic concept of human character. They helped him to understand the interaction between social groups and the individual, an interaction that structures the self and shapes society. They gave him his basic concept of human freedom and human slavery. Probably more than any other group of thinkers, they gave Farrell's naturalism its distinctive stamp. For his great theme was the making of Americans, a theme he dramatized with vivid particularity in depicting the separate but interlocking destinies of many selves, for better or for worse.

Also when Farrell began to write *Studs Lonigan,* he had witnessed the shame of wasted lives in Chicago. He had a sense of his own potential as an artist; but despite his formidable ego and the intellectual tools he had acquired at the University of Chicago, he had no certainty of success. His thoughts kept turning to his own past—often a miserable, humiliating past—as a subject for his writing. Like Danny O'Neill in *Boarding House Blues,* he wanted above all else "to find in himself some combination of words and ideas that would forever put to rest all that would not rest within him."[9]

What would not rest within him was not only the indignation and anger aroused by a past that he had to purge from his memory. Nor was the inner restlessness only the desire to bring about a social order that would favor the humane and the aesthetic rather than the materialistic and the acquisitive. It *was* these, but also it was the haunting awareness of the mystery of all human destinies, including the as yet undetermined direction of his own future.

All these considerations help to explain what made Jimmy run.

V

How far has Jimmy run? Not very far, say many critics. Stalinist spokesmen of the 1930s, New Humanists, censors and moralists, Catholic and Christian apologists, and academics of various persuasions have condemned Farrell in superlatives. One viewpoint, still heard forty years after *Studs Lonigan,* sees only destruction, decay, determinism, and death in Farrell's fiction. Thus Nathan Scott argued that because Farrell's novels lack myth they reinforce the faceless hostility of the world. Mike Gold called his novels *merdre*—shit. Alfred Kazin contended that Farrell was motivated by "grimy revenge" and hacked "his people to bits, stamping on them, scaling dead flesh."[10] Mark Schorer stated that Farrell's writing exhibits no technique whatsoever, so that "really, the thing is dead."[11] Leslie Fiedler, arguing that literary naturalism implies "a rigid philosophical determinism, which finds the individual insignificant or powerless . . . and therefore not responsible morally," called for the "ritual slaughter"[12] of the naturalist Farrell. Critics of a temperament less bloodthirsty have instructed Farrell how to write and what to write about. Farrell noted in 1961: "I began writing my own way, and I shall go on doing it. This is my first and last word on the subject."[13] Farrell is now seventy-two years of age, he has published forty-nine books, and he has others on the way.

Elsewhere, I have given my opinion that Farrell has gone very far indeed. His scope is impressive—journalist, essayist, social and literary critic, poet, short story writer, and novelist. With integrity he has explored a representative segment of middle American experience, with greatest distinction in *Studs Lonigan* and in the O'Neill-O'Flaherty pentalogy. His fictional world is remarkable for its authenticity, its singleness of vision, its fidelity to the development of a unifying theme, and the number of major characters who come fully alive. I agree with Blanche Gelfant[14] that Farrell's fiction is ultimately modern because it returns us to an examination of the world we live in. His writing speaks to all who struggle, for it dramatizes the impasses and the possibilities of American democracy. It demonstrates in detail not only the process of self-destruction but also the individual's search for self-definition and his achievement of self-autonomy through education, art, and action.

Farrell's fiction therefore has a prominent place within a distinctively American tradition of art and thought. According to the historian Frederick Jackson Turner, the interaction of the primitive and the civilized on the frontier made American social development a fluid process of perennial rebirth, whose chief outcome lay in the psychological and intellectual changes brought about in the new product that resulted—the changing American character. Like John Dewey, Turner thought of the self as being plastic and subject to creative development: the American was capable of transcending past circumstances and achieving a new identity.

As Henry Nash Smith recently has shown, James Fenimore Cooper's Natty Bumppo represents such a self-transcendence in the course of his development. As one example of this transcendence, Smith has written, Natty's skill in trailing becomes "an emblem of the response of man's mind to challenges from a new environment. It escapes all traditional categories and involves a harmony of senses, imagination, and reason" typifying "a release of the mind from predetermined patterns and constraints."[15] Bumppo uses his talent to solve problems arising from new sets of circumstances on or beyond the frontier. Then too, in a more general sense, as a mature woodsman he is a unique fusion of qualities derived from the cultures of both Indians and white men.

Look ahead several decades from the time of the Leatherstocking Tales to Mark Twain's *Roughing It*. The semi-autobiographical hero of that comic epic, the young man who makes the trip west, also undergoes a change that amounts to a transcendence of his past self. Former habits, preconceptions, and myths are brought to the test of experience and are abandoned or modified. Values never before questioned prove to be inadequate. The tenderfoot, fresh from a sheltered existence and a restricted environment, enters a fluid, open society. He comes up against new conditions, a new "sense of the other,"[16] as George H. Mead expressed it. He adapts, and the tenderfoot becomes the oldtimer and eventually a professional writer. Like Natty Bumppo, he personifies a novel synthesis of values, beliefs, and skills on *his* frontier. Mark Twain's Huck Finn undergoes another, more famous self-transcendence.

Stripped to its bare essentials, the story Farrell tells is much the same. His realism, however, is shaped by the intellectual climate of his times, and his young men never escape the modern urban environment. As for Studs, he pioneers on no frontier. Farrell once called him "the aftermath in dream of the frontier days."[17]   In his actions and in his dreams of the past, Studs perpetuates a barbaric, outmoded rugged individualism.   To use John Dewey's phrase, he strives to preserve a "cake of custom"[18] which will not sustain his own survival.   Like Studs, Danny O'Neill and Bernard Carr experience social tensions and moral conflicts. But that experience teaches them how to break with the past and to weave new patterns of feeling and thought.   Unlike Natty Bumppo or Mark Twain's young man in *Roughing It*, Bernard goes East, not West.   But his frontier is not essentially geographical, it is cultural and intellectual.   He is confronted not by a wilderness or by empty space, but by the harsh realities of a dense capitalist economy in depression and by the dogmatism of the Stalinists. Yet like Turner's pioneer, after meeting his new environment on its own terms and becoming partially assimilated to it, he emerges as an integrated self who goes his own way—a new product.   Both Danny and Bernard confirm Frederick Jackson Turner's insight that American experience offers genuine opportunity for innovation and creativity through self-transcendence.

*   *   *

"Jesus, we sure get paper on the floor here, don't we?" Jim said, seeing the paper stacked and piled under the dining-room table as he came into the room, wearing his old work clothes.

"Well, Jim, I always think this.   When the children are playing, I think to myself that if they got their health, it's good, and the paper they throw on the floor don't hurt the floor, not this floor full of slivers.   You couldn't hurt a floor in this dump," Lizz said, standing in the door.

"The floor's sometimes so covered with papers that we can't even see it," Jim said.

"Our Lord was born in a stable.   It isn't what the outside looks like.   It's what the inside looks like.   If your soul is clean, that counts more than if your house is.   Many there are in the world with clean houses and dirty souls.   And this morning, the souls in this house are clean.   This morning, everyone who's old enough to be in my house received the Body and Blood of our Blessed Lord," Lizz said, her voice rising in pride as she drew to the end of her declamation.

"Well, it isn't necessary to have a dirty house in order to

have a clean soul," Jim said.

"The children are playing in the yard now. I'm going to give them all a bath," Lizz said.

"Denny and Bob still sulking because of the whipping they got?"

"Can't you hear them yelling like wild Indians?" Lizz said.

"I didn't want to whip Denny. But after tanning his brother it wouldn't have been fair. By the time he came home from mass, I wasn't so sore as I was when I found the glue on the chair. But mind me, Lizz, if they ever pull a stunt like that again, God help them! God help them! I'm going to bring them up right, by God, if I have to put the strap to them every damn day of the year. Spare the rod and spoil the child? Not Jim O'Neill," Jim said.

Jim began sweeping the carpet.

"Mercy, the dust!" Lizz exclaimed.

"It's got to be raised a little, Lizz, if we want to get rid of it," Jim said.

"If those people of mine were any good and had any kindness in their bones, they'd hire a nigger to help me out, me with all these little ones," Lizz said.

"Lizz, there's nobody to rely on in this world but one's self. Forget the damn O'Flahertys for this Sunday at least. Let's have a happy Sunday with our family without any intrusion of the O'Flahertys. We nearly spoiled it once already this morning, and let's not go doin' it again," Jim said.

"I didn't spoil it," said Lizz.

"I know it," Jim said cursorily, still sweeping.

"I'm heating kettles of water for the children's bath," Lizz said, turning back into the kitchen.

Jim worked on, sweeping the dust into a corner, his nostrils irritated by it. He bent down and pulled papers from under the table, stacks of them torn and cut up, and dropped them into a wooden box he was using for waste. He thought that if the kids didn't tear up every newspaper he brought home, they could be saved and sold. Every little penny counted in this house, particularly when there was another mouth to come. He found an old pair of his suspenders in the papers, and held them up. He smiled. Things in this house were liable to be any place. And what was there that a regiment of kids couldn't get into? All kids were pretty much the same when they were young ones. They got into anything and everything. That was kids. But damn it, there was one thing they wouldn't do in his house. They wouldn't make a fool out of their father. They weren't going to play Katzenjammer kids on him. He swept the dust and dirt from under the table, thinking to himself that he'd bet even fellows like Al O'Flaherty and Dinny Gorman had been like other kids in their own days. Sure, they were. He swept under the table again. He moved the couch from the wall, and in doing it he saw the many punctures from BB's. What kids couldn't think of to do! Well, as long as they did no harm, he didn't care, and as long as they didn't do dirty things to themselves, what the hell! A few BB's shot into the wall of an old shack like this. Funny, he was calling this cottage an old shack already. When he'd found it and moved here from La Salle Street, he didn't call it an old shack. Well, it was an improvement over that other place. It was the best place they had been able to live in yet. But there were degrees in shacks and dumps as there were in everything in this world. And there sure were degrees of improvement ahead for the O'Neills. Would he ever be able to give his family a decent living, and his kids a chance to get ahead in life?

The dust almost choked him as he swept it from under the couch. Finishing his sweeping, he brushed the piles of dust into a large piece of cardboard which he used as a dustpan and dropped it on top of the newspapers in the wooden box. He put the sticks of furniture back in order, and looked at the room. It seemed a hundred per cent better, clean. Now, if the table were cleaned off and the trash on it put away, that'd be another improvement.

"Lizz," he called.

"Yes, Papa," Lizz replied.

"Bring me a damp cloth," he said.

He picked the trash off the table and dumped it on the couch. "Here, Jim," she said, coming in with a damp rag.

"I'm gonna fix this house up spick and span for once," he said, taking the rag from her.

"Oh, Jim, you work hard and you're a ruptured man. Don't do too much on your off day. I'll fix it up next week. You need your rest," she said.

"That's all right. I'll get it in tiptop shape this morning, cook *dinner, and then rest this afternoon," he said.*

He wiped off the oilcloth with the rag and then went over to the kitchen doorway.

"Oh, my, it's going to look nice," Lizz said as she noticed him glancing around the room.

"Now, if we can only keep this clean and a little bit in order," Jim said.

"We're going to," she said.

She went to him, embraced and kissed him.

"My rabbit, we're going to make a home that'll make us happy, and that's more than many with plenty in their pocketbooks can say," he said with feeling, holding her in his arms.

He kissed her again.

(Above excerpt is from section iii, Chapter 17 of Farrell's *No Star is Lost*, Vanguard Press edition, 1938. Reprinted by permission of the author.)

IRVING WALLACE: INDEPENDENT DRUMMER

RAY B. BROWNE

Irving Wallace the man and the writer is and always has been, to play on the title of one of his books, a square peg in a round society. He is a staunch individualist who though highly respecting society and holding out great hope for it has been intrigued by the quaint, the curious, the unusual. He is the type to appreciate the story told during World War II of Mrs. Franklin Roosevelt one night observing Winston Churchill, on one of his many visits, stalking up and down the hall of the White House dressed only in his smoking cigar. The story shows Churchill's unflinching individualism, his marching, in the words of Henry David Thoreau, one of Wallace's favorite writers, to a "different drummer." And Wallace steadfastly has marched in his own way and to his own rhythm. This trait in his personality accounts partially for his great appeal to the average reader.

The titles of many of Wallace's books reveal his bent: *The Fabulous Originals, The Scandalous Ladies, The Square Pegs, The Nympho and Other Maniacs.* And to a certain extent this interest is exemplified in all his other books, for they search out and develop the peculiar, unexplored, unexploited aspects of the human being or of society. At his best he has been remarkably farsighted. In *The Prize* (1960), for example, he pictured two doctors developing a serum that neutralized the body's rejection of a foreign organ being introduced into it. Six years later it was

*This essay in slightly different form appeared first in John Leverence, *Irving Wallace: A Writer's Profile* (Bowling Green, Ohio: Popular Press, 1974), pp. 431-42.

revealed that such experiments were underway, and the next year Dr. Christian Bernard succeeded in his first heart transplant.

Wallace early displayed and began to develop this interest in the unusual. As a high school student and writer for his Kenosha, Wisconsin, high school paper, the *Kenews,* he concentrated on the extraordinary. His first venture into commercial writing had to do with informing the public about the real location where Wild Bill Cody was buried. Wallace's first original story for the screen was about John Hix, a collector of odd facts. To a large extent the John Hixes in life have dominated Wallace's interest.

Another obvious characteristic of Wallace's writing is his great interest in accumulating and telling facts whether they are always relevant or not. This trait undoubtedly accounts for much of his appeal to the general public. To read one of Wallace's books is to peruse the shelves of a major library, to handle and glean facts from hundreds of books, and to talk to dozens of experts in the field being discussed. Wallace likes to repeat the facts and to give the anecdotes, even if he feels that he might be telling some of his readers more than they want to know.

Wallace's love of facts for their own sake, his desire to accumulate them, has been strengthened by his careful cataloguing and filing of them. Malvin Wald, a writer who knew and worked with Wallace when he first came to Hollywood, recalls that even then Wallace had his detailed filing system, and he, Wald, knew that eventually Wallace was going to succeed. He was simply too meticulous to fail. This method of working allows Wallace to document and make viable his philosophy. He is a humanist, a political liberal, who has always fought for the right to prove that "life is worth living, worth fighting for, worth defending against the forces of death."

This philosophy also undoubtedly accounts at least in part for Wallace's style of writing. Coming from a poor background, a fact that he has never forgotten, and never having graduated from college, through the years he has been determined to prove that he knows a great deal and can write his knowledge very well. This urge to transmit facts—to improve society—has always dominated his style. In his eyes the writer has a responsibility beyond his art. "It was because I believed in the responsibility of the writer to his art as much as I believed that he had other responsibilities beyond writing, it was because of this ambivalent feeling toward my work, that I determined that six days a week were enough to give of myself to avoid a debtor's prison. The seventh day of the week, I felt, belonged to me." He was especially pleased with his novel *The Man* because he felt it "affects the reader for the better, improves him, gives him more love and understanding of his fellows."

In his writing Wallace has never been slovenly no matter how great the royalties he has received, or out merely to make money. On the contrary, he has generally insisted on following his own Dream and writing in his own style. Even when he was penniless and skirting disaster he still determined to write his own way. As he said, he would whore around and write six days a week to live, but never on Sunday. That day he reserved for satisfying himself.

Part of his Dream has always been to learn and to teach. Wallace's reading and scholarship are staggering and shame many of his academic critics. He always has a paid researcher working for him, and often she will have many aids helping her. He will not write on any subject until he has learned everything he can about it, until he has lived with the experts in the field, and knows precisely that his resulting book cannot be faulted for its facts by any expert in the field.

Ignorance of a subject, if it appealed to him, has never been a deterrent to his accepting the challenge of a subject that he liked. He has set about informing himself, making himself into an expert. When he began writing *The Prize,* for example, his knowledge of the fields in which the Nobel prizes were awarded was better than average, but not precise enough for him to write about them with any expertise. He therefore set about informing himself. The result was that even experts praised him for his knowledge of fields that he should know little about.

Wallace once talked with Clifford Irving, long before he became notorious for his faked autobiography of Howard Hughes, who was complaining that he wanted to write a novel about lawyers but knew nothing about them or their profession. Char-acteristically, Wallace told him that all he had to do was to meet and talk with lawyers—live with them for a while—until he learned their business. Research, to Wallace, provides the answer to all questions—reading the printed word, talking with people, learning about new ways of life.

Naturally, then, when he was researching *The Prize* over a fourteen-year period, he sought out the recipients of the Nobel Prize—Albert Einstein, Pearl Buck and others—and asked them questions that would allow him to write on the subject knowledgeably. Wallace's files are always active and his memory retentive and responsive. If he ever learns anything it is subject to conscious or unconscious recall. His fiction, he says, demands "every resource of my imagination, my passions, my feelings," his nonfiction requires his "mind and intellect to do it well."

It is common knowledge that there is no single type of "popular writer." There are dozens of types that appeal to the vast body of persons known as the "popular reader." As a "popular writer" Wallace's intentions, like many others in his business, have been misunderstood. Because he does not write formulaic fiction (such as detective fiction, science fiction, the Western, or the like) he is not easily classified, and not being classifiable he is not easily pigeonholed. Wallace refuses to produce the same kind of story over and over, to write by formula. He gave up this kind of writing because he found that it wearied and restricted him even though he knew there is safety in formula fiction. As long as a popular writer sticks to his type he may be judged good. But once he tries to branch out or break through into something else he is severely criticized and is urged to get back into the groove he has worn for himself. The criticism leveled against Ross Macdonald for his latest book, *Sleeping Beauty,* is an excellent case in point. Macdonald has been told that he is a superb writer of detective fiction but should not try to write anything else.

Like Mark Twain before him, Wallace has written for the masses, for the millions. He knows, or thinks he knows, what appeals to them, and tries to reach that quality, because he feels, like W. Somerset Maugham whom he likes to quote, that a book is incomplete until it has a reader and the more readers the better. But he determines to be the cutting rather than the dragging edge of change, and will not—in fact cannot—sacrifice his independence of mind and action to coddle and cater to public demands that he does not agree with. Fortunately he does not have to.

A good example of Wallace's independence is found in the way he insists on structuring his novels. His plots are extraordinarily complicated and complex. Beginning with a problem, as Wallace sees it, they develop through conflict and drama, which he loves, in the characters. "Every human face has two profiles," Wallace says. "As a novelist, it is my duty to show not one but both." Wallace's interest is "in people and the hidden things in their lives," he once said in an interview for the New York *Herald-Tribune.* "My instinct is to take what's never been shown on the surface and to bring it to the surface. That's what makes a novel. . . ."

In development, Wallace's novels start from a large and ranging base. Then they grow pyramidally, gradually concentrating the plot and shedding sub-plots and details as they rise until eventually the top is reached and the problem is solved. These plots are rich and complex, or they are overly complicated and complex, depending on the reader's point of view. But Wallace, like John Barth, Truman Capote, Gore Vidal, Norman Mailer, Irving Stone, and dozens of other contemporary writers, must have room and time to develop his novels in considerable detail to get across his message.

Once this message has been developed, however, after the puzzle has been solved, Wallace seems to lose most of his interest in the book. He begins with a situation which seems to say, "What if . . .?" and goes on from there. "What if a Black man, through the force of events, suddenly became President of the United States?" "What would happen if suddenly a new portion of the Bible were discovered—how would the world, including religious leaders, be affected?" Wallace is fascinated by such possibilities, and although he is interested in the people who would be involved in such events, and although he realizes that characters make novels alive and memorable, he is actually mostly gripped by the themes themselves. Little wonder then that after the questions and answers have been demonstrated and worked out, the author rushes to close the book, apparently content to erase the characters once they have illustrated his point.

In *The Sins of Philip Fleming,* for example, Fleming, the protagonist, has been playing around with other women and has very nearly destroyed his writing ability and chance for a big job with a Hollywood producer. But he comes to his senses and returns to his wife, who understands and is waiting for him. In the final scene, at home with his wife to stay, he pulls back from her. " 'I'm hungry,' he said. 'Whip me up a couple of eggs. I've got a lot to tell you.' She started into the kitchen, and after a moment, he followed her." End of book. At the conclusion of *The Man*, Douglass Dilman has just become the first Black President of the United States and is assuming his duties the first day. Wallace concludes the book: ". . . Dilman lingered outside briefly . . . and then, feeling assured and purposeful, feeling good, he entered his Oval Office to begin the day's work."

Such endings have rightly been called fairy-tale, "They-lived-happily-ever-after," terminations. But Wallace has been explicit in answering the criticism leveled against them. An interview he gave on *The Prize* to the editor of *Information & Documents,* a French Cultural magazine, is revealing and should be given at some length (as quoted in *The Writing of One Novel,* pp. 185-6):

> "I've always been told I have a dangerous tendency toward happy endings, such as in *The Prize.* But I am at heart an extremely optimistic person. I am not childishly so. For it is also true that I have a balancing tendency to be cynical. I've seen so much that goes on behind people, their greed and hypocrisy. I am also dismayed by and curious about man's condition on earth—why he was put here, so uniquely, to have so much learning and passion poured into him, and then to be snuffed out of existence so quickly. Yet the very miracle of man's existence at all in the scheme of things excites me, and makes me believe that for every person's problem there must be a possible solution. I believe man is too complex and gifted a marvel not to be able to resolve his own or another's difficulties. . . .
>
> "As for coincidences, I believe life is filled with them. I feel it is nonsense to say 'we mustn't contrive a meeting, a situation which produces such and such because this is a convenience for the writer to make the story go ahead.'
>
> "A story creates its own truth. A novel does not have to represent real life, but one often has to go way beyond life to make it seem real."

Wallace assumes that after the problem raised in the novel has been settled, the world, which he does not see as having been really endangered, will rock on at about the same keel. Wallace's world is not as dark as those of many other writers—Mailer's or Capote's, for example. Like the British politician who said that one should never allow the threat of national calamity to interfere with a good night's sleep, Wallace can rest and awake to a world that he insists has some promise. Like William Faulkner in the speech he gave upon receiving the Nobel Prize in Literature, or Andrew Craig in his acceptance speech for the same award in *The Prize,* Wallace thinks the world will be safe because the individual, when developed into his full potential, is strong. Wallace believes that perhaps his best statement on the subject is Craig's speech, and readers of the novel will remember that it does have a fine ring:

> "This is the foremost of earthly honors that you have offered me," he found himself saying aloud. "I am moved and grateful beyond inadequate words. But I believe Alfred Nobel would have understood what I will say next. It is this—that all man's honors to man are small beside the greatest prize to which he may and must aspire—the finding of his soul, his spirit, his divine strength and worth—the knowledge that he can and must live in freedom and dignity—the final realization that life is not a daily dying, not a pointless end, not an ashes-to-ashes and dust-to-dust, but a soaring and blinding gift snatched from eternity. The ultimate prize is to know that each new day's challenge is meaningful and offered for use, that it must be taken to the bosom, and it must be used—and to know this, to understand this, is the one prize worthy as man's goal and all mankind's summit."

Wallace, unlike many other writers, reads his reviewers with interest.´ Perhaps he is unduly sensitive; maybe he reads the reviews because he wants to keep abreast of other attitudes. Anyway, he is quite aware of the obvious contradiction in this democratic America, where critics reviewing for the mass magazines usually impose elite standards that are essentially alien. All too frequently the American critic is so ashamed of the culture he lives in and so intent on improving it that he refuses to criticize a work on its own grounds, for its medium and for its audience. As Wallace commented on the subject to the reporter of *Politika,* the Belgrade magazine, he sounded almost as bitter as Mark Twain might have been:

> In America, it seems to me, there is a wide schism
> between what is wanted and loved by the professional
> reviewers and critics, and what is wanted and loved by the
> broad reading public. The critics, not all but the great
> majority, have shown a tendency to prefer precious writing,
> concave writing. The broad reading public, which for the
> most part ignores the critics, seems to prefer direct writing,
> plain writing, exciting writing, topical writing (that is,
> characters who bear some relationship to the lives of the
> readers).

Taken on balance, Wallace obviously has not suffered from
the critics of his published works. People from all walks of life
read and enjoy them. For example, the audience of *The Prize*
included among its millions of readers the typical housewife from
Wauseon, Ohio, the secretary on the University of Michigan
campus, the Nobel Prize-winning chemist H. C. Urey, who loved
it, and Martin Luther King. With each book, Wallace's reading
public, in this country and abroad, continues to grow.

Perhaps it may seem absurd to say that a writer like Wallace
is easily embarrassed by sex and likes to play it down. But the
statement must stand. Wallace is the first to admit that sex sells
books and that he wants to sell his works. But he also insists that
sex is life and that he, if he would be true to life, must demonstrate that sex is a dominant force. Freud, whom Wallace admires,
and the *Kinsey Report* have demonstrated, as have far more
sensational writers of the past few years, that sex is a vital part of
our daily lives. Further, as everybody is aware, and the Supreme
Court has recently ruled, there are the truthful though frank
writings about sex and there are the prurient exploitations of it.

Wallace correctly feels that he falls into the former category.
He is as explicit as he needs to be to demonstrate his point. But
he is never salacious. And searchers for the pornographic need
not look in his books. If his own restraints were not sufficient,
there is always his wife, Sylvia, whom Wallace characterizes as
"sharp, sensitive, perceptive, ruthless," who somewhat in the
manner supposedly played years ago by Olivia Clemens, Mark
Twain's wife, inhibits and redirects Irving's prose if it tends to get
racy.

Wallace grew up in a family that revered the old masters—Tolstoi, Dostoevski, Balzac. Throughout life he has read everything he could get his hands on. He dedicated *The Seven Minutes* to the authors John Cleland, D. H. Lawrence and James Joyce, the last two among literature's most respected craftsmen. Using such writers as models, he has worked as hard as any other dedicated writer to perfect his style, to choose precisely the word and phrase he wants. As he said in the Leverence biography, "The only way to become a writer is to write!" On *The Prize,* as he catalogued in the book *How To Write One Book,* he wrote 3,101 hours in a total of 582 days, or an average of more than five hours out of every twenty-four.

As a result of his dedication to the craft, through the years Wallace has developed an effective style. It is direct, carefully chosen and clear, never tortured and egoistic, as is the case with other contemporary writers. If at times it appears wordy, this is because of Wallace's insistence on getting the message across regardless of the method needed.

Wallace, like many others in this country and abroad, is a writer working in a genre and in a medium that need to be recognized for what they are, what they try to do, and not condemned for what they are not and do not intend to be. That is, Wallace is a "popular" writer, is proud to be one, and does not want to be among the "elite." Actually the differences between the two are more apparent than real—are shadings on a long continuum. But these differences have long generated much hard feeling.

The controversy goes back at least to the Classics. To Plato the non-elite people were "oxen," and their arts were dung. Aristotle, however, recognized that, "There is nothing in the intellect that is not first in the senses"—therefore all levels of life—and art—are important. Terence, the second-century B.C. writer of comedies, took all of life as his domain: "I am a human being; therefore nothing human repels me."

The real break between "elite" and "popular" art came, however, in the eighteenth century, with the rise of the Industrial Revolution, when wealth and poverty more sharply divided people, and when rapid printing presses developed a medium for mass communication. The controversy raged through the nineteenth and the first half of the twentieth century.

But now under the irresistible impact of the mass media and a liberalized new thinking, the whole concept of what constitutes "elite" and "popular"—"highbrow" and "lowbrow"—arts has been challenged. Despite the holding action of some influential critics the walls are tumbling down. Some critics have recognized reality all along. Howard Mumford Jones, one of America's most distinguished observers, rightly stated that to foreigners all of America's culture is "popular."

Abraham Kaplan used to argue that the popular arts should be considered as newly born artifacts that were growing toward maturity in a "higher" form. But such arguments are fast losing any influence. Susan Sontag, one of America's most perceptive critics, insists that there is a new attitude altogether creeping into our consideration of the so-called "popular" arts. These arts are a new dimension, having nothing to do with the presumed "higher" arts, and must be judged on their own merits and standards. "One cheats himself, as a human being," she says in *Against Interpretation,* "if one has respect only for the style of high culture."

Perhaps the most revealing, the most honest, statement of this kind was made by Ross Macdonald, the creator of the Lew Archer series of detective fiction. Macdonald, proud to be a popular writer, insists: "We learn to see reality through the popular arts we create and patronize. That's what they're for. That's why we love them."

Critics more and more are recognizing their proper function and are devoting their time and effort to the proper study of their proper subject. Robert Kirsch, book review editor for the Los Angeles *Times* and one of the more perceptive of the newspaper reviewers, was particularly acute in commenting on *The Prize* (as quoted in *The Writing of One Novel,* p. 58): "Irving Wallace is, in my opinion, a better writer than, say, Sinclair Lewis, and in time may emerge as a writer of real importance on the American scene. . . . In order to understand why these writers have found and kept a large audience, one has to examine what people want from a novel and what they have always wanted. It is, basically, entertainment." Entertainment—that is, telling a good story— was originally and always has been the primary purpose of the novelist, though many critics and academics tend to forget or to play down this perfectly honorable object. In so doing they try to frustrate human nature and so succeed in falsifying it.

Since *The Prize* Wallace has continued to explore new areas of investigation and to provide even more entertainment. *The Three Sirens,* his next book, was generally felt to be more readable than *The Prize,* as it surely is. *The Man,* Wallace's next work, the one he feels is his best, contained both readability and importance of topic; it is one of my favorites. In *The Plot,* his next book but one, Wallace expanded from a national to an international theme, yet did not succeed, in my estimation, in creating a more powerful book than *The Man.* In his next novel, *The Seven Minutes,* Wallace turned to a kind of interior monologue concerned with the problem of pornography and censorship. Here as elsewhere his research was exhaustive; the result is a stirring work with great impact. *The Nympho and Other Maniacs,* Wallace's next book, was in many ways a return to the author's interest in quaint and unusual persons, this time women. Although it is extremely well written and interesting, it fails to have the impact of his more conventional, larger, novels.

After these formidable achievements, Wallace produced his two finest books to date, *The Word* (1972) and *The Fan Club* (1974). In the former he was probing the very foundation of human nature—pondering the question of what would be the way society would respond if a new Gospel were discovered. Into the answer Wallace poured all his research, his talks with noted Biblical scholars, and his observations on mankind in general. The result is a powerful book which forces upon the reader the suspension of disbelief. Although the reader knows that no such Gospel has been discovered, he reads on, led by the immense amount of information presented and gripped by the power of the subject and the author's presentation. At the end, despite Wallace's apparent sunny attitude toward life in general and tendency to slight endings, a pessimistic conclusion consciously or unconsciously intrudes. In Wallace's view nothing is above man's exploitative nature; even the Word of God must be manipulated for man's personal gain.

The Fan Club (1974) was Wallace's most misunderstood book. It developed from a chance conversation Wallace overheard among a group of trainmen who fantasized about the ecstasy of spending a night with Elizabeth Taylor. Wallace asked himself his usual question and tried to work out the answer: "What might happen if a group of men tried to make this fantasy into reality?"

As Wallace developed the plot, four men decide to kidnap a Marilyn Monroe-type movie sex symbol named Sharon Fields, who, they think, once she gets to know the men will actually fall in love with them and will happily fulfill all their sexual desires. The four men represent a cross-section of society: Howard Yost is a middle-aged insurance salesman; Leo Brunner is an old accountant; Kyle Shively is a garage mechanic who thinks that sexually he is God's gift to women; and Adam Malone, an idealistic unsuccessful writer. After much plotting the four kidnap Sharon, hide her in the hills above Los Angeles, and because she will not respond to their declarations of love, rape her continually. At first Sharon is outraged and fights back. But she is smarter than the men attacking her, and soon decides to use their natural competitive spirit and envy to her advantage. She starts each to distrusting the other three, eventually bringing such discord that they turn on one another and, with the assistance of the Los Angeles Police Department, all are destroyed but Adam Malone, the writer. He has been the most sensitive of the whole gang all along, has in his way loved Sharon, and it is clear that Wallace has put the man in the book to voice the author's conclusions about the whole situation. The four men have been driven to their insane act by the world around them. Frustrated on every turn by the complicated and uncontrollable forces of life—poverty and deprivation—they engage their fantasies—moving into a never-never land where wildest dreams do come true. Adam Malone (who was in on the plot from the beginning and obviously named for a purpose) has seen his three companions degenerate into base drives and he himself has barely escaped the same fate. His three companions were killed. Sharon has spared Adam because she hopes that he might be salvaged. Wallace is undoubtedly a romantic. But he has seen too much of this world to be ingenuous. Here he unquestionably places his faith in human survival in woman. The four men—and men in general—are stupid. Sharon on the contrary—despite the fact that she has always been considered by the world as a fatuous sex-symbol unable to think and articulate anything that her press agents and directors do not tell her to say, triumphs. Here is Sharon Agonistes. The dedication of the novel is significant: "For all women and particularly one named Sylvia," his wife. And the conclusion is overwhelmingly clear. Adam returns to his apartment realizing that "The gold dust of fantasy could not be transmuted into the gold brick required by reality. It was too fragile, the stuff of dreams, and it evaporated and was no more." Yet once more inside his apartment, his Garden of Eden, which "looked good" and "cozy," Adam again cast aside common sense, "grateful to leave behind the painful, sick and violent world of reality and return once more to the euphoric and peaceful world of make-believe, where anything you want to happen happens, no more, no less, in that best of all possible worlds. After a good night's sleep, in which he forgets all his experience, he notes in some movie magazines the appearance of a new sex-symbol who is going to replace Sharon Fields. Immediately he wonders if he should "revive the Fan Club for her." And he finds himself "filled with excitement and purpose once more." And this time obviously he will be destroyed. Wallace's conclusion is uncharacteristically pointed and firm.

The book, as usual, received mixed reactions from newspapers and magazines. The Cleveland *Press* said that after the first half "the book gets going and we have the makings of a good story." The Associated Press called it "an ingenious plot." *Time* Magazine admitted "A reasonably good time might be had by all readers who like that sort of grisly fun. . . ." The Los Angeles *Times* called it "a tense, sensationally exciting, absorbing novel that should make all America members of Irving's fan club." The Philadelphia *Bulletin* called the plot "beautifully engineered" and concluded, "if you start you are almost sure to read it to the end, and you may well read certain passages twice."

Hostile critics, naturally, were not silent. *Newsday* called the book "prurient" and "corn pone," for example. Charges of "prurience" seemed to set the tone for most adverse criticism. The reaction to the sex, though somewhat anticipated by Wallace, his lawyer and publishers, was considerably more strident than expected. Many bookstores refused to sell the book because of its treatment of sex, though often the sellers had not read the book at all or had only scanned certain passages.

Such readings are superficial. The book uses sex, though not nearly as pruriently as many other books published the same year as *The Fan Club,* and uses it, though explicitly, for a larger purpose. It is unfortunate, therefore, when a serious critic, for one reason or another, misunderstands. Such a criticism was that of John Barkham: "For men it is a realization of the basic male fantasy—endless lovemaking with Venus herself. For women it is a callous exploitation of sexism with woman as simply a sex object." He ended his condemnation with the feeling that the novel "unabashedly treats [women] as sex objects all alike in the dark."

Few things could in fact be farther from the truth. The book undoubtedly reveals Wallace's true philosophy. Since truth, like beauty, is often in the eye of the beholder rather than the beheld, one wonders, to change the figure slightly, just how large and blinding the mote is in the eyes of some readers.

From the success of that novel Wallace turned to something as different as it could be. *The People's Almanac,* edited in conjunction with his son David Wallechinsky (his writing name) and growing from an idea that Mr. Wallechinsky had been working on for some two years, was an effort to do an almanac, one of the most popular kinds of book in America, as none other had been done before. Wallace's comments about the book reveal the range of his insatiable interests and his astonishing flexibility in writing books:

> I don't think a writer should be typecast. I think he should write whatever he wants to write if he feels like it. Some periods I like to dream up, invent story, and then I write fiction. Other periods I like to dig for facts and try to present them excitingly, and then I write nonfiction. I've always gone back and forth from fiction to nonfiction. I've published nine novels and seven nonfiction books— the *Almanac* is my eighth nonfiction. The fact that it proved to be a reference book was a wonderful change of pace for me. It required new disciplines. It was a lively change from purely imaginative writing. It was something fresh and new, and very exciting. Also a great educating experience.

If success can be measured in sales, then *The People's Almanac* is surely one of Wallace's triumphs. Reviewed sympathetically even in scholarly books, the volume has sold widely.

The R Document, published in the spring of 1976 just after *The People's Almanac,* is one of Wallace's hardest hitting novels. Not since *The Man* had Wallace addressed himself to a subject as nationally—or universally—important as he did in this latest work. Again he asks "What if . . . ?" Placing his novel prophetically in the future, he asks, "What if a Director of the FBI arrogated enough power from a duped public to be able to blackmail virtually everyone in the U. S. into passing a 35th amendment to the Constitution which would revoke the Bill of Rights?" Obviously Wallace's character is based on J. Edgar Hoover, who by now may be almost a stereotype of pernicious power. But Wallace's development is more living than stereotypical, and his concern is evident. In *The Man* Wallace had agonized over the presence in our society of cancerous bigotry and discrimination; in *The R Document,* like all thinking Americans, he joins in the general alarm against the usurpations of power by a government agency or individual. Though by now presumably we are all alert, Wallace in this book will bolster the caution of thousands of citizens.

Stylistically this novel is a reversal of Wallace's usual method in his recent works. Here he is not interested in sweeping backgrounds, nor in his usual gathering and presenting facts for their own sake. Instead this novel is stylistically terse, precise, direct and unrelenting—a *Billy Budd* to his usual *Moby Dicks.* The references to Melville are not gratuitous, for *The R Document* is unusually studded with literary and symbolic references. One of the main characters—who foils the villain's plot—is even named Ishmael.

The R Document is a timely book—an excellent addition to Bicentennial literature. But, in addition, it is a compelling novel in its own right, a powerful dramatization of Jefferson's caution that eternal vigilance is the price of liberty.

The books in Wallace's immediate future promise no lessening in variety and range. He is collaborating with his daughter, Amy, on *The Two,* a biography of the original Siamese twins, their wives and twenty-two children. And he is at work on another novel, called *The Pigeon Project.*

It is in the context of "popular" author—writer for the multitudes—that Wallace must be considered if he is to be judged fairly. Any writer who has sold 92 million copies of his books, who can expect to sell 2-3 million of any book he writes, must be doing something right. He is; Wallace is producing the kind of book that teaches and entertains—a hard combination to beat. To cavil and condemn him for doing this is foolish and beside the point. To criticize him for not writing other kinds of books is absurd. For what he attempts, he is one of the half dozen best writers working today.

While crafting his many works through the years, Wallace has marched to his own drummer as Thoreau did a hundred years ago. Wallace, in Thoreau's words, "steps to the music he hears, however measured or far away" or, perhaps better, Wallace creates his own music, a music that many people like. He is still the square peg in a round society. His four corners of independence have never been ground off: he has remained true to himself, to his way of life and philosophy, and beholden to no one. Those who lead lives of quiet desperation—as most of us do—have reason to thank him.

THE WINGS OF THE FALCON AND THE MALTESE DOVE

GEORGE GRELLA

In an essay on Henry James, James Thurber recounts a night in a "New York *boite de nuit et des arts* called Tony's," where Dashiell Hammett announced that "his writing had been influenced by Henry James's novel *The Wings of the Dove.*" Although confessing his inability to find "many feathers of *The Dove* in the claws of *The Falcon*," Thurber discovers a few useful parallels: a fabulous fortune at the center of both books, two designing women who lose their lovers, and a final renunciation scene. He concludes that "some strong young literary excavator may dig up other parallels." While those who know me may question the accuracy of those first two adjectives, I immodestly offer myself as the man to examine somewhat more closely the relationships between the two writers.

Hammett may seem the least likely writer to be influenced by the Master of the novel, and indeed the two seem to occupy no obvious common ground. The ace performer of the hard-boiled school surely doesn't derive his tight, terse style from the ornate convolutions of Henry James at the highest phase of his mandarin prose, in that stage of his career that earned him the title of James the Old Pretender. Aside from sentence structure and diction, however, there are some important matters of technique on which the two writers appear to agree. Perhaps more important, they share a similarity of subject and vision, a mutual sense of the evil possibilities in the world they portray and the characters with which they populate it. Though the idea may

108

shock some devotees of the Carr-Christie-Innes country house school of detective fiction, Dashiell Hammett is possibly the most Jamesian of all detective novelists.

The most obvious initial point of comparison between the two writers is their use of the image of the bird that broods so powerfully over their respective novels. In James the Dove of the title is Milly Theale, the doomed heiress who confers an ambiguous peace and absolution on the calculating lovers Kate Croy and Merton Densher. Milly sacrifices herself and achieves a kind of apotheosis—Kate Croy says, " 'she died for you then that you might understand her' " to Merton Densher—spreading her wings and bequeathing the gift of love. Hammett's bird, like James's, possesses certain religious connotations, but they are subverted by the greed and violence accompanying them. Although the falcon begins as a symbolic gift from a religious order to its patron, it becomes a symbol of the extents to which men will go to possess great wealth. A predatory creature, the falcon is the appropriate bird for a world which cannot know the peace and absolution of the Dove, and in which men prey on one another like beasts. The bird is a kind of reversed Holy Spirit, both evil symbol and fabulous object; the people of Hammett's novel will do anything to acquire the falcon and the falcon itself curses them into the inevitable process of doom and damnation. It precisely reverses the effect of James's bird: Milly Theale, as her name suggests, is the duckling who becomes a dove, while the fabulous bird of Malta metamorphoses into the cheap fake that has deluded its pursuers. One bird redeems a world, the other emphasizes its degradation. As if to underline his ironic parallel with James, Hammett has his bird delivered on *La Paloma*, the dove, whose captain dies from his contact with the fatal creature.

The images of the two powerful and symbolic birds lead to further affinities between the two writers. Both *The Wings of the Dove* and *The Maltese Falcon* deal with the subject of greed: the epigraph to both novels could be St. Paul's "*Radix malorum est cupiditas.*" The greed of Kate Croy and Merton Densher leads them to betray Milly Theale and each other, to cause her death and to destroy their own relationship. The greed of Brigid O'Shaughnessy, Casper Gutman, Joel Cairo and their cohorts creates an elaborate scheme of betrayal and deceit which draws in everyone they encounter, including Sam Spade. Brigid's apparent power over Spade and her obvious resourcefulness suggest her resemblance to Kate Croy; Spade's ostensible victimization resembles Merton Densher's. Both powerful and dominating women, Kate and Brigid manipulate the men around them to obtain the enormous wealth represented in the dove and the falcon. The greed that pervades *The Maltese Falcon* spreads over its world, driving Gutman, Cairo, Wilmer, and all the nameless pursuers of the bird before them, into any act that will guarantee the winning of the fabulous fortune.

Just as James sees, in most of his novels, the pernicious effects of money on even the worthiest individuals, so Hammett suggests that Spade can be duped and corrupted by the possibilities of great wealth. Spade can be seen, at least superficially, as the Merton Densher of the novel, or even—to take another example from James—as its Isabel Archer, the innocent caught up in a complicated, evil plot, victimized by the lies and falseness of everyone. Obviously, Spade turns out to be more than a match for the villains who seek to destroy him, but it takes him the entire length of the novel to make up his mind to do what finally seems the right thing. The world is so difficult and life so hard, that Spade, like any Jamesian hero or heroine, must be introduced to its problems by the process of betrayal and must decide for the right through the actions of sacrifice and suffering.

It is clear that both writers agree precisely in their definition of evil. Like Shakespeare, Hawthorne, Melville, and James, Dashiell Hammett appears to consider the violation and manipulation of selfhood the gravest human crime. To betray and exploit other human beings leads to destruction in almost all of James's novels; what makes Brigid perhaps the most evil character in *The Maltese Falcon*—worse than Cairo or Gutman—is her reflexive ability to manipulate anyone—Thursby, Jacobi, Archer, Spade himself—to attain the falcon. Her fate at the end is just: the falcon works its retribution through Spade's tortured resolve to turn her in. His most compelling reason, among the many he gives, is his refusal to "play the sap," to be exploited any further.

The characters and situations of *The Maltese Falcon,* even at times its onomastics, suggest again the Jamesian touch. The initial appearance of Brigid resembles the kind of situation that

James loves to create and then transform into endless possibilities. Miss Wonderly is the victim of the elegant Floyd Thursby—the names already are sounding like something out of a James novel— and desires the assistance of Samuel Spade and Miles Archer (who gets his first name from *The Turn of the Screw* and his last from *The Portrait of a Lady*).   As soon as the pact is made, the betrayals and metamorphoses begin: Miles dies violently, Thursby is shot, Miss Wonderly begins to metamorphose into Brigid O'Shaughnessy, who is somehow both innocent and wrong simultaneously, like any James heroine.   The wised-up Spade, though he tells Brigid that he knew she shot Miles all the time, begins to turn into the innocent hero (or heroine) of a James novel himself. With the advent of Joel Cairo—who is not only a homosexual but an International Jew—and Casper Gutman (curiously, his name derives from Caspar Goodwood of *The Portrait of a Lady*), Spade begins to seem the classic innocent American manipulated by the corrupt Europeans of any James novel—a Christopher Newman, an Isabel Archer, a Lambert Strether. Deceived and defeated at every turn, Spade is drugged, beaten, sent off on wild goose chases, and generally confused by the clever Europeans who work in league against him.

Spade saves himself from the destruction that somehow seems inevitable by remaining steadfast in his quest for the murderer of Miles Archer and in his desire to know what exactly the black bird means. Through bluff and pretense, he persuades his enemies that he knows as much as or more than they about the potentiality of evil (i.e., the Maltese Falcon); he demonstrates that he can be as coldblooded or manipulative as they when he discusses the need for a fall guy, a substitute victim for himself. Like Christopher Newman or Lambert Strether, he succumbs for a while to the dreadful powers of the Old World from which the falcon and its pursuers come, but triumphs through suffering and sacrifice over the Europeans. He asserts one of the most American of virtues in his litany to Brigid in their climactic scene—the loyalty to male comrades that transcends even the love of a woman. Even though, as Spade tells Brigid, " 'Miles was a louse,' " the detective has both a personal and professional obligation to track his killer down, to do what his world considers the right thing. Giving up the woman he loves for a noble ideal of conduct causes Spade considerable pain but insures his victory over the evil, European values with which he had been allied throughout the book. Like Isabel Archer rejecting Caspar Goodwood in *The Portrait of a Lady,* Spade recognizes that to be good he must suffer, that his fate must be renunciation accompanied by sorrow. The pain he endures is necessary: he has been chasing after strange gods, worshipping a graven image, and must pay the penalty of loss and regret in order to achieve even his partial redemption.

Among so many other themes, *The Maltese Falcon* employs a strongly Jamesian sense of renunciation. Thurber is the first to point out the superficial parallels between the two important Renunciation Scenes at the end of the two novels, suggesting that James handles his perhaps more delicately and skillfully. The two scenes may be alike in more profound ways than Thurber or others perceive. Kate Croy and Merton Densher find their relationship no longer possible on any terms after the death of Milly Theale, who has left Densher her fortune even after learning of his terrible duplicity. Densher now realizes the transforming powers of the Dove's wings and rejects both Kate and the wealth, choosing fidelity to Milly's memory, a faith in the redemption of the Dove. Kate ends the book with a terrible finality: " 'We shall never be again as we were!' " Spade, on the other hand, renounces the falcon and Brigid, but appears to be left in pretty much the same situation we found him in at the beginning. His fate, however, may in some ways be harsher than Densher's, who has at least the memory of Milly, who has shown him the transcendent possibilities of human love, to sustain him. Spade's renunciation, no matter how painful or noble, leaves him utterly alone. His faithful helper, Effie Perrine, recognizes the correctness of his action, but cannot accept what she sees as the human betrayal; she rejects him and wounds him terribly in the process:

> "Don't, please, don't touch me . . . I know—I know you're right. You're right. But don't touch me now—not now."

Spade is left, pale and shivering, waiting for Iva Archer to come in: one girl he loved is gone, another is repelled by his action, and the voracious woman he dislikes is about to smother him again. He is undoubtedly worse off and more alone than Densher; he must now live with his suffering, with nothing but his own resources to support him.

Integrally connected with the similarity of theme and subject in the two novelists is a shared interest in matters of technique. Hammett's novel demonstrates a careful attentiveness to the art of fiction worthy of the Master himself. *The Maltese Falcon* is a masterpiece of technical consistency, as bold and craftsmanlike a job as any of James's works. Its most striking triumph is its absolute fidelity to a fixed point of view, perhaps even more sternly and stringently adhered to than anywhere in James. We never see into anyone's mind at all, never are given even the least hint of the difference between what a character is saying or doing and what he is thinking; we are never treated to a lengthy consideration of the changes of mind, decisions and indecisions, causes and effects, internalized reactions, and so forth that James often proffers us in the reading of one of his novels. We know no more about any of the characters—including Sam Spade—than they know about each other. We must base our understanding of the people and events on the mere evidence of presentation, with no possibility of interpretation or assistance from the author. We see things from the point of view of Spade, we accompany him (and only him) everywhere, and our world and the world of the book is constricted to the narrow limit of his words and actions. The consistency is so well enforced that for all we know both the police and Iva may be entirely correct in their assumption that Spade killed Thursby: Spade is awakened at five minutes past two by the news of Archer's death and returns to his apartment at three-forty. We find out that Thursby was shot between the two times and, since we never see into Spade's mind and must guess at his thoughts and actions, we can believe with the others that Spade shot Thursby. The consistency and discretion of the authorial presence also limits the sense of that world—Spade can at least for a while be a murder suspect (he could even have killed Miles for all we know) in a world where nobody's actions are entirely clear or explicable. The difficulty and stringency of the narrative point of view make a Jamesian demand upon the reader and reinforce the harshness of Hammett's world.

Although the two novels resemble each other quite closely, there are, as we have seen, several points where the Hammett book seems to derive from other works of James. Ideally, a considerable study should be made of the entire corpus of Hammett, which would no doubt reveal further and more enlightening comparisons. There is a considerable amount of material drawn from James and from other authors in Hammett's novels and short stories. Next to James, for example, Hawthorne appears to be the most influential American writer for Hammett—the story of Flitcraft that Spade recounts to the uncomprehending Brigid, which seems to identify for so many critics the precarious nature of Spade's vocation, bears some significant relationship to Hawthorne's "Wakefield" and deserves further investigation. For the present, however, it should be sufficiently convincing to quote James's perceptive description of his work to see the pervasiveness of his influence on Hammett and the similarity of their vision: "I have the imagination of disaster," James wrote, "I see life as ferocious and sinister." The man who wrote that could very easily have written *The Maltese Falcon*.

JOHN DOS PASSOS AS CONSERVATIVE

DAVID SANDERS

"There's no place left in this world for a philosophical anarchist." ("Blackie Bowman Speaking," *Midcentury*)

John Dos Passos was a philosophical anarchist all his life and a conservative as well when he wrote *Midcentury* (1961). This novel, the last he would see published, expressed an idea that had appeared in most of his work: that individuals must contend forever with the gigantic systems they have invented for their self-government. Dos Passos's young ambulance drivers in *One Man's Initiation-1917* (1920) knew this as they vowed to fight the lies and the liars when they returned home after the war. The idea grew in *Three Soldiers* (1921), *Manhattan Transfer* (1925), and *U.S.A.* (1930, 1932, 1936), as Dos Passos described the union of big capital and big government during the war and their transformation into the dehumanizing big money of the nineteen-twenties. Dos Passos never ceased to believe in this idea. He became conservative the more he held to it because he came to believe that revolutions were not on the side of the individual, those of this century having created even larger and more oppressive systems than the regimes they had toppled.

What brought this home to him most dearly was the execution of his friend and translator, José Robles Pazos, by political security agents of the Spanish Republic in the first year of the Civil War. As Dos Passos understood the incident, his non-political friend had been killed because he was related to someone on the other side, a subversive because he was a displaced person. As Hemingway and others condemned him for putting friendship above anti-fascism, Dos Passos returned to the United States and

115

began a study of American history that should have surprised no one who had read *U.S.A.* carefully, especially the final sections of *The Big Money* where the "Camera Eye" poet (Dos Passos himself, of course) cries out that

> ". . . America our nation has been beaten by strangers who have turned our language inside out who have taken the clean words our fathers spoke and made them slimy and foul. . . ."[1]

Dos Passos wrote histories of the Constitutional period and the early American republic for the rest of his life, describing the "fathers" and the events in which they spoke the "clean words," and he continued to write novels about the passing twentieth century in which, he felt, that original chorus of self-government was becoming all but silenced. He never wrote a "Camera Eye" to explain this obsession with history, but all of his work after *U.S.A.* bears traces of the story that could follow the account of how a timid expatriate child grew up to write a novel which would characterize the America that had executed Sacco and Vanzetti. To discover this early American past was also to establish his own roots in America. No one could doubt this after reading his first history with its heartfelt title, *The Ground We Stand On* (1941).

This history is prophetic about Dos Passos's development as a conservative novelist. In the introductory essay, "The Uses of the Past," he tries to convey the urgency of everyone's studying the American past and then apologizes for having come to it so late himself. One must get back beneath one's cynicism and discover that there is some non-Marxist basis for future politics, Dos Passos insists. His answer is to define ground that free individuals (not too different from the Wobblies and the Spanish villagers of his earliest books) could stand on together, exercising self-government and mutual respect. He writes of Roger Williams founding New England towns that were "impregnated with the concept of the duties and liberties of every man alone," and then comes to what remains the commanding image of all his historical writing, Jefferson facing west from Monticello. Jefferson's facing west means less than his standing on his mountain, the learned continental traveller home to possess his land.

Dos Passos worked on this history at the same time as the novel, *Adventures of a Young Man* (1939), whose hero was shot by the Spanish republicans for being a counter-revolutionary. The few critics who read and condemned this book appeared to ignore the existence of *The Ground We Stand On,* and, chiefly for this reason, more has been written about Dos Passos as an anti-Communist than as a conservative. (Some reviewers noticed that he was still carrying that old grudge about Robles Pazos long after Franco had entered Madrid.) This is unfortunate because neither *Adventures of a Young Man* nor any other fiction that he has written about his disillusionment with the Communist revolution can stand comparison with such greater novels on this theme as *Bread and Wine* and *Man's Fate.* In *Adventures of a Young Man, Most Likely to Succeed,* and *The Great Days,* Dos Passos's characters complain about the party's subversions and fill pages with gloomy predictions about the advance of the Abominable Snowman of international Communism. In the novels by Silone and Malraux, a character's disillusionment with Communism leads to a transforming revelation. In *Man's Fate,* when the Comintern abandons the revolution in Shanghai, Malraux's hero, Kyo Gisors, affirms his belief that it is worthwhile to die for human dignity. Pietro Spina of *Bread and Wine* finds a brotherhood and a communion to replace a political organization which would have him serve the ends of Soviet foreign policy. To approach these works, Dos Passos would have had to write a novel which would have combined his disillusionment with the hope he expressed in *The Ground We Stand On;* in other words, the novel of triumphant conservatism he never wrote.

Instead, he wrote the novels that he and his publishers eventually decided to call "contemporary chronicles." Six of them follow *Adventures of a Young Man* and *The Ground We Stand On,* and at least four are good illustrations of John Dos Passos's work as a conservative novelist. *Number One* and *The Grand Design* are the remaining volumes of his second trilogy, *District of Columbia. Number One,* based in part on the career of Huey Long, is the highly imaginative story of such a demagogue's failure to wrest the Democratic presidential nomination from Franklin Roosevelt in 1940. *The Grand Design* is about all twelve years of the Roosevelt presidency from the bright hope of the first hundred days to Teheran and Yalta, where Dos Passos's characterization of Roosevelt exceeds in bitterness his portrait of Woodrow Wilson in *1919*. *Chosen Country* (1952) is a conservative novel in the sense of being the story of the writer's search for his roots; an autobiographical novel, whose most interesting disguise is the hero's choice to follow his father into law. Useful as any of these novels would be for the present purpose, I prefer to discuss *Midcentury* as an example of how age, politics, and the study of history affected Dos Passos's fiction. One reason is that it is, without question, his most conservative novel because it tries to build a story upon his eventual beliefs instead of spinning out the old plot of his disillusionment. It approaches the structure of the *U.S.A.* novels, restoring many of the actual techniques. Indeed, it is so reminiscent that when it does differ strongly or when some *U.S.A.* technique is missing altogether, one is tempted to recall Dos Passos's insistence long ago that content dictated form in his work[2] and blame a duller time for the disparity or the omission.

Midcentury, like *The Big Money,* is a novel about the United States in a postwar decade, and, like all of *U.S.A.,* its narratives are broken by a variety of non-fictional devices. These narratives are, as in *U.S.A.,* the stories of a few unexceptional Americans, whose lives are not necessarily representative. The "portraits" of *U.S.A.* are succeeded by *Midcentury*'s biographical sketches. *U.S.A.*'s "newsreels," which in typescript are actual paste-ups of clippings, headlines, and song lyrics, become the "documentaries" of *Midcentury.* There is no "Camera Eye" in *Midcentury,* no effective counterpart to those poetic memories which traced the education of a novelist and specifically the story of how John Dos Passos came to write *U.S.A.* Perhaps no comparable story could have been told of Dos Passos pursuing his education after *U.S.A.* In its place there are brief forewords to the major sections of *Midcentury* with Dos Passos entering his novel as "man walking his dog musing the century's decline."

Is it the mark of a conservative Dos Passos to stand so far from the events in his novel? The "Camera Eye" poet moved from the great distance of an expatriate childhood to the teeming center of the discontents in *The Big Money.* His innocence, the mysterious fragments of his education; the anger, despair, and

exhilaration of being in Europe at war, and even his young revolutionary hatreds are uttered with beauty, warmth, and insight
enough to make a despairing book also an exciting one. The angry
and bitter young man in Camera Eye 50 ("all right we are two
nations") seems to have existed more than a lifetime earlier than
the bitter and melancholy old man of *Midcentury.* That old
dog-walker remembers college lectures on the social insects who
enslave themselves in building their nests and hives just as man
does in building his institutions. Camera Eye sees everything at
hand in an agitation of forms and colors; it is also the inner eye of
memory and fancy, and sometimes it is the panoramic lens that
sweeps all the real and imagined occurrences in the narratives,
portraits, and newsreels. When the author of *Midcentury* is not
out walking his dog, he is back at his desk. He disdains any
illusion that would make the times his midcentury. His eye reads
Scientific American, rests on his script; his inner eye traces logical
connections between past lessons and current phenomena. In
these brief, despairing passages Dos Passos plays the role of an
historian without any explanation of how he became one.

The narratives of *U.S.A.* are much livelier than those of
Midcentury, even though the characters in both books confirm
Edmund Wilson's observation that "everyone loses out in Dos
Passos."[3] The greater vitality is partly due to the author's
mastery of a freshly invented technique in *U.S.A.* and his slackness
in trying to employ it twenty-five years later in *Midcentury.* The
stories of J. Ward Moorehouse, Eleanor Stoddard, Charley
Anderson, and all of the other *U.S.A.* characters are told in their
own language by the mocking author, who thereby measures the
weakness of their characters and the limitation of their sensibilities
with startling precision. It is caricature, perhaps Dos Passos's most
impressive satire. Some readers of *1919* may forget Joe Williams's
name, but never the last moments of his life on Armistice night:

> . . . Joe saw red. He pulled her away from the nigger who
> was a frog officer all full of gold braid and she said,
> "Wazamatta cherie," and Joe hauled off and hit the damn
> nigger as hard as he could right on the button but the
> nigger didn't budge. The nigger's face had a black puzzled
> smiling look like he was just going to ask a question. The
> waiter and a coupla frog soldiers came up and tried to pull

120

> Joe away. Everybody was yelling and jabbering. Jeanette
> was trying to get between Joe and the waiter and got a
> sock in the jaw that knocked her flat. Joe laid out a couple
> of frogs and was backing off towards the door, when he saw
> in the mirror that a big guy in a blouse was bringing down a
> bottle on his head held with both hands. He tried to swing
> around but he didn't have time. The bottle crashed his
> skull and he was out. (*1919*, p. 238)

The truth and anguish of the young Harvard poet of "Camera Eye"
come sharply to mind in the following passage from the life of a
fraudulent young Harvard poet named Richard Ellsworth Savage,
who has just dismissed the girl he has made pregnant:

> . . . He thought of Anne Elizabeth going home alone in a
> taxicab through the wet streets. He wished he had a great
> many lives so that he might have spent one of them with
> Anne Elizabeth. Might write a poem about that and send
> it to her. . . . (*1919*, pp. 396-7)

Dos Passos tells the stories of his *Midcentury* characters in
their own language from an omniscience more or less aware of their
limitations, but never with the mockery or the staccato pace that
succeeded in *U.S.A.* These gentler narrations are dull. Terry
Bryant, Jasper Milliron, and Will Jenks plod through detailed
sequences of events that are related to a postwar America of
corrupt labor practices and soulless business organizations. It is
easy to forget Jasper Milliron's occupation or his middle-age love
affair with someone reminiscent of Betty Crocker; it is even hard
to remember that Terry Bryant died, as Joe Williams did, of a
fractured skull. The most vivid fictional character in *Midcentury*
is Blackie Bowman, an old Wobbly who lies on his deathbed taping
his life story from birth to death through all of the old times and
places of *U.S.A.* Perhaps he, rather than the dog-walker, is
Midcentury's counterpart to Camera Eye: a dying man's well-
ordered memories recorded on the historian's tape.

The "portraits" in *U.S.A.* were written in the midst of Dos
Passos's political education. Most of them bear the mark of fresh
perception, some so fresh that Dos Passos's characteristic satire is
abandoned for something approaching lyricism, as in the last line
of his sketch of Veblen:

. . . his memorial remains riveted into the language: the sharp clear prism of his mind. (*The Big Money*, p. 105)

or in the conclusion to "The Campers at Kitty Hawk":

the Wright brothers passed out of the headlines but not even
the headlines or the bitter smear of news
print or the choke of smokescreen and gas or chatter of brokers
on the stockmarket or barking of phantom millions or oratory of
brasshats laying wreaths on new monuments
can blur the memory
of the chilly December day
two shivering bicycle mechanics from Dayton,
Ohio,
first felt their homemade contraption
whittled out of hickory sticks,
gummed together with Arnstein's bicycle cement,
stretched with muslin they'd sewn on their sister's
sewingmachine in their own backyard on Hawthorn
Street in Dayton, Ohio,
soar into the air
above the dunes and the wide beach
at Kitty Hawk.

(*The Big Money*, p. 285)

His portrait of Woodrow Wilson ("Meester Veelson") is a masterpiece of vilification placed in the exact center of *1919* so that Wilson's promises to keep the country out of war become the pivot in the century's dismal progress toward the Stock Market Crash. "The Body of an American," a portrait of the Unknown Soldier, is the bitterly appropriate conclusion of *1919*, every detail building to the pious fanfare at Arlington and the last line of the novel, perhaps the cruellest line Dos Passos ever wrote: "Woodrow Wilson brought a bouquet of poppies."

"Meester Veelson" is the most striking example of what Dos Passos achieved in the *U.S.A.* portraits. As one recognizes each brilliantly caricatured subject and the historical values Dos Passos assigns to him, one begins to see as much in every other part of the novel. One sees the film that *U.S.A.* might yet become, with the "Camera Eye" director ordering sequences of Wilson and Richard Ellsworth Savage followed by the incoherence of the newsreels.

The best *Midcentury* biographies remind one of the *U.S.A.* portraits, except that one cannot go on to imagine a *Midcentury* film. Instead, there could be a series of half-hour television programs before the *Today* show given over to the biographies alone, their unity established by an introduction which specifies that these are studies of "men alone" contending with "institutions they have built" and losing out in "the century's decline." All of the *Midcentury* biographies illustrate this thesis, whether they describe an anachronistic MacArthur or an up-to-date Walter Reuther. They are satirical except when Dos Passos gives way to invective or admiration; he remained a bright satirist to the end, but grew wearier in praising his heroes. He celebrates the virtues of General William Dean, whose strength as "one man alone" was severely tested in North Korea, and then exposes the self-pity and self-indulgence of James Dean, the actor. The actor is remembered in the nineteen-seventies much as he is presented in *Midcentury*, while those who remember him are now forgetting Commander Lloyd Bucher as they have already forgotten General William Dean.

No one hovers over *Midcentury* as Wilson did over *1919*. Neither postwar President, Truman or Eisenhower, is a biographical subject or mentioned beyond slight references in other sketches. The biography that comes closest to pervading the rest of the book is "Analyst," an attack on "Doctors X and Y," who derive from "Freud's poetry" a "twenty-five dollar an hour panacea." Psychoanalysis becomes a new horror to go along with the "Abominable Snowman":

> These are the brainwashers, the twin myths of Marx and Freud, opposed yet interlocking, as victory interlocks with defeat, which soared out of the scientific ruminations of the late nineteenth century to hover like scavenger birds over the disintegration of the Western will. (*Midcentury*, p. 30)

or merely ridiculed:

> Eros, erotic, erogenous zones: Dr. Y's patients find
> their subconscious an Ali Baba's cave full of an oriental
> profusion of erogenous whimsies, only to be sublimated
> at considerable expense,
> by art
> or by a beautiful redhead. (*Midcentury*, pp. 28-9)

Permissiveness rankles the philosophical anarchist, who would not destroy certain forms of authority, those of his parents and his conscience. Nor can he accept short-cuts to self-knowledge after having written "Camera Eye."

The documentaries of *Midcentury* begin with news of a nine-year-old child who thinks he is a machine and is unable to act until he is plugged in. A sixty-five-year-old man barks like a dog every ten minutes, frightening other commuters. Men develop "electrical power for a year in space," and the "economy shows few signs of weakness." Dos Passos appears to have ignored most of the political news in pasting up these pages. He scarcely refers to the Korean War or any other episode of the Cold War, including the death of Stalin, but dwells curiously long on congressional hearings dealing with unfair labor practices. Some of the juxtaposed headlines and snippets are hilarious and suddenly, as in *U.S.A.*, frightening when crazy, fragmented data confirm the worst that the writer has said himself.

After all of these comparisons between an earlier and a later book, the surest mark of Dos Passos as a conservative novelist is that he no longer wrote "Camera Eye." This is far more significant than the dullness of the later narratives. The conservative novelist Dos Passos repossessed the family farm on the Northern Neck of Virginia, commuted between there and Baltimore, and stayed home oftener than he travelled. He wrote as much history as fiction, and it is impossible to separate his vocation as a historian from his vocation as a novelist in the books he called "contemporary chronicles." At the end of his life, he was a learned, ironic philosophical anarchist at ease in his place in the world.

VACHEL LINDSAY: THE DANTE OF
THE FUNDAMENTALISTS*

PETER VIERECK

I

The end of an outer material frontier to explore in the west and midwest has helped cause the increasing inner explorations of the spirit. Vachel Lindsay represents a transition: apparently still an outer explorer, an evoker of picturesque place-names and loud American noises in the fashion of an older school; yet in reality an inward voyager of the religious imagination and the aesthetic imagination. Lindsay remains the finest religious poet produced by America's most local native roots. He is the Dante of the Fundamentalists (A Yankee Doodle Dante).

The comparison of Lindsay with Dante is intended not in terms of greatness, whether of poetry or thought, but in terms of voicing one's roots. In their respective religious communities, each was the poet who best voiced his particular heritage. The contrasting views of man in those two heritages will broaden the second part of this discussion from Lindsay to American culture as a whole.

Lindsay is the Dante of America's only indigenous church: Fundamentalist Bible-belt revivalism. For that church he wrote major poetry of mystical vision, as well as the jingly junk (boom-lay-boom) for which he is better known. Carrying further, church for church and relic for relic, the analogy with the Florentine poet of Catholicism, we may summarize: Lindsay's Rome was Spring-

---

*Page numbers after quotations refer to the excellent Macmillan edition of Lindsay's Collected Poems.

This essay appeared in somewhat different form in Storia E Letteratura: 107, Raccolta di Studie Testi; Essays Presented to Mario Praz (Rome, 1966).

field, Illinois; his Holy Roman Emperor was the specter of Abe
Lincoln; his Virgil-guide was Johnny Appleseed. His Beatrice was
"A Golden-Haired Girl in a Louisiana Town": "You are my love/
If your heart is as kind / As your eyes are now." His martyred
Saint Sebastian was Governor Altgeld (persecuted for saving the
Haymarket anarchists from lynching). His angel hosts were the
Anti-Saloon League and the Salvation Army, lovingly washing in
the "blood of the lamb" the stenos and garage mechanics of
Chicago.

To continue the analogy: Lindsay's version of the Deadly
Sins, as a middleclass Fundamentalist schoolma'am might see
them, were the beguiling depravities of "matching pennies and
shooting craps," "playing poker and taking naps." These two
lines are from "Simon Legree," a combination of a Negro spiritual
with a Calvinistic morality; the result of that combination can only
be called: intoxicated with sobriety. Dante's medieval heretics
partly corresponded to what Lindsay called "the renegade
Campbellites," a Fundamentalist splinter-group secession:

> O prodigal son, O recreant daughter,
> When broken by the death of a child,
> You called for the graybeard Campbellite elder,
> Who spoke as of old in the wild . . .
> An American Millennium . . .
> When Campbell arose,
> A pillar of fire,
> The great high priest of the spring . . .

But then, in the same poem, comes the sudden self-mockery of:

> And millennial trumpets poised, half-lifted,
> Millennial trumpets that wait. [p. 354]

Here the verb "wait," mocking the ever-unfulfilled prophecies of
Fundamentalist revivalism, is the kind of slip that occurs acci-
dentally-on-purpose. Such frequent semi-conscious slips represent
Lindsay's protest against his self-imposed, self-deceiving role of
trying to be more Fundamentalist than any Fundamentalist and
more folkish than the real folk.

That self-imposed role, which ultimately became his shirt-of-
Nessus, may have resulted from two tacit postulates. First, that

poetry readers have no more right to laugh at the homespun Fundamentalist theology of the old American west than at the subtler but perhaps no more pious-hearted theology of Dante's day. Second, that the American small-town carnival deserved as much respect as Dante's medieval pageants; it was as fitting a literary theme; it was no less capable of combining the divine with the humdrum.

Once you concede these two postulates to Lindsay, all the rest seems to follow, including such lofty Lindsay invocations as: "Love-town, Troy-town Kalamazoo" and "Hail, all hail the pop-corn stand." It follows that the Fundamentalist prophet, Alexander Campbell, should debate with the devil upon none other than "a picnic ground." It follows that real, tangible angels jostle Lindsay's circus-barkers and salesmen of soda pop. And certainly Lindsay has as much aesthetic right to stage a modern Trojan war, over love, between Osh Kosh and Kalamazoo as Homer between Greeks and Trojans. So far so good. But Lindsay often absurdly overstrains this aesthetic right, these old-world analogies. For example, he hails not an easily-hailed American *objet* like, say, Washington's monument but the popcorn stand.

Lindsay's motive for choosing the popcorn stand is not unconscious crudeness but conscious provocation. In effect he is saying: "By broadening the boundaries of aestheticism to include such hitherto-inacceptable Americana, my poetry is deliberately provoking, and thereby re-educating, all you supercilious eastern-seaboard-conditioned readers or Europe-conditioned readers."

But at the same time there is a suppressed saboteur within Lindsay, as within every exaggerated nationalist. That underground saboteur infiltrates Lindsay's poems via the most awkward-looking, absurdity-connoting letter in our alphabet, the letter "K." For whatever psychological reasons many Americans go into convulsions of laughter over the names of foreign towns like Omsk, Tomsk, Minsk, Pinsk, and nearer home, Hoboken, Yonkers, Keokuk, Sauk Center, not to mention those two Lindsay favorites, Osh Kosh and Kalamazoo. The core of each of those place-names is a throaty, explosive "K." Try to picture each of that same list, from Omsk through Kalamazoo, being spelt with a modest initial "C" or a chic final "que" in place of the "K"; in that case the names would lose half their comic effect on the ordinary American.

The letter "K" even *looks* lopsided, about to topple helplessly forward, an off-balance rube with metaphoric haywisps in its hair. More than any other letter it connotes the awkward yokel. The words "awkward" and "yokel" themselves would not connote half so much awkwardness, were they not so conspicuously spelt with "K."

Aside from above place-names and as further evidence for the hitherto unanalyzed role of "K" in American English, here are still other types of "K" usage with contemptuous connotations:

1. Awkward-looking alien animals: auk, aardvaark, kangaroo. In each instance, the animal's ridiculousness seems diminished if "c" or "que" are substituted for "K"; no awkward or comic connotation is attached to the Italian word for kangaroo, namely "canguro." An awkward-thinking as well as awkward-looking person, a crackpot extremist, is called a "Kook" in the American slang of the 1970's.

2. Epithets for allegedly crude aliens: yank (from southerners), kike, gook, chink, mick, kraut, bohunk (for Bohemian or Czech), hunky (for Hungarian or whitey), spik (for Puerto Rican), smoke (for Negro), snorky (for Swede). These are too many examples to be coincidental, despite the non-K terms of racial contempt that also occur. Since, except for sauerkraut, "K" is lacking in the source-words for these epithets (e.g., Chinese into Chink), it seems as if "K" were deliberately added—perhaps as an imitation of throat-clearing—to make a nickname more insulting.

3. Compare the old comic-strip spelling of "Krazy Kat" with the sarcastic spelling of "Kommunist Khrushchev" in a 1960 press release by the New York State Secretary, Caroline K. Simon (self-hatred of her own middle initial?), and with the 1960 appeal by Admiral Arleigh Burke, Chief of Naval Operations, asking us to spell "Communists" as "Kommunists" in order to make clear their "foreignism" and their "Kremlin bosses."[1] These absurdities (would "Cremlin Communists" evoke a more trustful response?) reflect a very American linguistic bias.

4. Unlike the plain "K," the combination of "ck" fails to connote "foreignism" or awkwardness. But it does still connote contempt. Indeed, "ck" has become the standard termination —explosively coughed out—of a surprisingly large number of

unprintable "four-letter words" (in some instances five letters), both nouns and verbs, as well as the longer compounds of noun plus verb. Curiously enough, this added connotation of obscenity enters only when a "c" gets prefixed to the "k."

Of course, no such deliberate linguistic analysis determined Lindsay's obsessive use of awkward town-names with "K." Rather, his use was determined by a blind instinct—a shrewdly blind instinct—for catching the very soul of spoken Americana. No one has ever equalled Lindsay's genius for manipulating the unconscious connotations of the colloquial, even though he perversely misused those connotations for the self-torturing purpose of provoking and then staring-down the ridicule of sophisticated audiences.

That willingness to provoke ridicule may produce his worst poems. Yet it is also the root of the moral courage producing his best poems, such as his elegy for Governor Altgeld of Illinois. Altgeld had defied a nineteenth-century kind of "McCarthyism" by his idealistic defense of slandered minorities. Political poetry, even courageous political poetry, is by itself merely a rhymed editorial, better written in prose, unless universalized beyond journalism and arid ideologies into the non-political realm of artistic beauty. Lindsay's Altgeld poem remains one of the great American elegies because it does achieve this humanizing process, transfiguring courage into lyric tenderness:

> Sleep softly . . . eagle forgotten . . . under the stone . . .
> The mocked and the scorned and the wounded, the lame
>   and the poor
> That should have remembered forever . . . remember
>   no more . . .
> Sleep softly . . . eagle forgotten . . . under the stone,
> Time has its way with you there, and the clay has its own . . .
> To live in mankind is far more than to live in a name,
> To live in mankind, far, far more . . . than to live in a name.

However, more frequently the heroes Lindsay's poetry presents as the American equivalent of old-world Galahads are not exactly Altgelds. For example, the subtitle of his actual poem "Galahad" reads: "Dedicated to all Crusaders against the International and Interstate Traffic in Young Girls." The subtitle of his poem "King Arthur's Men Have Come Again" was equally earnest and uplifting, namely: "Written while a field-worker in the Anti-Saloon League of Illinois." Of course, the moral heritage of rural Fundamentalism particularly objects to alcohol, along with "playing poker and taking naps."

These twin odes to the Anti-Vice Squad and the Anti-Saloon League are bad poems not because the evil they denounce is unserious but because their treatment of that evil sounds like a mock-heroic parody. To explain such bad writing in so good a poet, let us suggest the hypothesis that Lindsay's mentality included a demon of self-destruction, forever turning the preacher into the clown. This compulsion forced Lindsay, again and again in his verse, to strip himself in public of every shred of what he most prized: human dignity. Perhaps this inner demon was related to the compulsion that finally made Lindsay choose not just any method of suicide but the most horribly painful method imaginable: swallowing a bottle of searing acid.

When a poet consistently exalts whatever heroes, place-names, and occupations sound most ludicrous to his modern poetry audience (for example, Lindsay was an avid exalter of college cheerleaders), it may be either because he has no ear for poetry or because he has an excellent ear knowingly misused. The first explanation is easily ruled out by the beauty of the above Altgeld elegy. Aside from the self-destructive aspect, there is an important messianic-pedagogic aspect making the second explanation the more plausible one. For example, by inserting the pedantic adjective "interstate" in front of "traffic in young girls" and thereby incongruously juxtaposing the prosaic Mann Act law with the poetic word "Galahad," Lindsay says in effect:

> If you accept my hick-fundamentalist approach to morality, which I happen to consider the only true and autochthonous American religion, then you must also accept its humorless terminology, its ridicule-provoking bigotries. What is more, you must accept them with a religious spirit exactly as earnest as that with which Homer and Dante accepted their own autochthonous religious traditions.

Thus considered, Lindsay's poetry is not mere clowning, whether intentional or unintentional, but—in his own revealing phrase—"the higher vaudeville." The adjective "higher" makes all the difference; it means a medieval vaudeville, a messianic circus, a homespun midwest equivalent of the medieval fool-in-Christ.

II

In refusing to be apologetic toward the old world about America's own kind of creativity, Lindsay does have a valid point. In refusing to allow European legends, heroes, place-names a greater claim on glamor than American ones, he again does have a valid point. Likewise when he establishes the American gift for finding loveliness in the exaggerated, the grotesque. But the self-sabotaging demon within him tends to push these valid points to extremes that strain even the most willing "suspension of disbelief."

When Lindsay fails to make us suspend our disbelief, the reason often is this: he is trying to link not two compatibles, such as prosaic object with prosaic rhetoric or fabulous object with fabulous rhetoric, but prosaic object with fabulous rhetoric. Modern university-trained readers of poetry react unsolemnly to: "Hail, all hail the popcorn stand." Why? Because of a gap I would define as: the Lindsay disproportion. The Lindsay disproportion is the gap between the heroic tone of the invocation and the smallness of the invoked object. But Lindsay's aim, rarely understood by modern readers, was to overcome that disproportion between tone and object by conjuring up a mystic grandeur to sanctify the smallness of American trivia. That mystic grandeur derived from his dream of America as a new world free from old-world frailty, free from original sin. His dream-America was infinitely perfectable, whatever its present faults. Even its most trivial objects were sacred because incarnating the old Rousseauistic dream of natural goodness of man and eternal progress.

Lindsay believed, or felt he ought to believe, in the impossible America invented by the French poet Chateaubriand and other European romantics. Later, much later (nature imitating art) that invented America was sung by Americans themselves, by Emerson and Whitman. In poetry this utopian American myth culminated in Lindsay's *Golden Book of Springfield* and Hart Crane's *The Bridge*; in politics it culminated in the Populist and Progressive movements of the west.

But the laws of history and human nature permit no "new world" to be really new; Americans contain the same very human mixture of aspiration and fallibility as the old world. Europe's romantic expectation of superhuman achievements in democracy or in culture from America, an expectation that duped the Lindsays and the Hart Cranes as well as the European romantic school that invented it, has helped cause the current European disillusionment with America (even entirely aside from the lies of communist propaganda). Had Europeans not been so exaggeratedly pro-American in their hopes, they would not be so exaggeratedly anti-American in their despair but would see us as ordinary human beings like themselves.

The paradox behind European expectations of the new world appears in a supposed anecdote of the 1800's about Chateaubriand. He had arrived in America to flee old-world artificiality and to search for the unspoilt noble savage. And sure enough, as Chateaubriand was creeping through the wild jungle then filling northern New York State around Niagara Falls, he glimpsed a tribe of wild Indians between the trees. They were moving in a circle, as if in some primordial folk-ceremony. Bravely defying the dangers primitive America holds for older civilizations, he crept closer and closer through the thicket, to record for his friends in Paris an eye-witness account of unspoilt Americana in the midst of nature's wilderness. Suddenly he recognized what the redskins were dancing. Led by a little mincing French dancing-master, whom they had imported at great expense from Paris for that purpose, the Indians were pirouetting daintily through the latest steps of a formal Parisian ballroom number.

This anecdote is an allegory for European-American literary relations ever since. European critics are forever visiting our American literature to find a mystical, non-existent Noble Primitive. Instead they find some blasé professor, with a tweedy Oxford jacket and Boston accent, dancing with dreadful nimbleness through some complicated *explication de texte* of Proust. . . .

Instead of pouncing with shoddy glee on the absurd aspects of the Lindsay disproportion between tone and object, let us re-examine more rigorously the Chateaubriand-style dream of America behind those absurd aspects. That American myth is part of a romantic, optimistic philosophy seriously maintained, whatever one may think of it, by great or almost-great minds like Rousseau and Emerson. Therefore, it is unjust to dismiss that same philosophy contemptuously in Lindsay merely because his name has less prestige than theirs. What is wrong-headed in him, is wrong-headed in his preceptors also. He and they dreamed of a new world miraculously reborn without the burden of past history. That unhistorical myth of America distinguishes Whitman and Lindsay from Hawthorne and Faulkner in literature. It distinguishes Jefferson from John Adams in political philosophy. It distinguishes Fundamentalist revivalism, with its millennium just around the corner, and the hope of quick redemption that Lindsay's poetry hailed in the Salvation Army, from Niebuhrian pessimism within the American Protestant religion. While Lindsay is the Dante of the Fundamentalists, he differs from the old-world Catholic Dante by substituting a romantic, optimistic view of man for the tragic view held by traditional Christianity as well as by Greek classicism.

On this issue American literature has two conflicting traditions, the first romantic and progressive, the second classical and conservative. The first heartily affirms American folklore, American democratic and material progress. That Whitman-Emerson literary tradition cracked up in Vachel Lindsay and Hart Crane.[2] It cracked up not merely in their personal breakdowns and final suicides—let us not overstress mere biography—but in the aesthetic breakdown of the myth-making part of their poetry. The non-mythic part of their poetry, its pure lyricism, never did break down and in part remains lastingly beautiful.

A second American tradition is that of the literary pessimists, a new-world continuation of the great Christian pessimists of the old world, from Saint Augustine to Kierkegaard and Cardinal Newman. In America the second literary tradition is just as authentically American as the first one but has never received the same popular recognition, being less comforting. The most influential literary voices of our second tradition are Melville, Hawthorne, Henry Adams, William Faulkner. Its greatest political heritage comes from the Federalist papers and from the actual anti-Jeffersonian party of the Federalists, with their partly European source not in Rousseau but in Burke. Its most influential theological voices in America today are Paul Tillich and Reinhold Niebuhr.[2]   Note that all these literary, political, and theological voices are characterized by skepticism about man and mass and by awareness of the deep sadness of history. Therefore, their bulwark against man and mass and against the precariousness of progress is some relatively conservative framework of traditional continuity, whether in culture, literature, politics, or religion.

The necessity of tragedy, the necessity of recognizing human frailty, human limitation, the perpetualness of evil, a chastened skepticism about human nature and progress: such are the tenets of the primarily philosophical and aesthetic, primarily non-political movement sometimes known as the new conservatism (not to be confused with vulgarized current political "conservatisms" of the Goldwater Republican kind). These tenets seem partly confirmed by the failure of Lindsay's and Hart Crane's attempts to create a new, untragic kind of myth for America. As if original sin stopped west of the Alleghenies! As if the democratic American, like the noble savage of Rousseau, were immune from human frailty and immune from the spiritual price paid for industrial progress.

To be sure, the attitudes of Emerson and of Whitman (often more tragic and ambivalent than realized) were never so naive or unqualified as the above. But such was the over-simplified form their liberal American creed often took in their main literary heirs, including Lindsay and Crane. Note which two are the only American poets Lindsay names in his long "Litany of the Heroes":

> Then let us seek out shining Emerson,
> Teacher of Whitman, and better priest of man,
> The self-reliant granite American.

Emerson, it will be remembered, appealed to what he called "the great optimism self-affirmed in all bosoms." The germ of Lindsay's and Crane's attempts to force themselves to affirm industrial Americana lies in the following optimistic affirmation of material progress that Emerson noted in his journal for 1871: "In my life-time have been wrought five miracles—1. the steamboat; 1. the railroad; 3. the electric telegraph; 4. the application of the spectroscope to astronomy; 5. the photograph—five miracles which have altered the relations of nations to each other." The best rebuttal to this attempt to affirm "miracles" like the railroad, before having made sure whether they were man's master or slave, came from Emerson's friend Thoreau: "We do not ride on the railroad; it rides on us."

Anticipating the attempts of the Emersonian Lindsay to make a "Troytown" out of every Kalamazoo and to find a Helen in every Osh Kosh, Emerson wrote: "Banks and tariffs, the newspaper and caucus," were "dull to dull people but rest on the same foundations of wonder as the town of Troy and the temple of Delphos." There in one sentence stands the whole Lindsay crusade to rebaptize Americana with wonder, a crusade in itself justifiable but lacking, in both Emerson and Lindsay, the criteria for discriminating between which industrial Americana were wonder-worthy and which ones, being tied to mean goals, were wonder-destroying. Apropos the mean goals of so much mechanical progress, it was, once again, the profounder Thoreau who punctured in advance the Emerson-Whitman-Lindsay-Crane optimism by warning: "We are now in great haste to construct a magnetic telegraph from Maine to Texas; but Maine and Texas, it may be, have nothing important to communicate."

The optimistic progress-affirming and folklore-affirming voices of Emerson and Whitman cracked up in their disciples Lindsay and Crane when the crushing of the individual in modern mechanization became simply too unbearable to affirm. The modern poet of progress may try to keep up his optimistic grin for his readers while the custard pie of "higher vaudeville" drips down his face. But past a certain point, he can no longer keep up the grin, whether psychologically in his private life or aesthetically in his public poetry. Our overadjusted standardization becomes just one custard pie too many for the unadjusted poet to affirm, no matter how desperately he tries to outshout his inner tragic insight by shouting (in Lindsay's case) "Hail, all hail the popcorn stand" and by hailing (in Crane's case) the Brooklyn Bridge as "the myth whereof I sing." Lindsay and Crane committed suicide in 1931 and 1932 respectively, in both cases in that depression era which seemed temporarily to end the boundless optimism of American material progress.

Lindsay's *Golden Book of Springfield* and Crane's *The*

Bridge, though so different in other respects, are the two out-standing examples of trying to contrive an untragic myth of affirmation out of our modern industrial progress. Lindsay and Crane celebrated the American myth more enthusiastically than would the philistine kind of booster because, unlike the philistine, they were boosters not by temperament but by a self-coercion which their temperament was constantly sabotaging. The genuine booster will affirm not all but most Americana; Lindsay and Crane sometimes seemed to try to affirm all. Lindsay's idealizing of the Hollywood cinema and Hart Crane's romanticizing of what he called the oil-rinsed ecstasy of even such gadgets as ball-bearings were acts of desperation; they were forcing themselves to affirm even those crass aspects of American mechanization that they themselves suffered from most. In both cases the self-coercion proved literally unbearable; neither of our greatest literary opti-mists could *bear* staying alive on his own yes-saying terms.

Perhaps there is a profound lesson in the fact that both these poets of affirmation led miserable and so-called unsuccessful lives, ending in suicide, while T. S. Eliot, the fastidious no-sayer, who wrote the pessimism of *The Waste Land* instead of glorifying Springfield or the Brooklyn Bridge, has been thriving most successfully. Perhaps the lesson is that our modern industrial age is so unbearable that it drives its own boosters to insanity and self-destruction while acclaiming its knockers with Nobel prizes.

But even aside from our own particular age and the madness that strikes down the muse that would embrace its machines, it is a conservative fact of life that unqualified optimism about human nature results in disaster. Robert Penn Warren showed this in his long poem about Jefferson, *Brother to Dragons*. When events do finally force the excessive optimist to allow for human frailty, he ends up more disillusioned, more inclined to either self-destruction or terrorism than the conservative who was pessimistic from the start.

Lindsay's poems celebrate by specific references every single one of the main voices of American optimism: the Rousseau-Jefferson view of human psychology, the political utopianism of Jacksonian democracy, the economic utopianism of the Populists, the religious utopianism of Fundamentalist chiliasm, and the Emerson-Whitman literary tradition. All five of these often separate voices converge to produce one of Lindsay's most revealing couplets:

> God has great estates just past the line,
> Green farms for all, and meat and corn and wine.

The key line preceding that couplet is "Turn the bolt—how soon we would be free!" That line recalls the radical, anti-traditionalist slogan of that Bible of the French Revolution, Rousseau's *Social Contract* of 1762: "Man is born free and is everywhere in chains." Actually what makes man free is precisely those so-called "chains" of tradition, of established religion, of unbroken historical continuity; they free him from the *hubris* of his own nature, which becomes self-destructive if without traditional "chains." To vary the metaphor, freedom, in the older Christian and Burkean view, depends on a reverent conserving of traffic lights, not on a Rousseauist—optimist—radical smashing of them.

Despite coercing himself painfully into enjoying progress, Lindsay also had his bitter side about the relationship between the muse and the machine age. Our 1970's, like his 1920's, suffer from the pressure of overadjusted public life against the privacy of the free imagination. Resuming the analogy with Dante's *Divine Comedy,* we note that Lindsay's poetry had not only its Paradise, in his dream of his future Springfield, but its Inferno in the Springfield of his own day. His Inferno was the same as ours: the standardizing side of the America he secretly hated when he affirmed her, secretly loved when he rejected her. "Inferno" is not too strong a word for the soul-destroying commercialism whose symbols, in his poetry, were broken factory windows. This occasional bitterness about commercialism reflected the same kind of unadjusted poetic imagination as Baudelaire's bitterness about *l'esprit belge.* In Lindsay that anti-cash-nexus reaction produced two of the strongest, leanest lines ever written on the subject:

> Factory windows are always broken . . . ,
> *End of the factory-window song.*

Lindsay hoped a rooted, American Fundamentalist religion

from the midwest, would soon, in his own words, be "Building against our blatant, restless time / An unseen, skilful, medieval wall." This neo-medieval wall would overcome, he hoped, the secular materialism he attributed to the midwest of his day. He hoped to regenerate industrialism not by rejecting it pessimistically but by sanctifying it optimistically through a new religious era:

> Think not that incense-smoke has had its day.
> My friends, the incense-time has but begun. . .
> And on our old, old plains some muddy stream,
> Dark as the Ganges, shall, like that strange tide—
> (Whispering mystery to half the earth)—
> Gather the praying millions to its side. [p. 52]

Being also an amateur painter, Lindsay distributed on street corners his pictures of censers in the sky, swinging their "incense-time" redeemingly above Springfield, Illinois. To the open-mouthed, dumbfounded burghers of Springfield he distributed, as free messianic tracts, a poem called "The Soul of the City Receiving the Gift of the Holy Ghost":

> Censers are swinging
> Over the town . . .
> Censers are swinging,
> Heaven comes down.
> City, dead city,
> Awake from the dead! [p. 207]

Whenever Lindsay came to believe something, he believed it strongly enough to want to make all his neighbors believe it also. Risking mockery and rebuff he had the courageous idealism of giving unsolicited home-printed copies of his message to those who least wanted to receive it: "I flooded Springfield with free pamphlets incessantly." For such crusades he might be called either a crank or a genuine American saint. Instead of either of these alternatives, he pictured himself as following the foot-steps of his religious and folk hero Johnny Appleseed. Thus in his prose piece, *Adventures Preaching Hieroglyphic Sermons*, Lindsay wrote: "Johnny Appleseed, whom I recommend to all men who love visions, was a man of lonely walking, a literal Swedenborgian all his days, distributing tracts when occasionally he met a settler. . . . I am for Johnny Appleseed's United States." [p. xxii]

The more the forces of cash-nexus made Springfield secular, materialistic, overadjusted, the more did Lindsay (in his own words) "hand out to anyone who would take it in the street" the counterforce of his poem "Springfield Magical":

> In this, the City of my Discontent,
> Sometimes there comes a whisper from the grass,
> "Romance, Romance—is here. No Hindu town
> Is quite so strange. No Citadel of Brass
> By Sinbad found, held half such love and hate" . . .
> In this, the City of my Discontent! [p. 62]

How did his good neighbors respond to all this distribution of rhymed broadsides, this revivalist saving of their souls at street corners? Lindsay comments wistfully: "It was at this point that I was dropped from such YMCA work and Anti-Saloon League work as I was doing in the Springfield region." [p. xxxv]

Such was America's negative response to Lindsay's often valid gospel of beauty. Yet his faith in the American myth prevented him from becoming the type of the irreconcilable martyr-crank. If anything, he was reconciled all too easily to the commercialist society that rejected him. For example, he tried symbolically to beautify and thereby redeem the industrial revolution by his poem in praise of the electric-light ads on Broadway:

> The signs in the street and the signs in the skies
> Shall make a new Zodiac, guiding the wise,
> And Broadway make one with that marvellous stair
> That is climbed by the rainbow-clad spirits of prayer. [p. 39]

These flashing ad-signs of Times Square would indeed be, as Lindsay pretended, the most beautiful thing in the world if only (as Chesterton said) we did not know how to read.

Lindsay could not have continued writing, or even staying alive, in any society to which he could not be reconciled more easily than reality ever permits; he was too steeped in the boundless expectations of the Fundamentalist millennial spirit, the spirit he called "the Resurrection parade." Thus Lindsay quoted with approval Alexander Campbell's appropriately-named magazine *The Millenial Harbinger,* in which that Fundamentalist prophet wrote in 1865, "the present material universe . . . will be wholly regenerated." [p. 352] Himself a learned man and by no means "crude" in the more popular meaning of Fundamentalist revivalism, Campbell nevertheless fitted into the optimist-Rousseauist tradition by rejecting Original Sin and by rejecting baptism at birth as unnecessary and reactionary, evil allegedly not being present in human nature that early but added by corrupt society later.

What is shoddy in the American myth is not affirmation itself; classic tragedy affirms ("Gaiety transfiguring all that dread"). What is shoddy is not the hard-won affirmation that follows tragic insight but the facile unearned optimism that leads only to disillusionment. Here is a prose example of how Lindsay's valid crusade against the adjective "standardized" collapses suddenly into a too-easy optimism:

> I have been looking out of standardized windows of "The Flat-Wheeled Pullman Car." I have been living in standardized hotels, have been eating jazzed meals as impersonal as patent breakfast-food. . . . The unstandardized thing is the overwhelming flame of youth . . . an audience of one thousand different dazzling hieroglyphics of flame. . . . My mystic Springfield is here, also, in its fashion . . . a Springfield torn down and rebuilt from the very foundations, according to visions that might appear to an Egyptian . . . or any one else whose secret movie-soul was a part of the great spiritual movie. [pp. xxv-xxvi]

Note the typical Lindsay disproportion by which this moving passage ends with an appalling anticlimax, equating Hollywood's facile commercialized "visions" with the tragically-earned classic ones. Yet his best and worst writing are so intertwined that this "movie soul" gush is immediately followed by one of his finest prose passages about American democracy at its noblest:

> I believe that civic ecstasy can be so splendid, so unutterably afire, continuing and increasing with such apocalyptic zeal, that the whole visible fabric of the world can be changed. . . . And I say: change not the mass, but change the fabric of your own soul and your own visions, and you change all. [p. xxvi]

In Lindsay's Springfield Paradise of tomorrow: "civic

ecstasy." But in his Springfield Inferno of today: "Factory windows are always broken." Hence his outburst: "I went through the usual Middle West crucifixion of the artist." That outburst, so typical of the midwest artist of the 1920's and so rarely heard in the culture-vulture midwest of today, was valid enough for his time. It should not be snubbed as sentimental by later and sleeker artists, battening on fellowships and snob-appeal and producing art more elegant, less anguished than Lindsay's. But let us of the post-Sinclair Lewis generation note also the converse of Lindsay's outburst: namely, the usual verbal crucifixion of the Middle West by the artist.

When Lindsay was a child, an old duck-pond diviner pronounced this Delphic utterance about America's future laureate of Fundamentalism: "A child of destiny and also fond of sweets." This comment, in which the word "also" is particularly important, proved prophetic of Lindsay's combination of a messianic religious message with a lyrical aestheticism. In his messianic aspect of propagating the untragic American myth, he called himself a "cartooning preacher," a half-mocking phrase reminiscent of his phrase "the higher vaudeville." In his aesthetic aspect, preaching what one of his poems called "A Gospel of Beauty," he sometimes saw himself as a log-cabin Pater; it is often overlooked that, in such poems as "The King of Yellow Butterflies," Lindsay was more of a "pure aesthete" than most of the French Parnassians at their most ethereal. But Lindsay's aesthetic aspect was more frequently modeled on Ruskin's semi-moralized kind of aestheticism: "One of my crimes was a course of lectures at the YMCA on Ruskin's famous chapters on the nature of Gothic." [pp. 19-20] No wonder "there were days in my home town when the Babbitts . . . were about ready to send me to jail or burn me at the stake for some sort of witchcraft, dimly apprehended, but impossible for them to define"; that quotation reveals Lindsay's admirable courageous honesty about making no concessions to the anti-poetic cliches of his burgher audiences. But the darker undertone of the quotation also reveals his self-destructive compulsion to state his beliefs, in this case perfectly reasonable beliefs, in the terms most calculated to provoke incomprehension and ridicule.

Lindsay's authentic western Americana were never presented

for their own sake, never merely as quaint antiques for the tourist trade. Rather, they were presented for the more serious purposes of either his Whitman-messianic aspect or his Ruskin-aesthetic aspect, depending on whether the given poem happened to be fond of destiny or of sweets. The obsessiveness these two aspects had for him was best summed up in his own words: "Incense and splendor haunt me as I go." In the end the psychological and social meaning of his poems remains secondary to their lyricism, and indeed his poems achieve their occasional social effectiveness only via their lyricism, rather than apart from it. At his best, Lindsay incarnates for America the importance and dignity of spontaneous song: its ennobling and rehumanizing role in a standardized machine age.

Part of Lindsay's aesthetic compulsion, giving him the uniqueness only possessed by major poets, lies in his juxtaposition of the delicate and the grotesque: for example, in his phrase "the flower-fed buffaloes of the spring," subject of one of his purest lyrics. Running through his diversities of titles and subject matter, note also the delicate and the grotesque color-juxtapositions of "the king of yellow butterflies" with "the golden whales of California" and the semantic juxtaposition of "harps in heaven" with "the sins of Kalamazoo." Such gargoyle tenderness is a genre of sensibility explored by few other poets beside Beddoes and Rimbaud, the poets with whom Lindsay's unfulfilled genius, beneath its tough loud disguises, properly belongs. In a situation Beddoes would have cherished, here is a typical example of gargoyle tenderness in Lindsay; "The Song of the Garden-Toad" expresses the agony and hate of worms when the gardener crushes their soil, with unconscious cruelty, in order to plant airy flowers:

> Down, down beneath the daisy beds,
> O hear the cries of pain! . . .
> I wonder if that gardener hears
> Who made the mold all fine
> And packed each gentle seedling down
> So carefully in line?
>
> I watched the red rose reaching up
> To ask him if he heard

> Those cries that stung the evening earth
> Til all the rose-roots stirred.
> She asked him if he felt the hate
> That burned beneath them there.
> She asked him if he heard the curse
> Of worms in black despair. [p. 265]

Delicacy is not a noun most modern readers associate with Lindsay. Yet his sense of cadence was so very delicate that it disguised itself defensively, his time and place being what they were, beneath ear-splitting auditory signposts. His signposts deliberately pointed in the wrong direction, the loud indelicate direction. Living where he did and believing the myth he believed, he needed to conceal his bitter, introverted sensitivity beneath the extroverted optimism of American folklore. That is, beneath a tone deliberately coarse, chummy, whooping, the whiz-bang claptrap of poems like "The Kallyope Yell." In such curiosities of our literature, no poet was ever more perversely skilful at sounding embarrassingly unskilful. No poet was ever more dexterous at sounding gauche. What in Whitman was merely a would-be "barbaric yawp," does yawp with an unbearably successful barbarism in Lindsay:

> I am the Gutter Dream,
> Tune-maker born of steam . . .
> Music of the mob am I,
> Circus-day's tremendous cry:
> Hoot toot, hoot toot, hoot toot, hoot toot,
> Willy willy willy wah HOO!

Followed, as if that were not enough, with the dying fall, the final fading yawp of: "Sizz, fizz."

Consequently Lindsay's poetry is often defined as mere oratory, to be shouted aloud by a mob chorus. Part of him wanted this view to be held. Another part of him lamented: "I have paid too great a penalty for having a few rhymed orations. All I write is assumed to be loose oratory or even jazz, though I have never used the word 'jazz' except in irony." His best work, often his least known work, was produced by the part of him that once confessed: "All my poetry marked to be read aloud should be whispered . . . for the inner ear . . . whispering in solitude."

Admittedly Lindsay is to blame (via the pseudo-tough defense mechanism of his sensitivity) for the fact that his work is generally associated with an extroverted booming voice: for example, with his University of Kansas football cheers, his Salvation Army trumpets. Yet the truest voice of his poetry is its quietness. That quietness produced line after line of imaginative evocation. Line after line of it comes tumbling again and again—at random from a dozen unconnected poems—over that "inner ear" in all of us to which he "whispered." To which his lyricism still whispers today, quietly beautiful, in line after line like this:

> "The little lacquered boxes in his hands."
> "They shiver by the shallow pools."
> "I am a trout in this river of light."
> "Stealer of vases of most precious ointment."
> "Her ears became the tiniest humorous calf's ears"
>   (this of the Egyptian bovine deity of love, Hathor).
> "You will go back as men turn to Kentucky,
> Land of their fathers, dark and bloody ground."
> "Abraham Lincoln Walks At Midnight."
> "Sleep softly . . . eagle forgotten . . . under the
>   stone."
> "O empty boats, we all refuse, that by our windows
>   wait."

And even when an actual loud "cry" is described, what a dreamy inner cry: "We will sow secret herbs and plant old roses" while "Green monkeys cry in Sanskrit to their souls." Many poets have written of the "sounding sea"; none has made it sound so hushed, so inward as this:

> Useful are you. There stands the useless one
> Who builds the Haunted Palace in the sun.
> Good tailors, can you dress a doll for me
> With silks that whisper of the sounding sea?

Here is an entire poem of delicate quietness:

> *Euclid*
>
> Old Euclid drew a circle
> On a sand-beach long ago.
> He bounded and enclosed it

With angles thus and so.
His set of solemn graybeards
Nodded and argued much
Of arc and of circumference,
Diameter and such.
A silent child stood by them
From morning until noon
Because they drew such charming
Round pictures of the moon. [p. 231]

This Lindsay parable of the two meanings of circles purges the modern reader of arid, abstract rationalism and re-humanizes, re-lyricizes, de-mechanizes him. The poem avoids coyness and cuteness, even if only by a triumphant hair's breadth, and thereby achieves not the facile but the difficult kind of simplicity.

Like Yeats, Lindsay transforms sentimentality into true art by means of the accompanying anti-sentimentality of nervously sinewy rhythms. Note, for example, the craftsmanship with which the lean rhythmic rightness of these two Lindsay quatrains redeems their otherwise sentimental rhetoric:

Why do I faint with love
Till the prairies dip and reel?
My heart is a kicking horse
Shod with Kentucky steel.

No drop of my blood from north
Of Mason and Dixon's line
And this racer in my breast
Tears my ribs for a sign. [pp. 352-3]

Such poetry is a pure art for art's sake. Yet the same author could also be a poet of urgent social polemic. Here is Lindsay's higher-vaudeville imitation of how a sixteen-year-old Bryanite Populist Democrat in 1896 would have viewed the revolt of western mass egalitarianism against the traditionalism and aristocracy attributed to America's eastern seaboard:

Defeat of western silver.
Defeat of the wheat.
Victory of letterfiles
And plutocrats in miles
With dollar signs upon their coats

And spats on their feet.
Victory of custodians,
Plymouth Rock,
And all that inbred landlord stock.
Victory of the neat . . .
Defeat of the Pacific and the long Mississippi . . .
And all these in their helpless days
By the dour East oppressed . . .
Crucifying half the West,
Till the whole Atlantic coast
Seemed a giant spiders' nest . . .
And all the way to frightened Maine the old East
        heard [them call . . .]
Prairie avenger, mountain lion,
Bryan, Bryan, Bryan, Bryan,
Smashing Plymouth Rock with his boulders from the
        West. [p. 96]

Let us consider that extraordinary Bryan poem first aesthetically, then politically. Note the sensuous concreteness of imagery. Instead of characterizing Bryan's enemies with the abstract, unlyrical word "the rich," Lindsay says concretely: "Victory of letter files / And plutocrats in miles / With dollar signs upon their coats." His self-mocking sense of humor, the subtlety of his pseudo-crudity, explains the surrealist fantasy of pretending, with wonderful preposterousness, that plutocrats literally wear dollar signs on their coats.

Taken in its political symbolism, Lindsay's aesthetic image of the Populists "smashing Plymouth Rock"[3] tells more than many prose volumes about the psychology of this recurrent American form of social protest. The invocation "avenger, mountain lion," brings out the motivating importance of revenge in Populism, revenge for having been humiliated and patronized by "that inbred landlord stock" of Plymouth Rock. The same emotion of revenge-for-humiliation is often shared by recent immigrants in Boston and the east as well as by the older American stock in the west, including Wisconsin. Therefore, the emotion portrayed in Lindsay's Bryan poem helps in part to explain the neo-Populist nationalist demagogy of the early 1950's, known as McCarthyism. No wonder McCarthyism was, in part, a demagogy of social inferiority complex that resented primarily not the Communists, whom it denounced, but the social elite (Ivy League colleges,

State Department of Groton-Harvard Acheson), whom it implicated.

In Lindsay's day, the midwest dream of messianic "civic ecstasy" in politics (really, Fundamentalist revivalism secularized) still had a touching youthful innocence; his Bryan poem, despite its doctrinaire social message, could still succeed in being movingly lyrical; American optimism was cracking but not yet cracked up. In contrast, the neo-Populist nationalism of our own day can find no voice, whether poetic or social-reformist, of Lindsay's cultural or moral stature. For meanwhile American standardization plus Ortega's "revolt of the masses" have transformed salvation-via-mob from innocent dream to sordid nightmare. And from genuine economic needs (such as Populist farmers exploited by railroads) to economic hypochondria.

Even the early Lindsay had not been able to celebrate without tragic qualms (disguised as comic hamming with K's and popcorn stands) this utopian faith in the mass-instinct. After his death, this pure young optimism of the west degenerated into a frustrated and scapegoat-hunting optimism, a soured and hence lynch-mob-minded faith in the avenging People. On the biographical plane Lindsay himself partly succumbed to this process in the final paranoid[4] fantasies accompanying his suicide. On the plane of social psychology: it is the process whereby soured left-wing radicals, the Populists and La Follette Progressives of yesteryear, have become right-wing radicals (would-be conservatives) while significantly still retaining their basic Populist-folksy-isolationist resentment against eastern-Anglophile elites.[5] Ponder, for example, the isolationist-Anglophobe career of a Senator Nye or a Senator Wheeler, forever "smashing Plymouth Rock"—first from left, then from right—"with his boulders from the West."

Here are two examples far more extreme. Father Coughlin, starting out as a western free-silver radical of the old Populist left, became a pro-Nazi, Anglophobe, anti-semitic radical of the "right" without ever having to change his (and his mass-movement's) true emotional bias, the bias against fancy eastern city slickers and international bankers. Likewise Ezra Pound's wartime broadcasts for Mussolini, against Jewish and British international bankers, have their true psychological and social origin in the mid-western free-silver Populist background of Pound's earlier tracts on economics and on the "conspiracies" of the Wall Street gold standard.

From this salvation-via-mob dilemma, with its false choice between leftist and rightist mob-hatreds, Lindsay himself pointed the way out. The way out was love; not that philistine-humanitarian love of progress (so aptly refuted by Edmund Burke and Irving Babbitt) whose hug squashes individuals into an impersonal mass; but the creative lyric love that flows healingly from the inner integrity—the holy imagination—of great art. In short, when Lindsay did voice deeply enough the roots of the human condition, he became a fundamental poet, rather than merely the poet of the Fundamentalists. His poem "The Leaden-Eyed" describes perfectly the human price paid for unimaginative standardization and at the same time, through the very act of being lyrical, demands the rehumanizing of the machine age:

> Not that they starve, but starve so dreamlessly,
> Not that they sow, but that they seldom reap,
> Not that they serve, but have no gods to serve,
> Not that they die but that they die like sheep.
> [pp. 69-70]

Such a rehumanizing-through-creativity as Lindsay achieved at his best, seems the only way out from our age of the three impersonal M's: masses, machines, and mediocrity. This great, absurd, and holy poet of America's native religious roots merits the adjective "God-intoxicated" because he found the redeeming religious imagination everywhere, everywhere—in the absurd as well as in the high:

> Once, in the city of Kalamazoo,
> The gods went walking, two and two.

And finally (after boomlay-booms are forgotten) there remains his noble seven-word line that expresses the exhausting yet creative tension between the outer ethical demands of society and the aesthetic demands of inwardness; let us conclude, then, with Vachel Lindsay's quietest line:

> Courage and sleep are the principal things.

MEYER LEVIN'S *COMPULSION*

LOUIS FILLER

In his introduction to Nathan Leopold's *Life Plus 99 Years* (1958), Erle Stanley Gardner, acting in his favorite role as the Court of Last Resort, protested against what he called the over-publicization of the Loeb-Leopold affair. He believed this made it difficult for Leopold to receive a proper hearing—one enabling him to hope for a parole. Loeb was long dead—sadistically murdered by another prison inmate—and Leopold was a manifestly rehabilitated man. Yet everything he did automatically became front-page news, reminding the world of the atrocious crime he had committed in 1924. In the almost thirty-five years which had passed, numerous other crimes had been committed, some even more atrocious, many more purposeful than the Loeb-Leopold attempt to perform a "perfect crime"—an ambition reflecting on the rationality of the then nineteen- and eighteen-year-old boys. Yet all such subsequent deeds, and their perpetrators, had been forgotten. The "crime of the century"—an often-repeated phrase Gardner found distasteful, continued to bemuse journalists, historians, and the public.

It did not occur to Gardner that the book he introduced was itself contributing to recollection, to the stream of writing on

Believing in the power of dialogue, the writer leans backward to express the viewpoints of others. This essay gains by having been read by David Madden of Louisiana State University, who is in full disagreement with its premises. His comments in the footnotes are identified as by "Caveat." Although Dave did not have the opportunity to study the book his responses, set down with his permission, are spontaneous and informed in the area, and must be regarded seriously.

the subject. True, Leopold's book in 1958 sought to change his old image of murderer. Leopold ingeniously cast his story to begin *after* the event which changed his life. But he knew, even as he wrote, that he was naked before the world, and that anything he set down might as readily anger the reader as evoke his sympathy. Leopold had no choice, if he was to appeal for mercy at all. And he, no more than Gardner, understood what distinguished him from numerous others who had committed crimes, but somehow won sufficient anonymity to qualify them for pardon or parole.

According to Leopold, he was importuned by Meyer Levin for aid in writing his novel, but turned him down again and again. Levin's persistence even caused Levin to print a public appeal that Leopold's family make available to him details he felt were needed to write a full, accurate account of their scapegrace relative. Leopold knew Levin had been a contemporary of his on the University of Chicago campus in 1924, but he rather patronizingly noted that there had been "about ten thousand students in attendance when I went there, and I certainly did not know or remember him." Leopold had been of an elite set; Levin had been a working boy with no social credentials.

Levin was a well-known author when, in 1956, he published *Compulsion.* His two most substantial earlier novels were *The Old Bunch* (1937), a tale of his youth and associates, and *Citizens* (1940), an equally lengthy narrative of the 1937 so-called Little Steel Strike in the Chicago area, and especially of the Memorial Day clash between strikers and police which resulted in a number of union dead. Both these novels merit analyses of their own, and may well receive them in due course.[1] For the moment it perhaps suffices to note that they, like *Compulsion,* are in the realistic tradition, and, as such, require assessment in terms of the qualities realism projects, or projected.

A word from Levin himself on this subject is in order:

> It has become customary to introduce realistic novels with the statement that their characters and events are imaginary.
>
> I shall not attempt a discussion of the relations between fiction and reality here, except to point out that the realistic novel by its very nature depends upon the use of

human materials, and it follows that those materials must in every case fall within the possibilities of human experience.

Perhaps people who lived in the time and places described will expect to identify themselves with the characters in this story. Such identity is entirely mistaken. Certain human traits, problems, and life patterns are recurrent within the society that I have attempted to depict. The use of this kind of material is within the granted province of the novelist.

I can say that to my knowledge no real individual is the counterpart of any character in this novel, with the exception of those who are named by actual name. And even they appear in their legendary rather than in their living aspect. Believing that such figures as Samuel Insull, Big Bill Thompson, and Al Capone have become part of the legend of Chicago, I have taken the liberty frequently used by writers of realistic fiction, and introduced their presence. I think that my furthest liberty is to have caused Mr. Insull to appear at a wedding of one of my characters. . . .[2]

It might be added that although theoretically method can be independent of subject matter, in practice method discriminates subjects and materials chosen for attention. Thus, realists and naturalists such as Theodore Dreiser, John Dos Passos, and James T. Farrell found such critics as H. L. Mencken, John Chamberlain, and Farrell himself to praise the mountains of detail which authors of their persuasion displayed, in order to focus attention on their commonplace characters, in order to demonstrate the determinism which ruled their lives, in order to describe their animal natures, to mimic their speech, or arraign their inadequate society, and achieve other goals of realistic or naturalistic type.

Such critics lost prestige in post-World War II years; explication took over, not in order to review the findings of their predecessors, but to supersede them entirely, determining not only method but proper topics worthy of their method. Henry James enjoyed a splendid season of explication, attracting critics seasoned in the genre, and also others who had just recently been endorsing the literature of social significance and naturalism. Dreiser lost much of his charm for critics; Lionel Trilling, in a 1955 essay, accorded him every expression of contempt, as artist and personality. Dos Passos's turnabout from communist sympathizer to anti-communist lost him critical status without increasing clarification of his art before or after his transformation. Farrell suffered in public esteem as novelist and critic. And Meyer Levin, of the younger generation, endured a number of experiences at the hands of critics and others which at one time contributed to making him consider giving up his American citizenship.

One should hasten to add that explication had a number of virtues which, properly controlled, were calculated to throw true light on the intentions of artists and the validity of their art. The T. S. Eliot apotheosis should have done no more harm in literature than the inordinate concern for Angela Davis should have done for social philanthropy. The difficulty with criticism had been that, as in leukemia, the white corpuscles of explication tended to eat up the red corpuscles of impressionism, social significance, ethnicity, and other human values which affected esthetic perception. Charles Shapiro, in his *Theodore Dreiser: Our Bitter Patriot* (1962), nicely utilized some details of explication in order to demonstrate, to his satisfaction, the validity of Dreiser's prose in many instances. It may well be that a reconstructed criticism will find elements of esthetics and communication which will prevent criticism—whether explicatory or otherwise—from becoming too constricted in its range of interests and techniques.

In any event, it seems fair to generalize that Levin has been seen as undiscriminating in his detail, obsessed with social justice at the expense of art, and parochial in his concern for Jewish communities.[3] Certainly, in method, he is the opposite of a Hemingway, when, at Hemingway's best, he is being strict in economy, evocative in symbols, and all but declassed and without nationality in connotation. The question is whether the Hemingway technique, for instance, could have brought out the points and point of view which interested Levin, and, of course, whether these points were worth eliciting.

The image of Levin as merely pounding out words on the typewriter is not quite accurate. It is not generally realized, for example, that Levin was something of a prodigy in his own right, having graduated from the University of Chicago at age eighteen, and, while yet a student, having been a working journalist on the

Chicago *Daily News.* In that capacity, he covered the Loeb-Leopold case for his paper. He brooded over the case's meaning, to himself, to others, during the more than thirty years which followed. *Compulsion* was not the work of a season.

He identified himself with Alvin Goldstein, another young Chicago journalist, who won the Pulitzer Prize for having unearthed evidence which helped solve the Loeb-Leopold case.[4] But Levin's fictional Sid Silver drew feelings and attitudes from his own personality as well. Levin interposed Silver as a classmate and campus acquaintance of the well-favored Loeb and Leopold. Indeed, he made one of their girls, Ruth, a liaison figure between Judd Steiner, the fictional Leopold, and Silver. Ruth develops deep feelings for Judd, somewhat at the expense of Sid, whom Judd sees as a "smart-aleck reporter." Sid is somewhat associated in the novel with Loeb's counterpart, Artie Strauss, though he has nothing of the latter's social charisma. Both Sid and Artie are deemed brilliant, the youngest students ever to graduate from the University. But Sid resents Artie as shallow and corrupt: a heartless liar and cheat, as the original Loeb in fact was. There are many passages in the novel to indicate that Levin was not merely exploiting the case,[5] but assessing a generation which had professed to wage a war for democracy, but which had, in the process, nourished the gross egotism of a Loeb and the neuroses of a Leopold—a process which put the latter's genuine brilliance at the disposal of the intrinsically shabby Loeb.

The boys' heads are filled with puerile Nietzscheism. Their fantasies range from sex to murder, replete with 1920's slang and wisecracks: ishkabibble, kiddo, screw you. But this is no mere decor—it is the dregs of patriotism, national pride and purposes, Wilsonian rhetoric. In one passage, Judd conjures up the image of a Hun, but as a mere aid to his erotic compulsions and sense of inferiority, which have enslaved him to Artie's arrogance, his will to use and misuse:

> The Hun and the girl, the war poster in the hallway when he was at Twain [School]—the young Frenchwoman with the dress half torn crouching against a wall, her arm up in defense, and the Hun with the slavering mouth coming toward her, then grabbing her by the hair and doing it to her. Then the almost naked body of the woman, the

limbs all awry, broken, in a field of grass. . . .[6]

Americans were supposed to have been virtuously inspired by such visions, but it is an old fact of literature, and especially of popular literature, that moral stances have often been a cover for the mental excitements conjured up by fallen women, opium dens, whipped slaves, and the like.[7] Levin is not dabbling among depraved or stupid people. His protagonists are among the most esteemed, most respectable elements of American society, and have the attention and concern of patently useful and decent people. Levin's plot is thus not peripheral to key issues in American life; it touches on the very nature of American civilization.[8]

The story moves swiftly between the scene of the crime in the wild, natural areas of South Chicago, today wholly filled with suburbs, to the university campus, the homes of Artie and Judd in affluent neighborhoods nearby, local and city police stations, and a variety of streets and parks in which the boys conduct their erratic pursuits and poisoned personal relations. Could anything have been gained by reducing the tale to tight symbols and interpretations? With much of Chicago now dead, and with a new life needing to be born for its troubled citizens, I would doubt it. That vibrant world of students, adults, and law enforcement officers needs to be seen as it was, if one is to understand[9] how they progressed until they became ourselves.

It is well known that despite the carelessness and blunders of Loeb and Leopold—which Clarence Darrow, at their trial, emphasized in order to portray them as inept and incapable, rather than of essentially "superman" qualities—despite all this, the crime would not have been solved had it not been for an impossible accident, one which made Leopold a devout Orthodox Jew who prayed daily for the soul of the murdered Bobby Franks. Had it not been for the glasses Leopold carried to Hegewisch in south Chicago—glasses he did not need and scarcely used, but which fell from his pocket—had it not been that the hinge which connected the earpiece to the nosepiece had just been introduced in Chicago and to but one firm, and that the firm had used it upon only three pairs of glasses, two owners of which could account for their whereabouts—had it not been for this detail, Leopold and

Loeb would have gone on to graduate schools and careers to become pillars of society. Leopold especially, with the incredible brain which enabled him to pick up languages at will and to be an authority on bird life while in his teens, doubtless would have made his mark as he chose.[10] Thus, his dreadful deviation from humanity could not only have seemed endorsed by the success of his murder prank. It might well have influenced his social attitudes and role in life, giving him comradeship with others whose criminality was not detected, and who went on to respectable and influential lives. The script is the exact opposite of the American dream of virtue triumphant, evil crushed in the dust. It fits very well the destiny of the doomed protagonist of Franz Kafka's *The Trial*, published, by coincidence, in 1924.[11]

A passage from *Compulsion* will illustrate the view of life which Leopold, or Judd, had felt free to indulge. A game-warden has noticed his class in ornithology. He knows that his glasses have been found. He is pleased to find himself calm, when he has been picked up at home for questioning. Artie would admire his aplomb. There seems to be no suspicion of him; he is involved in a routine checkout. He answers questions with apparent candor, though weighing the words against future possibilities.

> Then the captain just sat there as though trying to think of more questions. Judd didn't want to appear anxious to leave. He was indeed beginning to enjoy the situation, beginning to form an account of it in his mind, for Artie. Still, the silence became somewhat tense, and he allowed himself to glance at his watch. "As a matter of fact," he remarked, "I have a date to take a girl birding this afternoon, but I guess we won't be going to Hegwisch." The captain's flesh wobbled with his chortle. "That's a new name for it. Birding!"[12]
>
> Judd took a full breath.
>
> "Okay," the captain said, pushing a sheet of paper toward him. "Tell you what, son. You write me out a little statement, all you just said, the facts you just stated, for the record."
>
> As he opened his fountain pen, Judd felt in himself, perhaps a little more faintly, but still quite recognizably, that shiver of elation he had experienced when he had first read in the papers of the glasses being found. For he had after all come under suspicion. This had been a mild third

degree. He had acquitted himself. He had gone through the sieve.

"I'll have the boys drive you home, so you won't be late for your date—birding." The captain chortled again.

Judd watched himself, so as not to write too much. A paragraph. He wrote fast in a careless hand; one thing was sure, this wouldn't match his lettering on the envelope of the ransom letter. "This all right?" He passed the sheet to the captain.

The officer read it over slowly; he was a lip-reader, but concealed it by mouthing a cigar. He nodded, pushing the paper under a corner of the blotter on his desk.

"I'm afraid I haven't been of much help," Judd said, rising. A clear, mathematical conviction of superiority had come back to him. Against such people, it was a certainty he and Artie had to succeed; they could not be caught, any more than two and two could make five.[13]

"Well"—the captain leaned back—"it's a downtown job now. But we've all got to give them all the help we can."

Judd went to the door, opened it, even enjoying a fluttery feeling that a peremptory voice could still halt him. . . .

The two cops dropped him at the house. The maid rushed forward as though she had been waiting at the door. Judd laughed at her. "I'll bet you were scared I'd never come back."[14]

"Oh, no."

"It was just some routine junk about my bird-watching classes," he said, so she wouldn't be spreading stories.

He went upstairs. There was an elation in him now over the way he had handled the interrogation. His victory was like a confirmation of his entire code of behavior. He was right, right, right![15]

Leopold found the novel upsetting, and feared it would hurt his chances at his next hearing. In time, he concluded the novel—and Levin's personal appeals in his behalf—had probably helped. But his own views of the work add further evidence that it was an artistic triumph,[16] as well as what Leopold saw to be an amazingly accurate reconstruction of the time and circumstances. Forty percent fact, and sixty percent fiction, he judged. But the sixty percent obviously referred to the character and psychology of the people involved, himself included. He protests that Levin has written fiction rendered insidious by his seamless, consummate artistry.[17] Out of his emotional upset and confusion, Leopold accuses Levin of having imputed to him thoughts and crimes which had never occurred to him. "My God," he cries, "what I did is horrible enough and the load of guilt I bear on my conscience is already heavy enough without this additional source of turmoil."[18]

Yet in the passage of the book following, Leopold feels himself "as I suppose a man would feel if he were exposed stark-naked under a strong spotlight before a large audience." Leopold is not always aware of the implications of his own words. His entire effort has been to reveal himself as totally separate from the wretched youth who had made his bloody imprint on social history. His body, he insists, has over and over again sloughed off all his physical self; there is not a cell in him which was there in 1924. Years of remorse have altered all his views and feelings.

Yet . . . he recalls that, on having been jailed, following his confession, his next cellmate, a lad of his own age, was gracious and considerate of his feelings.

> The meals were good enough [he recalls]. There was just one hitch: no liquids or semi-liquids could be sent in. One day I remarked idly that I had a yen for some real chop suey; I wished that could be sent in. The next visiting day, Augie, without saying anything to me, must have asked his mother to send him some. That night after lockup a big cardboard container full of succulent chop suey arrived. Piping hot, too. Did it ever taste good.[19]

That the unreconstructed Leopold could have enjoyed his chop suey with Bobby Franks desecrated and cold in his grave can be understood. Less comprehensible is Leopold's mental pleasure in the dish more than thirty years after.[20]

Yet it is unlikely that Leopold's insensitivity—for, despite his brilliance in material phenomena and categorical information, he was grossly immature emotionally and esthetically[21]—it is unlikely that all this hurt him significantly with the parole board or the public. Numerous critics observed that part of the impact of Dreiser's *An American Tragedy* (which, like Levin's book, also featured a full-length trial) resulted from a general awareness by readers that there but for a bit of luck or alternate circumstances

went they themselves to the electric chair. The defense which
enabled Clarence Darrow to gain for his clients Loeb and Leopold
life imprisonment instead of the death penalty was based solely on
anti-capital punishment grounds: a faith that Americans would
not condemn to the uttermost the issue or their own loins and
lives.

There is a Freudian thread throughout *Compulsion* engrossing
child-parent relationships, childish fantasies, homosexual tenden-
cies, and abortive male-female congress. Levin's Sid Silver, in a
species of postscript, reviews the tragedy with a friend of college
days who is now an analyst. They reconsider the relations of
Artie and Judd, and find meaning in the white concrete pipe in
which Bobby's body had been thrust, in Judd's Madonna fixation,
and in other details. I myself do not find these interpretations
too enthralling, or persuasive. What does seem to me impressive
is the emergence of such investigations, the multiplying of clinics,
case studies, therapy, all reflecting the need of Americans to
understand the source of their compulsions, and to control them.
All of this was and is socially necessary in a nation which offered,
and continued to offer a degree of opportunity and permissiveness
unexampled in history. *Don't Shoot,* a worthy study of recent
youthful desperadoes tells us, *We Are Your Children.*[22] We do
indeed need to understand ourselves and each other. But we need,
in addition, to perceive the difference between the therapy of
psychoanalysis and the therapy—or catharsis—of esthetics. Levin's
Compulsion contributes to the latter.

I offer the following passage from it as testimony.[23] Artie
has just been arrested, and imprisoned:

> He didn't feel out of place. The closing door, the
> turning lock had familiarity. Artie looked to his cellmate
> with an almost mischievous glance, as though they were
> two kids: now the game begins. But the cellmate was a
> dull-witted farm lad, who didn't even seem impressed by
> who Artie was. After brief exchanges of what they were
> in for—the cellmate had done a robbery with a gun—Artie
> stretched on his bunk.
>
> He had seen himself often, lying behind solid dungeon
> walls. After Miss Nuisance had tucked him in tight and
> placed his teddy bear beside him and gone out, shutting
> the door as the lights went off, he would turn to the bear,

whispering the magic word, and it came to his lips now, the magic beginning, "*and now, Teddy . . .*" But here the light never really went out; some greasy kind of half illumination hung over the cell floor.[24]

And now, Teddy they got us. But we can figure out a way to lam. We always did it and we can do it again. Like from the house in Charlevoix, climbing out of the window and swiping the car and driving like all hell—too bad there was the collision.

But the master criminal, the greatest of them all, cannot be held by locks and bars. Shall it be the special key that fits all locks, smuggled in by our moll? No, Teddy, this place is easy—you saw that guard, that screw, give me the eye, the one at the main gate. He's in our pay; he's part of the master criminal's gang. And in a few days, as soon as we're ready, we'll tip him the wink, and the gate will accidentally be left open and we'll walk right out of here.

Meanwhile, we'll play the game just like we did with Miss Nuisance. We will be model little boys, model prisoners who never tell a lie. They will trust us, and we'll wander around and get the layout—the rainpipe we can slide down, things like that.

But Mumsie hasn't come. Mumsie hasn't come to say good night to poor Artie. Only Miss Nuisance. Mumsie is busy with her baby. A new baby must be taken care of by Mumsie. *All right for you!*

Is Nuisance gone? Good and safe and gone? Safe in her room? Sneak the flashlight from under the mattress. The detective book. The master criminal kidnapers. Snatch the baby right in his own house, and bring him up to the hiding place in the garret; everything works perfectly. That Italian organ grinder outside plays the signal-tune that says the ransom is ready. Only we work it with care. A car horn. Hear that horn—*shave and a haircut, ten cents?* That means ten grand is ready.

No, we'll do it differently. We'll pretend to play cops and robbers with little brother. Yes, Mumsie, I'd love to play a game with Baby.

Shh, Teddy, here's the plot. That little stupe believes everything you tell him. You pretend you're on his side, helping him catch the master criminal, and I will be lying in wait at the top of the stairs. You bring the little bastard up, and *pow!* I've got him! It was an accident! Nobody knew the pistol was loaded. Poor baby, oh, my sweet little kid brother!

Then, punishment. They never spank you. They lock you in your room.

Revenge! Do the same to them! . . . "Now Artie, this is your new governess, Miss Newsome, and you must be very nice to her." There she goes into her room! Turn the key on her! Listen to the prisoner pound on the door! "Oh, Artie, Arthur! You naughty—!"

Then Miss Nuisance made him sit on a chair. Mumsie didn't save him from her. Mumsie said obey Miss Newsome. All right for you, Mumsie, I'll get even with you. In some dark hallway, *pow!*

They were leading him to the scaffold and Miss Nuisance was walking behind, reading *A Tale of Two Cities* out loud to him. . . .

Turning over on his pallet, feeling something crawling under his clothes, Artie sat up. Bugs, lice.[25]

B. TRAVEN AND *THE DEATH SHIP* AS HIGH CULTURE

ROBERT OLAFSON

The fiction of B. Traven has garnered a vast worldwide readership. For almost half a century, for example, *The Death Ship* has been in the mainstream of popular literature. The novel first loomed large on the literary horizon in the spring of 1926, when the Gutenberg Book Guild published 91,000 copies. The novel subsequently has been published in scores of countries. *The Death Ship*'s most recent port call in the United States was in 1973 as Hill and Wang (Traven's current publishers) printed a hardback edition in New York. This marks the third appearance of the novel here: *The Death Ship* (New York: Knopf, 1934; Collier Books, 1962; New York: Hill and Wang, 1973).

Commonly B. Traven's sales record is the *major* recommendation of his fiction. The Collier Books' paperback carries this backcover blurb:

> B. Traven, one of the mysterious literary figures of the twentieth century (his true identity has long been a closely guarded secret) is the author of *The Treasure of The Sierra Madre*. His twelve novels, published in more than 500 editions in 36 languages, have sold millions of copies. *The Death Ship* . . . has sold more than a quarter million copies in Europe and Latin America and more than a million in Russia.

Although these statistics may be inflated, two facts are indisputable: B. Traven has striven to remain anonymous[1] and he has written best sellers. Several of these best sellers have also achieved further popular success as motion pictures in Germany, Mexico and the United States. *The Death Ship* was filmed in Germany with Horst Buchholz and Elke Sommer; *Macario* and *The White Rose (Rosa Blanca)* were set to the screen by the Mexicans; and, of course, *The Treasure of The Sierra Madre* has become one of the American film classics, on the strength of Humphrey Bogart's fine acting and John Huston's superb directing.

B. Traven's popular success has not been accompanied by voluminous critical success, especially in his native United States. American critics seldom have gone beyond labeling the few works they *have* read of Traven as interesting adventure yarns, not too far removed from the fiction of popular pulp magazines. Frequently the author is cited as having a rough, uneven style, of being a proletarian writer more interested in the message than the medium, of being essentially a low culture writer, possessing few of the skills of the accomplished novelists.

Even the two most recent champions of Traven, American critics Charles Henry Miller and Walter M. Langford, have not come fully to grips with Traven's use of form in his fiction. Each critic recognizes some elements of Traven's art, yet each man does not escape fully from the common notion that there are many aspects of "artlessness" or popular low culture in the fiction.

Charles Miller's essay "B. Traven, Pure Proletarian Writer," in David Madden's *Proletarian Writers of the Thirties,* Carbondale: 1968, defends cogently Traven's philosophy and some elements of his style and prose strategies but fails to give final due to the author as a careful shaper of form in the novel. On the plus side for Miller, he defends Traven's diction, particularly in *The Death Ship,* as ". . . work language [with]. . . powers of suggestion, allusion, and eloquence." Miller continues:

> His death ship is a "tub . . . a bucket . . . a coffin . . . a deathmobile . . . a bobtail. His fellow workers speak a bit of all the languages of the globe they sail. The ship is a floating babel, and Gales [the narrator] is concerned with language, soliloquizing on the captain's too-correct grammar and the differences between real and literary English. Gales speaks common American English. The captain is "the old man," the workers "knock off" and "bring in the grub." The language is dated but effective. It is the dialect of the underdog; it is part of our vital, melded, American idiom.

On the negative side, Miller in his desire to prove that Traven is the "pure proletarian writer," again especially in his reading of *The Death Ship,* overemphasizes his belief that the novel is primarily made up of raw autobiographical experience and underplays possible literary sources.

Although Miller recognizes Traven's many uses of literary allusion, he sees them more as ballast than as important cargo in the novel. Miller observes:

> But the sailors, stokers, jailbirds, farmers, workers, petty officials, and cops whom Traven describes and to whom all his books are directed are not concerned with lofty literary names, and the author is primarily concerned with his proletarians and with ideas which apply to their condition and destiny.

Miller, good as he is on Traven, places *experience* above *imagination* in his reading of the fiction and ultimately fails to give credit to Traven's artistic genius.

Walter Langford in his recent, *The Mexican Novel Comes of Age* (Notre Dame: 1971), focuses on B. Traven's contribution to the Mexican literature of the *campesino* (peon) and the search for Traven's true identity. Regarding the former theme, Langford writes, ". . . no writer, Mexicans included, has better understood the *campesino* of that country or defended his cause in more fiery manner."

After praising B. Traven as a champion of the underdog with keen insights into both the American and Mexican cultures, Langford comments on Traven's art: "As a writer, Traven is no great stylist and he worries little about the structure of his novel." Again, as with Miller, Langford really doesn't try to see him as a truly creative, imaginative artist.

This view of Traven which sees him as a rough, uncut diamond in literature is similar to the critical treatment often given his contemporary, Theodore Dreiser. Both novelists have been tarred with the same brush. Yet Dreiser's stature as an artist continues to rise as more and more perceptive critics turn to serious study of him. So we may predict, B. Traven will undergo a similar recognition in the future.

The evidence of Traven's wide mass appeal, with very little

accompanying critical acclaim, in no way relegates him to the camp of the low culture writers, who write formula pieces for popular success. B. Traven is no Mickey Spillane, Alistair MacLean or anyone so inane—pardon the rhyme!

Leslie Fiedler provides a definition which distinguishes between serious and popular art which is applicable to B. Traven:

> Works of "literature" depend on their success primarily on form (organization, selection, subtlety of pattern, precision of diction and detail); popular art, on the other hand, lives chiefly by its *mythic* appeal, its ability to hit upon the pattern story and image which can transmit to everyone, simple or sophisticated, what they need to know, without making them aware that they are learning anything or, God forbid, improving themselves or enriching their lives. (Leslie Fiedler, *The Art of The Essay*, 2nd ed., Part III, "The Discovery of Popular Culture," New York: 1969.)

The Death Ship, subtitled *The Story of an American Sailor*, on the surface, does have many stock patterns of sea adventures (the missed ship, a mysterious captain, outcast crews, gun-running, ship-wreck, etc.) and elements of the myth of the homeless man, the sailor without a country, the victim; but it goes beyond a simple pattern story of the sea and the underdog. From the uncomplex plot of the sailor who misses his ship, loses his identification papers, is deported from several European countries and finally gets a berth on a death ship—Traven creates a complex work of art.

The genre of the novel is picaresque first person narrative told in vernacular slang, the detail is realistic description of a work world, still known all too well by the world's underprivileged and exploited workers on the fringes of "respectable" jobs. All is welded together carefully by Traven.

Yet few of the millions of the readers of *The Death Ship*, including Charles Miller and Walter Langford, think of it as an "arty" book. Paradoxically, however, it is ladened with a heavy manifest of literary allusion, of subtle patterns of organization and brilliant selection of detail. In a word, the novel has form. The same assertion can be made for *The Treasure of The Sierra Madre, The Rebellion of The Hanged, The White Rose, The Bridge in The Jungle*—for that matter all Traven novels—they are works of literature, each with its own unique principles of organization, selection, subtlety of pattern, etc. B. Traven may not always be successful in his creation of literature, but he is always a highly conscious artist. For purposes of brevity, this essay examines the form of *The Death Ship*.

B. Traven strives to write a realistic novel of the sea, of the tramp steamers that ply it and of the men who sail it. In the first chapter of the novel, only four pages long, Traven pointedly attacks both romantic and popular literature repeatedly. "All the romance of the sea that you will find in magazine stories died long, long ago." His narrator, Gerard Gales,[2] the sailor out of New Orleans, leaves the *Tuscaloosa* for shore leave in Antwerp because: "I was sick of reading true confession stories and ranch romances." He says a few lines before this:

> . . . the song of the real and genuine hero of the sea has never yet been sung. Why? Because the true song would be too cruel and too strange for people who like ballads. Opera-audiences, movie goers, and magazine-readers are like that. They want to have everything pleasant, with a happy ending. The true story of the sea is anything but pleasant or romantic in the accepted sense. The life of the real heroes has always been cruel, made up of hard work, of treatment worse than animals of the cargo get, and often of the most noble sacrifices, but without medals and plaques, and without mention in stories, operas and movies. Even the hairy apes are opera-singers looking for a piece of lingerie.

As Traven heaps up these attacks on sea romances of "the China Sea" (Joseph Conrad), "hairy apes" (Eugene O'Neill), "success stories of the builders of our nation" (Horatio Alger), and "ranch romances" (Zane Grey), it becomes obvious that the opening chapter of *The Death Ship* sets forth Traven's artistic credo. The references to Conrad, O'Neill and Alger reoccur in subsequent chapters frequently. Allusions are also made to Kafka, Shakespeare, Goethe, Dante, Melville and Cooper in the novel.[3] Despite Charles Miller's belief that *The Death Ship* is highly autobiographical, few works of modern literature are as source ridden as this novel. Indeed, it is B. Traven's use of these allusions that gives the *form* to *The Death Ship*.

Divided into three books with a total of fifty chapters, section after section of the novel reveals Traven's complex and subtle use of sources. For instance in Book I, containing twenty-two chapters, chapters one through eighteen are deeply influenced by Franz Kafka's art, as Gales goes through numerous bureaucratic horrors in his attempt to establish his identity. Gerard Gales, who is now nameless, like Kafka's K is disoriented, distressed, and disliked by a series of bureaucrats who are highly evocative of similar figures in Kafka's nightmare visions of modern man. Clearly Kafka's *The Penal Colony* (1919), *The Trial* (1925) and, possibly, *The Castle* (1926) are Traven's sources. Another Kafka story, "The Stoker" (1913), published in the magazine *Der jüngste Tag,* may also have influenced B. Traven. "The Stoker," which eventually became the first chapter of *Amerika,* is a simple tale of Karl Rossmann's meeting a stoker below decks of his liner when it reaches New York. He hears the stoker's story of woe and defends him before the captain. When Karl asks the stoker if he likes his job, the stoker replies: "I don't like it. I don't suppose you're thinking seriously of being a stoker, but that's just the time when you're most likely to turn into one." This, of course, is exactly what befalls Traven's sailor when he boards *The Death Ship:* he is a coal-drag (stoker) by accident.

The major theme of Book I, however, is Gales' inability to effectively communicate with bureaucrats, to be regarded by them as a human being. Examine this example of the Kafkaesque bureaucratic snafu in *The Death Ship:*

> The whole affair passed by quicker than the time it had taken me to get the idea about seeing His Holiness the American consul at all.
>   "You are American?"
>   "Yesser."
>   "Where is your sailor's identification card?"
>   "I have lost it, sir,"
>   "Passport?"
>   "Nosser."
>   "Citizenship papers?"
>   "Never had any. Born in the country. Native state—"
>   "Never mind. Well, what do you want here?"
>   "I thought maybe, sir, I mean I was thinking, since you are my consul, that maybe you might—what I was going to

say you perhaps might do something to get me out, because, you see sir, I am stranded, to make it short.

He grinned at me. Rather nasty. Strange that bureaucrats always grin at you in a nasty way when they want to thumb you down.

Still grinning, he said: "Your consul? My good man, let me tell you something: if you wish to address me as your consul, you will first of all have to prove that I am really your consul."

"I am American, sir. And you are the American consul."

"Right-o. I am the American consul. But who are you to tell me that you are American. Have you got any papers? Birth certificate? Or passport? Or authorized sailor's identification?"

"I told you already that I lost it."

"Lost. Lost. Lost. What do you mean lost? In times like these one does not lose such important papers. Ought to know that, my good man. You cannot even prove that you have been on the *Tuscaloosa*.

He pronounced "have" like *hauve* and "know" like *knouw,* trying to make us poor Middle West guys believe that he came from Oxford or Cambridge or I don't know what.

"Cawn you prove thawt you hauve been on the *Tuscaloosa?*"

"No."

This scene takes place in Rotterdam, similar confrontations occur, with European and American officials, in Antwerp and Paris. The Kafkaesque motif of frustration even takes on allegorical significance. Although Charles Miller does not relate it to the model of Kafka's allegorical method, he does fathom Traven's allegory. Miller writes:

> The first documented idea is that most societies, including our American one, tend to be criminally careless about lowly members on the outer fringes. And the strongest thematic idea is the young hero's apocalyptic vision of death, the real horizon toward which all of us are sailing, with oppressed proletarians outsailing the rest of us. (In "B. Traven, Pure Proletarian Writer.")

Chapter Five ends:

> There is a good reason for being the way he is. The state

cannot make use of human beings. It would cease to exist.
Human beings only make trouble. Men cut out of cardboard do not make trouble. Yesser. Excuse me, I mean:
yes, sir.

The second major source lending structure to Book I becomes
operative in chapters nineteen through twenty-two—which ends
the first book.   Traven consciously names the filthy, battered
hulk of a death ship, which Gales boards in Barcelona, the
Yorrikke.   Hamlet's famous lines commemorating Yorick, the
king's jester, as he holds his skull in the open grave, undergird
these chapters:

> . . . Alas, poor Yorick! I knew him, Horatio: a fellow of
> infinite jest, a most excellent fancy: he hath borne me on
> his back a thousand times; and now, how abhorred in my
> imagination it is! my gorge rises at it.

When Gales first sees the *Yorrikke* in chapter nineteen, he
reacts, "The whole thing was a huge joke." The crew standing at
the rails strikes him as half-dead clowns in outlandish makeshift
clothes (Chapter 21). And the narrator's "gorge" will rise again
and again as he comes to know the death ship.
     Book II restates allusions to Conrad (Chapter 25) and Alger
(Chapter 26), while introducing allusions to Herman Melville and
amplifying ones to O'Neill's play *The Hairy Ape*. The reference
to *Moby Dick* is clever and witty—yet minor; the reference to
The Hairy Ape is major. Indeed, Traven's reaction to *The Hairy
Ape* (1922) is the controlling structural device in Book II.
     First the reference to Melville: Gales, unwilling to use his
real name on the *Yorrikke,* calls himself Pippip before the
captain—a fine descriptive touch by Traven as Gales, working as
a coal-drag in the stoke-hold, spends his life covered with soot
and working like a slave. The model of Pip, the black boy, in
Moby Dick is effectively evoked. (Dickens's Pip in *Great
Expectations* may also be evoked here, ironically of course,
because Pippip has *no expectations.*)
     Now to O'Neill's play:

> We wore only pants. On his feet the fireman wore a sort of
> cloth slipper. I had shoes. Now and then the fireman

jumped back with a curse and shook the cinders that leaped
upon his bare arms and naked chest. There were no hairy
apes around with lurking strains of philosophy for stage
purposes. No time for thinking and looking under dames'
skirts. Five seconds lost thinking of anything else but your
stoke-hold might cause twenty square inches of your sound
flesh to be burned away. A stoke-hold in a stage-play or in
the movies is something different, at least more pleasant.
People in evening dress would not like to see the thing as it
is and still pay for it. (Chapter 30.)

The allusion is to the scene in which Yank sees Mildred at
the end of Act I, scene iii. Traven obviously feels that O'Neill
does not capture the black gang with sufficient realism. Yet it
can be argued that Traven learned from O'Neill in the use of
language and expressionistic techniques. Gales' speech patterns
are similar to Yank's and certainly the descriptions of the cramped
and filthy interior of the *Yorrikke* parallel O'Neill's expressionistic
descriptions of the set in *The Hairy Ape*.

Other parallels to the play are found in Traven's references
to the Wobblies and remote and uncaring shipowners. You will
recall O'Neill's similar themes:

> Long: . . . They dragged us down 'til we're on'y wage
> slaves in the bowels of a bloody ship, sweatin', burnin' up,
> eatin' coal dust! Hit's them's ter blame—the damned
> capitalist clarss! (Act I, scene i)

and:

> Voices: Douglas? That's the president of the Steel Trust,
> I bet.
>
> Sure. I seen his mug in de papers.
>
> He's filthy with dough.
>
> Voice: Hey, feller, take a tip from me. If you want to get
> back at that dame, you better join the Wobblies. You'll
> get some action then. (Act I, scene vi)

A lesser leitmotif of the *Morituri te salutamus* theme of the
slave-gladiator's salute to the Roman Emperor also runs through
Book II, supporting B. Traven's vision of modern slavery. Traven's
horror of and preoccupation with the new kind of slavery (a debt-

slavery: fashioned out of a system that beats down the workers economically, psychologically and physically—they invariably owe their souls to the company store) emerges clearly in *The Death Ship*. This theme is Traven's major artistic preoccupation: it is the theme of all his major novels. Before 1930 Americans are frequently featured in his fiction as the victims or victimizers, after this date the Mexican Indians are the victims and the *ladinos* (Mexican white supremists) are the slavemasters. Traven's novelistic studies of *peonage* and other forms of forced labor occur in a six-novel series set in the time of the iron-rule of the dictator, Porfirio Diaz, before the Mexican Revolution of 1910.[4]   *The Carreta* and *The March to the Monteria* are two examples.

Coal-stokers, cotton-pickers, oil-riggers, ox cart teamsters, loggers, miners, coffee-harvesters all are portrayed in Traven's fiction as virtual beasts of burden, often literally worked to death by unscrupulous employers.

Book II of *The Death Ship* documents this view of the down-trodden worker carefully.   Gales says of replacing fallen grate-bars in the ship's furnace:

> . . . to put them back into their berth not only cost blood, not alone flesh torn off, large pieces of skin scorched, but cost bleeding sperm, shredded tendons, and painfully twisted entrails.   (Chapter 31)

Gales continues the theme:

> Within four hours the fires of the *Yorrikke* swallowed about sixteen hundred well-filled large shovelfuls of fuel. The fuel was in many instances so far away from the boilers that these sixteen hundred shovelfuls had to be thrown in four shifts before they reached the fireman, so that the real hauling for the drag was not sixteen hundred shovels, but sometimes close to seventy hundred shovels. (Chapter 31)

Yank in *The Hairy Ape* may have felt at home in the hold of his ship, may have felt pride until he reacts to Mildred's stare of revulsion, but Gales can never feel comfortable as a beast of burden.

Book II also contains the story of the Pole, Stanislow Koslovski of Poznon, who through the caprices of World War I has become a displaced person, his home country fell to political expediency at the Treaty of Versailles. His tale told to Gales replays the Kafka theme of bureaucratic horror in the novel.

Finally Book III, chapters forty-six through fifty, concludes *The Death Ship*. Here the structure of the novel is not as heavily dependent upon explicit literary allusion. Many implicit ones surface, however, in a close reading of Book III. Gales, as Pippip, and Stanislav are shanghaied aboard another death ship, the *Empress of Madagascar* and B. Traven begins to employ "echoes" or buried allusions (similar to T. S. Eliot's techniques in *The Waste Land*).

Gales-Pippip survives shipwreck in images that evoke Ishmael in *Moby Dick*. Stanislov hallucinates with thirst as do Coleridge's seamen in *The Rime of the Ancient Mariner*. Drowning sailors battle the sea as in Conrad's *Typhoon*. Pippip and Stanislov survive briefly the first hectic efforts to abandon the ship and return to the *Empress* as she lies hard upon the reef; they take inventory of the ship's stores in scenes that evoke Defoe's *Robinson Crusoe*. Pippip has a dream-vision that even presents river and raft imagery akin to that in Twain's *Huckleberry Finn:*

> Now I could see quite clearly the river-banks both sides. We were still drifting down the river. It might be the Hudson or the Mississippi.

B. Traven does not emphasize or amplify these "echo" allusions in Book III. He is more concerned with creating an image of a journey from Hell to Heaven in the conclusion of the novel. The men, Pippip and Stanislov, fall to the depths of Hell (the hold of the ship) and rise to salvation (in Stanislov's case to heaven) and to actual new life in Pippip's.

Gales-Pippip ends the novel with these lines on the drowning of Stanislov:

> He had signed on for a long voyage. For a very great voyage.
>
> I could not understand this. How could he have signed on? He had no sailor's card. No papers whatever. They would

kick him off right away.

And the Great Skipper said to him: "Come, Stanislov Koslovski, give me your hand. Shake. Come up, sailor! I shall sign you on a fine ship. For an honest and decent ship. The finest we have. Never mind the papers. You will not need any here. You are on an honest ship. Go to your quarters, Stanislov. Can you read what is written above the quarters, Stanislov?"

And Stanislov said: "Aye, aye, sir. He who enters here will be forever free of pain!"

As the final line echoes Dante, B. Traven ends *The Death Ship,* a novel structured as consciously and carefully as any vessel ever created by master shipwrights. B. Traven is an artist very much in tradition of the novelists of high culture.

STEPHEN VINCENT BENÉT'S "HAIR-RAISING DEFECTS"?

WILLIAM J. HARRIS

> "John Brown's Body" has merit enough; it has hair-raising defects; and yet it deserves to be widely read and, within reason, praised.
>
> Allen Tate, *The Nation,* September 19, 1928

Stephen Vincent Benét, a winner of two Pulitzer Prizes for poetry, an author who was one of the most popular of serious writers in America, a man of letters who wielded a great deal of literary power, has been forgotten by the American literary world. He is no longer attacked for his "hair-raising defects" by some stern and serious critic but, rather, is simply ignored. He is not included in Richard Ellman's 1973 edition of *The Norton Anthology of Modern Poetry* (somehow Masters, Sandburg and Lindsay have survived him) nor is he included in Albert Gelpi's *The Poet in America* (1973), and, perhaps even more significantly, he is excluded from Louis Untermeyer's *50 Modern American and British Poets* (1973). Benét was included in Untermeyer's earlier anthology *Modern American Poetry* (1962). Not only the anthologists ignore Benét but the critics do also: Roy Harvey Pearce (*The Continuity of American Poetry,* 1961), Hyatt H. Waggoner (*American Poets,* 1968), and Walter Sutton (*American Free Verse,* 1973) never mention Benét.

I would not be very troubled about Benét's literary misfortunes if he had only written *John Brown's Body* and "The Devil and Daniel Webster," his most famous works. I would not care that he has been damned to the high schools if he still even occupies that circle of Hell. Yet he has written a few short stories that should not be forgotten—"Johnny Pye and the Fool-Killer" and "A Death in the Country," in particular—and written an important and successful epic poem, *Western Star.*

John Brown's Body, the poem for which he is famous, is a cartoon of the Civil War: with Jack Ellyat, the Northern hero, finding and losing love in the middle of the war and with Clay Wingate (can you believe that name?), the Southern hero complete with a cardboard Southern mansion, a cardboard Southern mammy and a cardboard Southern family. "Yeah, Steve," I can almost hear part of Benét's mind say, "this ain't going to sell if you don't put a love story in." In this poem Benet's imagination sinks to the level of a best-selling novelist like Frank Yerby or Irving Wallace. There is not one living three-dimensional character in the whole book. That part of his imagination that could write hack and conventional stories has won out over the more serious part. Yet it is a poem of a humane man who could see goodness in both the North and the South but could not imagine a living universe. It is not Benét's heart that fails in this work but his imagination.

"The Devil and Daniel Webster" is not a product of a "cheap" imagination but it is too fragile a vehicle to handle its profound message about the brotherhood of man whether he be damned or saved. Benét's imagination becomes profounder in both prose and poetry as the poet grows older. *Western Star,* his last poem, published posthumously and unfinished, is a serious epic which presents a humane and peopled history of America's first years.

Even though *Western Star* is different from our standard modern epic poem—*The Cantos, Paterson, The Waste Land*—it should be accepted into the canon of modern literature. In fact, the canon—our conception of literature—should be expanded. The roots of the modern epic can be found in Whitman's *Leaves of Grass.* It is subjective, plotless, philosophical, optimistic and lacks any real characterization beyond the poet-narrator. For our time, *The Waste Land* is the prime example of the modern epic: it is difficult, obscure, rich in world mythology, fragmented, plotless; it lacks characterization and it is dispairing. Whitman's roots have been somewhat twisted and mutated by the twentieth century: the epic has darkened.

Western Star has characters we grow to know and even care about; it is easy to read; it is not esoteric in any way; it has a plot and its history is either familiar or Benét gives the reader any background information he might need. And it is a poem of praise,

praise of the ordinary people who established this country. But Benét's praise is different from Sandburg's, our other champion of the common folk. He does not praise the people, the mob, an abstraction:

> I am the people—the mob—the crowd—the mass.
> Do you know that all the great work of the world is done
>   through me?

(Complete Poems of Carl Sandburg, p. 71)

Rather, Benét praises concrete individuals from all classes who were involved in the early history of America. He does not praise the masses but praises Dickon Heron, the teenage apprentice; Matthew Lanyard, the carpenter; Mother Billington, the earthy woman; and Henry Shenton, the seeker.

> Not for the great, not for the marvelous,
> Not for the barren husbands of the gold;
> Not for the arrowmakers of the soul,
> Wasted with truth, the star-regarding wise;
> Not even for the few
> Who would not be the hunter nor the prey,
> Who stood between the eater and the meat,
> The wilderness saints, the guiltless, the absolved,
> Born out of Time, the seekers of the balm
> Where the green grass grows from the broken heart;
> But for all these, the nameless, numberless
> Seed of the field, the mortal wood and earth
> Hewn for the clearing, trampled for the floor,
> Uprooted and cast out upon the stone
> From Jamestown to Benicia.
> This is their song, this is their testament,
> Carved to their likeness, speaking in their tongue
> and branded with the iron of their star.

(Western Star, p. vii)

To paraphrase Parry Stroud, the author of the only full-length study of Benét of work, Benét has extracted from the archives of libraries living and therefore convincing individualized characters (Benét, 145, 147-48). In a letter to Paul Engle Benét unconsciously sets forth his purpose in Western Star.

> I have been doing a lot of reading for *Western Star*—
> Pilgrims, Puritans, Virginians, etc.—and at least know some-
> thing more about early America than when I started, and
> hope it will come out some day. The diaries and letters
> and such are wonderful—why in hell aren't they better
> taught in most histories—why don't they let the people
> come through?

> (*Selected Letters of Stephen Vincent Benét*, p. 302)

The people come through in *Western Star*.

More than plot or obscurity, what most separates *Western Star* from the modern epic is that it is not a poem of despair but of praise. *The Waste Land* has provided the dominant image of our modern literature, an image of sterility which has haunted the literary landscape from *The Waste Land*'s publication to the present, from *The Great Gatsby* to *The Dead Lecturer*. Today, to praise seems naive. I am not trying to say that *The Waste Land* is false—that this has been a great century and this is the best of all possible worlds. *The Waste Land* is a great and influential poem which has documented a great spiritual crisis of our civilization: the death of God, the destruction of traditional values for many sensitive individuals. Yet many sensitive individuals have not felt the death of God or values. Many sensitive people either do not care that God died or believe he is alive and well. Benét is an artist who does not really care much about the existence of God but does care about the conditions of man on this earth; he is a humanist and, as Parry Stroud (*Benét*, Preface) implies, he is a liberal who believes in the pursuit of life, liberty and happiness. In fact, Benét's world is not religious but historical and political. Like Kenneth Patchen he is concerned about the community of man.

By the end of *Western Star* we care deeply about the people in the poem. Unlike in a poem by Eliot or Pound we know the characters: they are not fragmented people who seek a tradition and a replacement for God in a city of fog and uncertainty; they are people involved in the struggle for their own existence. There are no existential blues in Benét! We learn to know Dickon Heron very well. We watch him as an apprentice to Master Knapp in London; we learn of his love of the sea; we see him go to America; we see him grow from being a boy to being a man; we see him realize his dream in the new world—we see him marry and gain the land and we are saddened when he is killed by the Indians. This is a man we know and his death is important to us. Dickon Heron's death is moving in a way that no death is in *John Brown's Body*. I didn't care when Jack Ellyat was wounded; he never walked the earth and cast a shadow. Benét, the reasonable and compassionate man, moves from a cartoon civil war to a real world which deserves his reasonableness and compassion.

In *Western Star* we get to know the Puritans as people. We follow Matthew Lanyard from England to Holland to America. We see him not as an ancestor but as an individual. He is a man who loves his wife who is more devoutly Puritan than he. A while after she dies he reluctantly remarries because his daughter must have a mother. The new wife, Kate Lanyard, also a Puritan, wants to be a good wife but cannot fully love this other woman's child. This is not a Hollywood movie about the Puritans but real life. Benét is not trying to whitewash either the Puritans or American history. He shows that Lanyard was a good man and that Kate was a narrow woman. He illustrates the Puritan's weakness of knowing they are next to God and that they know God's will.

> So she [Kate] thought and crushed the cut worm upon the
> leaf
> For it ate what it should not eat and it knew not God
> And so she would do to any who knew not God.
>
> (*Western Star,* p. 175)

And Kate would crush Humility's husband, Henry Shenton, because he was a seeker, a man who wanted more than the official religion, wanted something truer.

Benét's interest in religion is not salvation (like Eliot's) but freedom. There is the same concern about freedom and sanity in *John Brown's Body* as in *Western Star;* it is only more humanly realized in the later poem. John Vilas—the hider from war and man's insanity, a Thoreau of the wilderness—to a degree fore-shadows Henry Shenton, "the seeker, the man who is not content," in *Western Star.* Shenton wants to escape man's insanity —not war this time but narrow and rigid ideas about religion. Unlike Vilas he does not flee to a romantic hiding place beyond war and history but to Roger Williams' Rhode Island where he can exercise religious freedom.

"The Devil and Daniel Webster" contains Benét's vision as completely as any of his works: damned or not men are brothers and there is the possibility of decency in every man. It is the liberal vision of man. I believe the message but though Daniel Webster may be able to melt the hearts of the jury from hell Benét does not manage to melt my heart with his tale. The telling of the story is too cute. In the first two paragraphs of "The Devil and Daniel Webster" we can see its almost arty folksiness:

> It's a story they tell in the border country where Massachusetts joins Vermont and New Hampshire.
> Yes, Dan'l Webster's dead—or, at least, they buried him. But every time there's a thunderstorm around Marshfield, they say you can hear his rolling voice in the hollows of the sky. And they say that if you go to his grave and speak loud and clear, "Dan'l Webster—Dan'l Webster!" the ground'll begin to shiver and the trees begin to shake. And after a while you'll hear a deep voice saying, "Neighbor, how stands the Union?" Then you better answer the Union stands as she stood, rock-bottomed and copper-sheathed, one and indivisible, or he's liable to rear right out of the ground. At least, that's what I was told when I was a youngster.
>
> (*Thirteen O'Clock*, p. 162)

It's too self-consciously an American folk tale with its "Dan'l," "Union stands as she stood, rock-bottomed and copper-sheathed," and "he's liable to rear right out of the ground"; it's too preciously colorful; the paragraphs are too contrived with their opening and closing lines, shouting this is a gen-u-ine American Tall Story.

"Johnny Pye and the Fool-Killer" says all men are fools because they must die. We have another seeker after the truth to add to our list, Johnny Pye. Johnny Pye spends his life trying to escape the Fool-Killer, a supernatural agent of death. At the age of eleven he runs away from home and over the years apprentices himself to a variety of "wise" men: a con man, a businessman, a congressman and others. He hopes that one of them will give him wisdom. Eventually he discovers that all men are fools and there is no way to escape death. In fact, in his early nineties he welcomes the Fool-Killer.

"Johnny Pye and the Fool-Killer" has a resonance that "The Devil and Daniel Webster" does not. The Fool-Killer is authentic. I gather from reading "A Death in the Country," one of Benét's best stories, that the Fool-Killer is a "real" boogieman from his childhood. Grown-ups told their children that they better watch out for the Fool-Killer. Benet has taken this childhood boogieman and has transformed him into an excellent personification of death. There is nothing arch about him. As LeRoi Jones says: "The most powerful way to deal with an image is to make sure it goes deeper than literature. That it is actually 'out there.' " (*Home,* p. 129) The Fool-Killer is more "out there" than "Daniel Webster." Yet by the time of *Western Star* Benét is able to make history "out there," to make history as living as his personal experience.

Allen Tate, in *The Nation,* said of *John Brown's Body* shortly after its first appearance that "it has hair-raising defects" and I agree with Mr. Tate. Earlier I spoke of what a poor story *John Brown's Body* told and as a poem it is almost as bad. There are good individual sections, like the "Invocation," but there is much flat language in it. But to dismiss *John Brown's Body* should not mean the dismissal of Benét. I do not find very many hair-raising defects in *Western Star* and "Johnny Pye and the Fool-Killer": they are moving and effective works. Not only are the characters better drawn in *Western Star* than in *John Brown's Body* but the poetry is better. Even though *Western Star* is generally simple and direct it is effective because it is suited to its subject matter. Here are a few lines from a description of the famous John Smith:

> . . . this skin-changing stepchild of Ulysses,
> On fire, yes, fed or fasting, to see new things,
> Explore, map out, taste, venture, enjoy, astound
> And look, look, look with a fly's remembering eye,
> A child's delight in marvels, a liar's gorgeousness,
> And the patient, accurate pen that mapped two great coasts.
>
> (*Western Star,* pp. 72-73)

This is not great poetry—the language does not excite. In the above there is only one surprising phrase: "with a fly's remembering eye." This poetry would not make Emily Dickinson "feel physically as if the top of [her] head were taken off." However, it is workmanlike verse that is good for telling a story and presenting characters. This is the style of most of the poem but at times the poetry does become more lyrical. For example, in these lines about the English conception of the settling of the New World:

> Tick-tock,
> Tick-tock,
> Cross the seas or stay,
> Men will live and women bear
> And time will pass away.
> Tick-tock,
> Tick-tock,
> Plant the tree or die,
> We will hear the tale of it,
> Hear it bye and bye.
> Plant it if you can, then,
> Plant it with a will,
> Every root and every shoot
> Must be England's still.
> Tick-tock.
>
> (*Western Star*, p. 77)

Western Star generally avoids the weaker lines that Tate so deplored in *John Brown's Body*. Here are two of Mr. Tate's favorites:

> Now the scene expands, we must look at the scene as a
>   whole,
> How are the gameboards chalked and the pieces set?
>
> (*John Brown's Body*, p. 171)

I cannot truly say how highly Benét should be ranked in comparison with other modern American writers—it has been an incredibly rich century for literature—but I think Benét has written at least a very good poem and a few stories that deserve to survive. His work is an excellent expression of the liberal imagination. *The Waste Land* must make room for *Western Star*. The world of the religious and the spiritual must make room for the world of the political and social. The Anglo-Catholic church is one solution for modern man's problems but another is the community of man, Benét's answer. We are all brothers faced with the Fool-Killer and we have the potential if not of an "earthly paradise" at least of a workable democracy. But we need new Daniel Websters in order to find this democratic decency in our hearts.

NORMAN MAILER TO POSTERITY

DIANNE F. SADOFF

Critical evaluation of Norman Mailer and his work varies from outrageous praise to outrageous damnation. Norman Podhoretz says, for example, that Mailer is a "major novelist in the making," that he has "extraordinary technical skill," and that his mind has "boldness and energy."[1] Irving Howe proclaims that Mailer is enormously, even outrageously talented;[2] Richard Poirier, one of Mailer's staunchest supporters, thinks Mailer's work "constantly comes alive with extraordinary accumulations of intensity and brilliance."[3] Alfred Kazin, when asking himself and us "How Good is Norman Mailer?" concludes that he is "one of the most variable, unstable, and on the whole unpredictable writers I have ever read. He has a remarkable intelligence, . . . a marvelously forceful and inventive style; great objective gifts as a novelist. On the other hand, his intelligence, though muscular, has no real ease or quietly reflective power; he is as fond of his style as an Italian tenor of his vocal chords."[4] Diana Trilling offers a measured and realistic assessment of Mailer's career:

> While Mailer has neither stopped writing nor succumbed to the temptations of Hollywood, he has had his own gifted way of co-operating in our more cynical expectations for him as a novelist and of obstructing the development that might once have followed upon the early flowering of so much talent. After the extraordinary triumph of *The Naked and the Dead,* he not only deserted the "naturalism" of his first novel but more and more moved from fiction to nonfiction, and of a polemical sort. And

181

> increasingly he has offered the public the myth of the man
> rather than the work of the writer. . . . It is scarcely
> surprising that his career is now shadowed in dubiety.[5]

If Trilling sensed this "dubiety" so clearly in 1962, how much more so must we in 1974, after Mailer's coverage of moon walks and his cribbing from two other authors the text for a picture book of Marilyn Monroe nudes?

The question of Mailer's "career" is one I'd like to examine from dual viewpoints; temporally, and as epitomized in one novel, *An American Dream*. Richard Poirier, in his essay, "The Literature of Waste: Eliot, Joyce, and Others," defines a "literature of waste" as one "in which a writer displays not so much an external waste land as the waste which is his own substance"; Poirier defines the mind that works in this mode, the "de-creative imagination," and he thinks Mailer an "especially revealing example of [this] literary-cultural-psychological complex."[6] Mailer himself is aware of such temporal issues of growth and degeneration, but sees his own career in terms of multiplicity, even literary virtuosity; he says of journalism:

> It can be terrible for your style. Or it can temper your
> style. . . . In other words you can become a *better* writer
> by doing a lot of different kinds of writing. Or you can
> deteriorate. . . . But if what you write is a reflection of
> your own consciousness, then even journalism can become
> interesting. One wouldn't want to spend one's life at it
> and I wouldn't want ever to be caught justifying journalism
> as a major activity (it's obviously less interesting than to
> write a novel), but it's better, I think, to see it as an essen-
> tial betrayal of the chalice of your literary art.[7]

Journalism to the novelist, then is like sparring to a prize-fighter.

But Mailer's desire to keep in shape by doing many things well, by creating out of his talent a multi-faceted influence on our culture, can, like the issue of multiplicity versus careerist goal-orientation, be seen in many ways, the least interesting and intelligent of which is to simply choose one alternative over the other. Irving Howe discusses Mailer's continual experimentation in very positive terms, therefore choosing the multiplicity term of our agon, but he also understands that acts occur in time and that multiplicity for the sake of multiplicity achieves nothing; Mailer demonstrates, he says, an "unwillingness to settle into his achievement, an impatience with a style as soon as he comes close to mastering it, a devotion to restlessness as a principle of both life and art." On the other hand, however, Mailer's "fear of stasis" may lead him into "self-delusion and self-incitement," into a love of restlessness and violence for its own sake.[8] And this is where Poirier's insight into a "literature of waste" becomes impossible to ignore; Mailer's multiplicity merely wastes his substance, it relieves him of the responsibility of novel-writing, it pays his bills (*Marilyn* was done for money, Mailer freely admitted on various network talk shows). And so we wait on for the next "big" novel, remembering that the last "big" novel turned out to be *Advertisements for Myself.*

Keeping in mind our metaphor of career-as-waste, *An American Dream* appears to be Mailer's most characteristic novel. When it appeared in 1965, its obscenity, its concern with filth and waste, outraged critics like Elizabeth Hardwick, who called it a "dirty book," and Phillip Rahv, who called it a "crime without punishment." Stanley Edgar Hyman deplored Mailer's obsession with smells and his outrageous use of metaphor, and proceeded to reduce the novel to its basest banality by simply retelling the often absurd narrative.[9] But Leo Bersani, chuckling over the "quaint resurgence of neoclassical canons of taste" among the reviewers, calls *An American Dream* "a dazzling performance, a recklessly generous yet disciplined exercise in self-exposure and self-invention . . . [which] sins continuously against the rules of propriety and verisimilitude, and the clarities of *bon sens.*"[10] The book *is* dirty; the book *is* dazzling: my students find it repulsive, but love reading it. And so all the arguing comes down to whether Mailer's values are indeed repulsive, and if so, whether we can condemn the novel on the basis of Mailer's values.

The center of *An American Dream* is its experience of waste. The omnipresent concern for the foul smell of everything represents Mailer's obsession with excrement displaced upward to a civilized organ, the nose. Deborah exudes a "powerful odor of rot and musk and something much more violent. . . . It was like the scent of the carnivore in a zoo. This last odor was fearful—it had the breath of burning rubber."[11] Deborah smells rotten, like waste, but she also smells powerful, and power becomes associated throughout the novel with smells, waste and excrement. The desire to become powerful and to be manipulative makes other people into the excrement the manipulator feels like himself. The smell of waste also reveals Deborah's primitive violence; and this dark, animalistic side of the "great bitch" frightens Rojack, since she attempts to manipulate him as he does her. But Deborah's smell like a "wild boar full of rot" is supplemented by another smell—"her perfume perhaps, a hint of sanctity, something as calculating and full of guile as high finance, that was it—she smelled like a bank, Christ . . ." (p. 68). As Freud, Jones, Ferenczi, Brown—and, yes, Mailer—know, money and excrement are equals in the childish unconscious, as well as in the conscious mind of the anally-fixated personality. Rojack goes on to equate the smell of waste, the need for power, and animalism with Deborah's female sexuality: "I used literally to conceive of a snake guarding the cave which opened to the treasure, the riches, the filthy-lucred wealth of all the world" (p. 38). Deborah usurps all things masculine; when hunting she "shoots from the hip."

All characters in the novel who attempt to overpower Rojack exude fearful smells. The detectives at the police station release the "smell of hunters sitting in overheated hut at dawn," since Rojack "was game to them at this moment" (p. 73); when Rojack meets Tony, "hatred came off him like scent, dull and powerful" (p. 109); Kelly, like Deborah, brings together many of the novel's smells: "Beneath a toilet water of punctilio and restraint . . . a deep smell came off Kelly, a hint of a big foul cat, carnal as the meat on a butcher's block, and something else, some whiff of the icy rot and iodine in a piece of marine nerve left to bleach on the sand. With it all was that congregated odor of the wealthy . . . a whiff of the tomb" (pp. 203-04). Rojack's fear of Kelly's power, money, and brutality reveal themselves to the reader through animalistic, wasting, rotting smells—the decaying of flesh, the smell of death. And at the center of the obsession with waste and rot lies death; death is what the power-hungry Rojack fears most. His experience at the morgue brings together all the fears we have seen working throughout the details of smell in the novel: "There was now new silence, a dead silence, some stretch of the void with no sense of events beneath, just a silence of the waste. My nostrils hurt from the antisceptic and deodorant and the other smell (that vile pale scent of embalming fluid and fecal waters) insinuated its way through the stricken air" (p. 76). The motif of smells demonstrates that to Rojack the world is full of excrement, and he fears everyone tries to bury him in it.

Rojack encounters waste everywhere, but most intensely when having intercourse with a woman. Poirier believes Mailer's "highly moral allegory of sex does involve a contest between the powers in him of God and the Devil, between sexual acts that create life and sexual acts that cannot, a contest, to be specific, between vaginal and anal intercourse."[12] By "moral," I can only assume Poirier means "Puritanical"; he certainly cannot mean "ethical." For while Poirier implies that Mailer chooses the correct sexual philosophies, he makes explicit his belief that Mailer assumes this sexual pose, this "chic literary formula," merely to cast it off and demonstrate its falsity. You are all familiar, of course, with the great buggery scene in *An American Dream*. After attempting to purge the rot from his innards by murdering his wife ("I was feeling good, as if my life had just begun" [p. 43]), Rojack runs out to bugger the maid, whose name is a fine pun on Rojack's sexual activity and "prowess." The scene brings together all the complex motivational elements of the novels. Ruta smells: "a thin high constipated smell (a smell which spoke of rocks and grease and the sewer-damp of wet stones in poor European alleys) came needling its way out of her," and that smell reminds Rojack of money, of cost. But after Rojack humiliates Ruta sexually (which of course she adores), her smell of ambition and stubbornness is "replaced by something tender as the flesh but not at all clean, something sneaky, full of fear, but young, a child in soiled pants." Filthy lucre becomes directly tied to buggery, as Rojack goes "dropping down for more of that pirate's gold." The scene also works to equate Mailer's God-Devil battle with his excremental vision; Rojack feels as if he "were gliding in the clear air above Luther's jakes and she was loose and free, very loose and very free, as if this were her finally natural act: a host of the Devil's best gifts were coming to me"; "I was gone like a bat and shaking hands with the Devil once more." After the bugger, Rojack tells Ruta " '*Der Teufel* asked me to visit!' " Throughout the scene, the vagina is associated with "the creation," and when Rojack spills his seed, wasted, in her anus, he has a vision of the desert; later he thinks of that "empty womb, of that graveyard which gambled a flower and lost," of his semen "perishing in the kitchen of the Devil," of his "seed expiring in the wrong field" (pp. 46-52).

Of course all this appears to be a dialectical exploration of good and evil; D. H. Lawrence used the very same sexual metaphors to create that metaphysical dialectic. But Lawrence does indeed explore the very basic human need to experience corruption and filth in order to transcend it, although even he fails to resolve the dialectic convincingly in favor of creative transcendence. Mailer totally fails to create creation since his dialectic is fake to begin with. All Rojack's "creative" urges in his sexual exploits are tied not to life forces embodied in creating a child, but to deathly and obsessive needs to recreate the self through the child. Rojack is so saddened by his failure to "cast a baby into Ruta" (p. 54) that he tries her again after calling the police. This time "something in her leaped to catch that child" (p. 57). This same obsessive desire to create a child makes Rojack despise birth control, makes him search for "that corporate rubbery obstruction" which he must pull out of Cherry and fling away in order to have good sex with her. After having intercourse with Cherry, Rojack thinks they have conceived a child: sex is meaningful only if the possibility of conception exists.

Mailer's notion of the mysterious, life-giving womb—Freud clearly missed such male manifestations of "womb envy" because of his negative view of women—relates back to motivations of power and fear in sexuality. Throughout the novel, sexual encounters become duels for power. Rojack believes that all women are killers; for Deborah, as for all women, sex is an extreme form of "hunting" or castration and humiliation of the male. In a famous line from the novel, Rojack generalizes that "women must murder us unless we possess them altogether" (p. 97); while buggering Ruta, and therefore initiating her into her "natural," Nazi, anal self, Rojack thinks "she was becoming mine as no woman ever had, she wanted no more than to be a part of my will" (p. 48). Even Rojack's "good sex" begins with "hunting," stench, and power: "But we did not meet as lovers, more like animals in a quiet mood, come across a track of the jungle to join in a clearing, we were equals"; Rojack has "some distant awareness that [his] breath could hardly be good and her lungs breathed back an air of ashes and the tomb"; Rojack is "aware of nothing but [his] will, that casing of iron about [his] heart, and of her will anchored like a girdle of steel about her womb." Only when the "iron will" of the diaphragm is removed can male ego, the smell of death, and power-hunger be purged from sexual experience; normally, however, sexuality partakes of all these wasteful and filthy psychological interactions.

The basis of Rojack's need for power over women is his fear of them, and here Mailer's peculiar brand of existentialism combines with sexuality and the excremental vision. "When I was in bed with a woman," Rojack realizes, "I rarely felt as if I were making life, but rather as if I were a pirate sharpening up a raid on life, and so somewhere inside myself—yes, *there* was a large part of the fear—I had dread of the judgment which must rest behind the womb of a woman. A small perspiration came out along my back" (p. 115). Rojack's sexual encounters are existential battles because he must "perform," he must be a good lover in the standard destructive masculine notion of sexuality as male demonstration, because otherwise, as Mailer tells us in *The Prisoner of Sex,* the female will deny his seed the right to fertilize her egg. This fear of women, this womb-envy, relates to woman's power over life and death. Rojack and Cherry discuss both death and sexuality before they go to her room to make love:

> To be not afraid of death, to be ready to engage it—sometimes I thought I had more of a horror of dying than anyone I knew. I was so unfit for that moment. . . .
> "You say you're afraid," she said, "do you mean of women?"
> "There comes a moment when I don't believe I belong in them." (p. 114)

The same fear of death lies within every womb for Rojack; all women are murderers, and "women who have discovered the power of sex are never far from suicide" (p. 57).

Rojack's metaphysics feed and support his fears of death. He is a television personality, ex-politician, and professor of "existential psychology with the not inconsiderable thesis that magic, dread, and the perception of death were the roots of motivation" (p. 15). Despite the self-indulgent, self-deprecating tone of that confession, Rojack really does believe in death as the center of motivation, as, I believe, does Mailer. Nearly all Rojack's actions in the novel are basically confrontations with death. Rojack proves his worth—and, he thinks, saves his life—by standing up to Tony and by beating up Shago Martin; Shago says to Cherry before the fight, " 'I be damn. . . . You got yourself a stud who can stand' " (p. 173). Rojack proves himself by talking his way out of a murder rap, by outwitting the city detectives and by confronting gangsters; ironically enough, Rojack escapes arrest only because the mob wants to protect itself against any investigation into Deborah's spying.

Rojack's most symbolic confrontation with death occurs, of course, during sexual intercourse; if conception *can* occur, he may win, and, creating life, live himself. But when he discovers he loves Cherry, Rojack finds that "good sex" cannot overcome his experience and knowledge of death. Since he "believed God was not love but courage," love for Rojack comes "only as a reward." On his way to confront the Mafia, Rojack remembers the vow he took in Cherry's bed: "No, if one wished to be a lover, one could not find one's sanity in another. That was the iron law of romance: one took the vow to be brave" (p. 191). Because love forces Rojack to go on confronting death in yet another way, it does not protect the lover from death, but instead exposes him to it more violently: "Now I understood that love was not a gift but a vow. Only the brave could live with it for more than a little while. . . . It had always been the same, love was love, one could find it with anyone, one could find it anywhere. It was just that you could never keep it. Not unless you were ready to die for it, dear friend" (p. 156). Cherry who shares Rojack's fears, thinks she will not live long after experiencing orgasm during heterosexual intercourse, and she dies shortly thereafter. And so, love, like existence, is gratuitous, and the battle to be brave goes on, and Rojack constantly confronts situations filled with the fear that makes him nauseous: " 'The root of neurosis is cowardice' " (p. 235).

Rojack's most explicit confrontation with death and his own cowardice, his well-known walk on the parapet over a Manhattan street, links death with sexuality and the obsessive need to create a child. Rojack thinks that by jumping off the parapet, by committing suicide and allowing himself to die the death he has always feared, he will create himself anew by insuring the life of the child he thinks Cherry has conceived: "And I had a sudden thought, 'If you loved Cherry, you would jump,' which was an abbreviation for the longer thought that there was a child in her, and death, my death, my violent death, would give some better heart to that embryo just created, that indeed I might even be created again, free of my past" (p. 210). But Rojack cannot jump, and so he ritually enacts a substitute version of death-confrontation: his walk around the parapet. In the walk Rojack battles his fear and trembling, his dread of failure, and his sense of personal weakness: "My will slipped away from me, and I stood motionless, trembling and a blubber. I might have wept like a child if I were not afraid even of that. 'Every cockroach has the memory of a revolting failure,' muttered something, some-where, whether in or without my mind I hardly knew" (p. 240). Having walked nearly around the parapet, Rojack's need to over-come his fear makes him decide to walk around again, but Kelly's withdrawal to another room draws Rojack off the parapet, and so he fails. For Rojack, cowardice wins, both because of his own weakness and cowardice, and because of the corruption of the world around him—especially personified in Kelly and the gang. Rojack does indeed get away with murder, but not very happily so.

The pattern of fear and the desperate need to confront that fear through willful and power-hungry personal interactions and rituals finds its counterpart in the novel in a pattern of cathartic acts. Because all his confrontations involve a testing of his will, they ultimately do not satisfy Rojack's needs. The best act for Rojack is a purgative act; personal catharsis relieves him of the feeling of rot, waste, and deathliness, and also liberates him from his manipulative will. In a novel of this kind, cathartic needs are often expressed through bodily metaphors and motivations:

> I vomited with all the gusto of a horse on a gallop, crude, violations, the rot and gas of compromise, the stink of old fears, mildew of discipline, all the biles of habit and the horrors of pretense—ah, here was the heart of the puke!—

came thundering out with the fluid intent downrushing
sounds of a stream tearing through the wood to recover its
river, I felt like some gathering wind which drew sickness
from the lungs and livers of others and passed them through
me and up and out into the water. . . . Oh here came
Leznicki, up from the belly, up, up, and the presence of
Roberts up and *splat!* Pea beans and shreddings of puke
came up from the basement of my belly, the police were
saying good-by to my body. (p. 98)

The self needs voiding because, paradoxically, it is a void which
has been taken over by other rot. When Deborah tells Rojack
quietly that she does not love him, he "thought again of the moon
and the promise of extinction which had descended on me. I had
opened a void—I was now without center. . . . I did not belong
to myself any longer. Deborah had occupied my center" (p. 32).
And that void, that emptied self filled with waste, becomes
obsessed with vomiting it out.

Sexual experience is another of Rojack's cathartic acts, but
only when the "iron will" breaks down and allows orgasm to
become purgative: "For the first time in my life without passing
through fire or straining the stones of my will, I came up from my
body rather than down from my mind" (p. 122). Rojack experiences purgative sex with Cherry because the two partners meet, if
you recall, as equals: equal animals, equal manipulators, equal
hunters. Rojack and Cherry fit perfectly in bed because they are
equally tainted and filthy, and therefore in equal need of
catharsis. Cherry's background creates part of her taint; her
parents having died, she was raised by an incestuous brother
and sister; she has had sex with Kelly, the leader of the mob,
himself a practitioner of incest with his daughter, Deborah; she
has been begrimed by her relationship with Tony—which expresses
itself through Tony's smell, "an essence of that taint [Rojack]
felt in Cherry the moment [he] came near to passing out"
(p. 109). For two such filthy characters, sexuality successfully
purges the dirt of the past.

Violence is also cathartic for Rojack, and violence becomes
associated motivationally with sexuality, especially male domina-
tion over women during intercourse: "There is something manly
about containing your rage. . . . The exhilaration comes I

suppose from possessing such strength." Besides, murder offers the promise of a good orgasm; it relieves the body of unwanted matter and aggression. Murder, sexual intercourse, vomiting, defecating, all become cathartic acts in *An American Dream,* or are desired to become such. The novel's structure alternates macho confrontations with death, and purgative, usually bodily, acts, and part of the reason the pattern must repeat itself so continually results from the lack of transformation actually achieved through catharsis in the novel. Despite his obsessive confrontations and his attempted purgations, Rojack cannot transform his filthy life or the corrupt world he lives in.

The final questions about *An American Dream* center on how seriously we should take its mumbo-jumbo, macho, excremental, and existential dread. We realize that Mailer creates his excremental vision seriously and sincerely; the excremental obsessions of *The Presidential Papers* on waste and the "Metaphysics of the Belly" from *Advertisements for Myself* tell us that. Reading Mailer's review of Bertolucci's *Last Tango in Paris* in the *New York Review of Books* also reveals his immersion in and obsession with the excremental vision: he loves the buggery, the obscenity, and looking death up the ass.

Part of this same question is our desire to discover whether Stephen Rojack is really Norman Mailer. Does Mailer condemn his hero for his inability to deal with his dreads and excremental deathliness, or does Mailer enjoy them too much to care about condemning them? The novel's tone, we discover, is so seductive, so positive that we find it difficult to dissociate Mailer from his hero. Although Rojack becomes conscious of his failures, his weaknesses, and his cowardice, he so thoroughly enjoys the buggeries, fights, and outwittings that we must believe he—and his author as well—glories in the indulgence of them. Although Rojack seems to desire purgation of his inmost rots, Mailer informs us that indulging ourselves in filth does not mean we will transcend it. Our experience of the novel is primarily one of waste, degradation, and the omnipresence of filth; instead of transformation or transcendence of this corrupt world, Mailer emphasizes transformation downward: back to filth, not away from it. Thus the novel reveals Mailer's conscious attempt to create a cathartic novel, but manifests his unconscious drive to wallow in the filth he purports to transcend. For this reason, we find it difficult to accept Rojack's sudden conversion from macho manipulation of women to willess loving of Cherry: in the context of the novel, it appears to be just one more self-deluded, insignificant, and unsuccessful attempt to vomit when the stomach gets existentially nauseous.

In conclusion, we must act as if Mailer and his obsessions are all self-inflated posturings. Kate Millett decides that because the seemingly perverted values of *An American Dream* are upheld and substantiated by the journalism, we must accept the values of the novel as Mailer's.[13] This is a very acceptable literary judgment, yet even in reading *The Prisoner of Sex* which displays all the same outrageous macho claims and womb-envies as does *An American Dream*, I get the sneaking suspicion that Mailer is putting me on, that his journalism, like his novels, are exercises in the creation of false selves. Using *personae*, creating masks, has always been a valid literary endeavor: Browning did it to demonstrate the relativity of judgment, the disjunction between sympathy and judgment, and the inherent irony of epistemology; Swift did it to satirize and therefore reveal the corruption of a society in which norms could be inferred and understood because of an assumed and widely accepted system of community values. But Mailer's satire, if it is satire, does not reveal an author able to identify widely with human values, but an author able only to identify with perverted and obsessive values which waste his substance. If none of Mailer's writing reveals his real values, he is empty and essentially valueless: an author without a center. If Mailer's journalism truly reflects his values (and therefore upholds the values of *An American Dream*), he is a sensationalistic, adolescent, anally-fixated man.

EDNA ST. VINCENT MILLAY: NOTES TOWARD A REAPPRAISAL

FREDERICK ECKMAN

> Let sanguine healthy-mindedness do its best with its strange
> power of living in the moment and ignoring and forgetting,
> still the evil background is really there to be thought of,
> and the skull will grin in at the banquet.
>
> —William James

> Dark, Dark, is all I find for metaphor.
>
> —Millay, "Interim"

I

The year 1912 is well enough remembered in modern literary history as that *annus mirabilis* which marked the founding of the Imagist Movement and the first appearance of *Poetry: A Magazine of Verse.* At the time, however, neither of these events seemed so auspicious to the American literary world as the publication of Edna St. Vincent Millay's precocious visionary poem, "Renascence" in a widely-publicized anthology, *The Lyric Year.* Though the poem had received only fourth place, and no prize, in the anthology's national competition, the book's readers, its editors (after agonizing post-publication reappraisal), and even its prize winners, all agreed that "Renascence" deserved much better than a runner-up position.

For the next twenty-five years or more, Edna Millay, the tiny auburn-haired woman from Maine, enjoyed a combination of popularity, public notice, and high esteem unmatched by any other American poet in this century. Even though Millay's critical reputation has languished since her death in 1950, at least a few of her poems hold a sacred place in the hearts of the American reading public hitherto occupied only by the most familiar verses of Poe, Longfellow, Whittier, and Dickinson. In Hayden Carruth's

193

The Voice That Is Great Within Us, a 1970 anthology of American poetry since Frost, only two of the twenty-four women poets represented (H. D. and Denise Levertov) have more poems than Millay. Even in the trend-conscious 1973 *Norton Anthology of Modern Poetry,* she is represented by ten poems, one more than Stevens, H. D., and Wilfred Owen; only one less than Marianne Moore, and a mere two less than either Whitman or Auden. Her poems continue to appear in high school and college textbooks, as well as specialized anthologies: poetry by women, poetry for children, social-protest verse, and love poetry. Cloth-bound editions of her *Collected Sonnets* (1941), *Collected Lyrics* (1943), and *Collected Poems* (1956) have remained constantly in print since their publication.

It should not, however, surprise anyone familiar with patterns of American popular taste to find that the public, the beloved, the prestigious poet is not the *essential* poet. In literature, as in music and art, Americans exercise their democratic rights: rather predictably they choose the sunny, the funny, the sentimental and nostalgic, the pleasantly instructive, and the mildly scandalous. Even grim works, when not truly terrifying but merely scary, can delight American readers. Partisan considerations of "high culture" and "developed taste" aside, the general reading public is quite as selective, according to its lights, as the most discriminating connoisseur. Interestingly enough, the legends it forms about its favorite writers are almost identical to those formed by the highbrow reading public.

What appealed to readers in "Renascence," I suspect, was the image of none other than Howells' ideal reader of a generation before, the saintly "girl of sixteen," given a voice and a habitation. Even the young woman who emerged immediately thereafter in the most widely quoted and reprinted of her "Jazz Age" poems was a logical 20th-century transformation: the clever, vivacious, slightly wicked (but still sensitive and intelligent) Greenwich Village soul-sister of Daisy Buchanan, Lady Brett Ashley, and Lorelei Lee. Probably no other poet in recorded history has acquired a more enduring public image from six lines than Millay did from these two epigrams in her second volume, *A Few Figs From Thistles* (1920):

FIRST FIG

My candle burns at both ends;
It will not last the night;
But ah, my foes, and oh, my friends—
It gives a lovely light.

SECOND FIG

Safe upon the solid rock the ugly houses stand;
Come and see my shining palace built upon the sand!

These two "figs," along with certain other poems in the volume, not only revived a moribund tradition of light verse in America, through the work of such disciples and contemporaries as Dorothy Parker, Samuel Hoffenstein, Richard Armour, Phyllis McGinley, and Ogden Nash; they fixed in the American mind a simulacrum of the modern woman poet that has only recently begun to change into the troubled likeness of a Sylvia Plath. Yet, as later portions of this essay will imply, the poetic imaginations of these two poets—questions of relative excellence aside—are a good deal more alike than their public images.

II

The first impression that comes from reading Millay's *Collected Poems* from beginning to end (as I have done three times in as many months) is that she is so totally a *literary* poet. One expects the early work of any writer to reflect various admirations and influences. Most poets at any age are bookish, if not always imitative or allusive. But Millay's poems simply never stop drawing from the imagery, language, rhythms, forms, and allusions of other poets. If there is truth in Eliot's mock-solemn dictum that major poets commit grand larceny while minor poets are guilty only of shoplifting, then Millay is indisputably major. In another, more serious context, Eliot discusses this matter:

> Immature poets imitate; mature poets steal; bad poets deface what they take, and good poets make it into something better, or at least something different. The good poet welds his theft into a whole of feeling which is unique, utterly different from that from which it was torn;

the bad poet throws it into something which has no cohesion.

At best, certainly, Millay makes her thefts from Shakespeare, Shelley, Keats, Tennyson, E. B. Browning, the Pre-Raphaelites, Housman, the Georgian Poets (especially de la Mare), Yeats, Frost, Sandburg, MacLeish, Jeffers, and such women contemporaries as Anna Hempstead Branch, Elinor Wylie, and Sara Teasdale into "something different." She is a true and good mockingbird. Allen Tate's conclusions on this aspect of Millay's poetry are more perceptive than anything I could hope to write:

> Taking the vocabulary of nineteenth-century poetry as pure as you will find it in Christina Rossetti, and drawing upon the stock of conventional imagery accumulated from Drayton to Housman, she has created out of shopworn materials an interesting personal attitude: she has been able to use the language of the preceding generation to convey an emotion peculiar to her own. . . . She has been from the beginning the one poet of our time who has successfully stood athwart two ages: she has put the personality of her age into the style of the preceding age, without altering either.

There can be little doubt that Millay's constant echoing of the familiar has done much to increase her popularity. By Pound's much harsher standards of excellence, she is the sort of "diluter" who is often preferred by a casual reader of poetry to the genuine article. But both Eliot and Tate make a distinction about derivative work that Pound—himself a compulsive borrower—failed to make: the difference between imitation and transformation. And though Millay's poems cannot always stand up to this test, she is quite often able to employ another's style in the best interests of her own poem.

III

The next, and deepest, impression that comes to me from reading Millay's poetry *in toto,* and the central topic of this essay, has already been hinted at in my epigraphs: its overwhelming, obsessive concern with death and desolation. Frequently it is human death, in the most literal, naturalistic sense: graves, tombstones, decaying corpses, drowned bodies, shrouds, skulls, and skeletal bones. Even her ubiquitous nature imagery—which arises from the precise, loving observation of a person totally at home in the natural world—is strongly impelled toward falling leaves, bare fields and hills, stagnant pools, withered flowers, slain or hunted wild creatures, snow, frost, cold winds, floods, blighted grain, weeds, maggots, voracious dogs and wolves, venomous snakes, and gnawing rodents. Likewise, her domestic imagery always seems to be moving away from the warm, comfortable, and secure, toward burnt-out fires, empty cupboards, blank and hostile windows, gaping doors, shabby furnishings, rancid and sour household odors, decayed food scraps, irritating daytime and ominous night noises, funerals, sickrooms, dim or extinguished lamps, cobwebs, broken or unwashed crockery, leaking roofs, and mortgages. Since Millay is seldom a poet of verbal paradox or irony, we can usually accept this accumulation of images at face value. And more important than their conventional sign-values is their totality of impact from poem to poem, over the entire canon.

At this point I would like to brush away all temptation to indulge in amateur psychoanalytic criticism, especially that of the Freudian persuasion, which seems always to end with patronizing moral-esthetic judgments that reduce both poet and poem to mere curious objects of pathology. Death is, after all, one of the givens of the natural world; in the human realm, coming to terms with it is such an agonizing central struggle that, existentially speaking, we are better served by suspecting as abnormal the person who boasts of not being disturbed about it. As a critic I am not at all interested in determining whether the woman Edna St. Vincent Millay had a death wish, an immature horror of death, or even a creepy fascination with decay. I *am* interested in trying to demonstrate that themes of death and desolation in her poetry are evidence that her work needs reassessment, deliverance from the stock opinion (largely unchanged from her earliest reviews) that she is primarily a poet of praise, affirmation, and celebration. It is possible, of course, to select from such a large body of work enough images, or even complete poems, to prove almost anything. And I am well aware that death, dying, desolation, loss, and grief can, routinely employed, be no more than empty literary postures.

More convincing to my argument than any of the numerous poems *about* death are those in which such imagery works to another purpose. A simple instance is the lyric, "Passer Mortuus Est" from Millay's first volume:

> Death devours all lovely things;
>   Lesbia with her sparrow
> Shares the darkness,—presently
>   Every bed is narrow.
>
> Unremembered as old rain
>   Dries the sheer libation;
> And the little petulant hand
>   Is an annotation.
>
> After all, my erstwhile dear,
>   My no longer cherished,
> Need we say it was not love,
>   Just because it perished?

In this elegantly clever little poem, the "turn" of the third stanza serves to remind us that *carpe diem* is, after all, grounded in a darker view of existence than its surface frivolity would indicate. We note also that the oft-borrowed Catullan tag in the title and first stanza is put to an altogether original use.

Another poem from the early 1920's employs a personified Death, to purposes beyiond mere mortality:

SIEGE

> This I do, being mad;
> Gather baubles about me,
> Sit in a circle of toys, and all the time
> Death beating the door in.
>
> *White jade and an orange pitcher,*
>   *Hindu idol, Chinese god,—*
> *Maybe next year, when I'm richer*
>   *Carved beads and a lotus pod . . .* ·
>
> And all this time
> Death beating the door in.

From the traditional form of the "mad song," a splendidly compact and original poem emerges. On a first level, it is a personal parable of the poet, collecting at great cost a small hoard of rare and beautiful artifacts against, or in defiance of, the ravages of mortality. At another level, the poem can be read as a statement about the human necessity to create order—any order—against the chaos of existence. Read as a woman's poem, it would seem to refute Thoreau's sneer at "the ladies of the land, weaving toilet cushions against the Last Judgment." Whatever the reading, Death cannot be dismissed as a stock poetic device: he is hammering down the door like a storm-trooper or a National Guardsman; whether the speaker's lack of response to him comes from indifference, preoccupation, or defiance might be arguable, but one is not obliged to make a choice.

IV

In Millay's fourth volume, *The Harp-Weaver and Other Poems* (1923), there appears a remarkable seventeen-poem sequence entitled "Sonnets From an Ungrafted Tree." Only one critic, to my knowledge, has paid it more than cursory attention; and I am in total agreement with Sister Mary Madeleva's 1925 opinion that it is a really outstanding work. In its language, rhythms, and imagery, the sequence is heavily indebted to Frost; yet somehow Millay managed to repay her debt by making Frost's familiar idiom sound as if it were her own. The plot of the narrative is about dying and death, but the central concern is with the altering consciousness of a survivor. A woman has come back to her estranged and dying husband, after an indefinite absence, to care for him in his last weeks. For most of the sequence, the dying man is only an object in another room; the real focus is on the woman and the house, with glimpses of the New England village where the story takes place.

> So she came back into his house again
> And watched beside his bed until he died,
> Loving him not at all. The winter rain
> Splashed in the painted butter-tub outside,
> Where once her red geraniums had stood,
> Where still their rotted stalks were to be seen;

The details are lovingly rendered, perhaps from memory: early in 1912 Millay had gone to care for her seriously-ill father, who had been divorced from her mother for a dozen years. Although the father recovered, her memories of the event—especially her own ambivalent emotions—must have remained fresh and poignant over the ensuing decade. The woman in the sequence hears the grocer's delivery man outside; in panic she flees to the cellar until he has left:

> Sour and damp from that dark vault
> Arose to her the well-remembered chill;
> She saw the narrow wooden stairway still
> Plunging into the earth, and the thin salt
> Crusting the crocks; until she knew him far,
> So stood, with listening eyes upon the empty
>   doughnut jar.

The theme of a marriage gone sour, along with Millay's uncharacteristic bending of the sonnet form, suggests another debt: George Meredith's *Modern Love;* but again, the borrowing becomes a transformation. An entire tract on the randomness of choice in marriage could not cover more ground than this quatrain:

> Not over-kind nor over-quick in study
> Nor skilled in sports nor beautiful was he,
> Who had come into her life when anybody
> Would have been welcome, so in need was she.

The boy has attracted her attention by flashing a mirror in her eyes at school. Soon there is an episode of swimming and seduction at the lake:

> So loud, so loud the million crickets' choir . . .
> So sweet the night, so long-drawn-out and late . . .
> And if the man were not her spirit's mate,
> Why was her body sluggish with desire?

Thus they marry, and the sequence moves back into the grim present:

> Tenderly, in those times, as though she fed
> An ailing child—with sturdy propping up

> Of its small feverish body in the bed,
> And steadying of its hands about the cup—
> She gave her husband of her body's strength,
> Thinking of men, what helpless things they were,
> Until he turned and fell asleep at length,
> And stealthily stirred the night and spoke to her.

Her days become dream-like and hallucinatory. Fact and fantasy, in her deathbed attendant's routine, become confused:

> Upstairs, down other stairs, fearful to rouse,
> Regarding him, the wide and empty scream
> Of a strange sleeper on a malignant bed,
> And all the time not certain if it were
> Herself so doing or some one like to her,
> From this wan dream that was her daily bread.

I hesitate to summon again the august shade of Mr. Eliot, but passages like these inevitably suggest his concept of the "objective correlative": "a set of objects, a situation, a chain of events which shall be the formula of that *particular* emotion. . . ."

The heroine of this sequence is not unusually perceptive or even, beyond her household and nursing chores, able; what makes her heroic is her honesty. When the doctor asks her about preparations for the inevitable funeral,

> She said at length, feeling the doctor's eyes,
> "I don't know what you do exactly when a person
> dies."

Finally, viewing her husband's dead body from the bedroom door,

> She was as one who enters, sly, and proud,
> To where her husband speaks before a crowd,
> And sees a man she never saw before—
> The man who eats his victuals at her side,
> Small, and absurd, and hers: for once, not hers,
> unclassified.

So the sequence ends. I have not been able to give more than fragmentary glimpses of a suite of poems where emotion is skillfully controlled—dammed up, as it were, by precisely-rendered and composed details; and where dramatic power is released smoothly in the flat, lucid flow of the narration, like Williams' "river below the falls." Throughout the poems, images of death and loss are in the employ of answering that ultimate question posed by Frost's oven bird: "what to make of a diminished thing." That is to say, of existence itself. If the answer here seems to be no more than the stoic formula, "See things through," then we must be reminded that extracting messages and "paraphrasable content" from poems is only another intellectual game: the poem *is* the message, and ever so much more than the message.

V

Any reassessment of Edna Millay's poetry, then, should come from the poetry itself—the body of work. All but a few of her critics are useless, except perhaps as bad examples. John Crowe Ransom, the most eminent critic of that moment, chose in 1937 to set her record straight through a review of Elizabeth Atkins' critical study, published a year earlier. The essay, surely the silliest, most pretentious and patronizing thing Ransom ever wrote, attacks the poet—through her perhaps equally silly champion—for (a) being a woman in the first place, (b) her "lack of intellectual interest," and (c) not being John Donne or a modern facsimile thereof. His method is the usual New-Critical strategy of attack: to pick apart, word by word, a few chosen poems, then set bleeding and mutilated passages beside those of poets he admires. About Ransom's first objection, a writer in our time can only shake his head sadly; about the second and third, he may reflect nostalgically on fashions in critical taste, wondering if perhaps the New Critics are by now at least as shopworn as Millay's Jazz Age flippancies. But from Ransom's method one can surely draw a lesson: that no poet (with the necessary exception of Chidiock Tichbourne) ought to, or need to, have a lifetime of accomplishment balancing on the point of one poem—or two, or even three.

My discussion of "Sonnets From an Ungrafted Tree," then, is intended only to point a direction. If a poet can be read first of all in terms of the large patterns in the work, then a critic may well proceed, depth by depth, to what is at once the most important and the most elusive of critical goals: a true understanding of the individual poetic imagination in all its range and complexity. Such a study as I have outlined might well show us that Millay's imagery of death and desolation gives her more in common with the contemporary poets we now most prize—Roethke and Berryman, Plath and Sexton—than with the Roaring Twenties bohemians, the Depression radicals, and the quivering sensibilities of small-town poetry societies, where she is usually found nowadays.

RAINTREE COUNTY REVISITED

JOSEPH BLOTNER

The arrival of one recent attempt to write the Great American Novel was almost as unique as the book itself. In July, 1947, six months before publication, Ross Lockridge, Jr.'s 1,066-page *Raintree County* won the $125,000 Metro-Goldwyn-Mayer Novel Award. When the book was published it was made the January selection of the Book-of-the-Month Club, adding $25,000 more. Financial success was assured before a single copy had crossed a bookseller's counter.

The chorus of yeas and nays that followed from the critics seemed to contain enough favorable notes to assure critical success as well. It was called "an achievement of art and purpose, a cosmically brooding book full of significance and beauty."[1] Dissents were just as emphatic: one writer declared that "the total effect is failure."[2] *Raintree County*'s antecedents were scrutinized as closely as its text. It was said to descend, legitimately and illegitimately, from Joyce, Sterne, Twain, Whitman, and Wolfe. Other forebears assigned to the book included the frontier humorists and the American myth-makers. A temperate, perceptive appraisal of the novel was published by William York Tindall in November, 1948.[3] But in December, *Time* magazine, reviewing the year's books *ex cathedra*, delivered its final judgment:

> Nobody harpooned the . . . mythical white whale
> known as the "Great American Novel." Indiana's Ross

Reprinted by permission from *The Western Humanities Review,* Vol. X:1, Winter, 1955-1956.

Lockridge (who later committed suicide) made a stab at it;
he brought home a huge, *Ulysses*-like animal named *Raintree County,* which was hailed by critics as a monumental
attempt and then floated away in embarrassed silence.[4]

Now one notices only occasional references to the novel.
Sales, which mushroomed to over 400,000 copies by the end of
1948, had dwindled by 1953 to a few hundred. Just how good is
this book which to one was "a novel of rare stature for these
days"[5] and to another "an amalgam of undigested Wolfe, murky
Faulkner and watery Whitman"?[6]   What are *Raintree County*'s
ancestors and achievements, its myths and meanings? Across the
moderate space of eight years it seems time for a reappraisal of
what may well be one of the five or six most important novels of
this era.

The story of the book is this. The small town of Waycross,
in Raintree County, Indiana, holds a special Fourth of July celebration in 1892. The day-long patriotic program is seen through
the eyes of John Wickliff Shawnessy, a 53-year-old-schoolteacher
and prominent citizen of Waycross. Three of his boyhood friends
—a newspaper man, a senator, and a financier—return for the day.
Through their arguments and reminiscences, and through fifty-two
flashbacks, the most important events in John's life are recreated.
This chronicle includes the strange courtship and loss of his first
and greatest love, his seduction by his first wife and the tragic
events which follow it, and his turbulent wooing of his second
wife, with whom he finds peace. These flashbacks give the story
of one man's life, but they also form a pageant of American history
through fifty tumultuous years. The flashbacks are alternated,
chronologically for the most part, with the speeches, parades, and
fireworks of the Waycross celebration. The novel's denouement,
following a climactic mob scene, finds John alone. His friends
have departed and Waycross has gone to bed; he is alone with the
night and Raintree County. This is more than the story of John
Wickliff Shawnessy; through him it is the legend of Raintree
County, of America, and of man upon this earth.

Such a book is rarely a literary virgin birth. Lockridge's
debt to others includes elements of concept and style, matter
and manner. There are so many similarities that the influence of
James Joyce's *Ulysses* is unmistakable.   Like Joyce, Lockridge

used the single-day framework, multiple symbolism, mythology, and the dream-fantasy. Johnny, as the poet-hero, resembles Stephen Dedalus. Like him, trying to "forge in the smithy of my soul the uncreated conscience of my race," Johnny has labored to "become the epic poet of his people,"[7] to be "an image-bearer of the Republic" (p. 977). Consecrated to their tasks, these two are marked by special and ancient names: Stephen is the Celtic "Kinch"; John is the Indian "Shakamak." Shawnessy is contrasted with Jerusalem Webster Stiles as Dedalus is with Leopold Bloom, and as Dedalus has his Buck Mulligan, so Shawnessy has his Garwood B. Jones. A linguist like Joyce, Lockridge too fused words for special effects: "timesmoothed," "homeremembering," "memoryhaunted."

Ross Lockridge freely admitted the influence of Thomas Wolfe on his work, but he felt that his own historical background was stronger. A boyish declaimer at American shrines and writer of historical pageants, he had hymned America all his life. In *Raintree County* he wrote

> Of mounds beside the river. Of threaded bones of lovers in the earth. Of shards of battles long ago. Of names upon the land, the fragments of forgotten language . . . Of the people . . . of their towns and cities and the weaving millions. Of the earth on which they lived—its blue horizons, east and west, exultant springs, soft autumns, brilliant winters. And of all the summers when the days were long (p. 1060).

Walt Whitman's name is mentioned twice in *Raintree County*, his poetry is quoted, and his influence is clear. Lockridge sings of all the people who made America,

> Of their vast and vulgar laughters, festive days, their competitions, races, lusty games. Of strong men running to a distant string . . . Of their plantings, buildings, minings, makings, ravagings, explorings. Of how they were always going with the sun, westward to purple mountains, new dawns and new horizons. Of the earth on which they lived (p. 775).

He writes of the pioneers, endlessly moving west, and speaks of "Young men, my comrades" (p. 669), many of whom, with

Johnny Shawnessy, are borne to the hospitals that receive the backwash of the war.

If the frontier humorists left their mark upon the author's mind, so did Mark Twain. Lockridge makes Flash Perkins representative of the frontiersman; his code is that of "the backwoodsman or river man . . . the code of breezy cocky men, who had no fear in heaven or earth they would admit to" (p. 174). The book is shot through with the humor of this Western man, and the battle vaunts of Flash and Johnny could almost be transposed with those of the raftsmen in *Life on the Mississippi.*

The footsoldiers of all wars have much in common, and anyone who writes of the infantrymen's lot will necessarily treat elements others write of. But Johnny Shawnessy's ordeal in the slaughter of Chickamauga and the vicious charge up Missionary Ridge immediately suggest Henry Fleming's baptism of fire at Chancellorsville in Crane's *The Red Badge of Courage.* Each experiences the shame of flight, the confused exaltation of victory, and the aging that comes with both.[8]

Besides these various debts, there are episodes which recall Fielding, Smollett, and Sterne. Lockridge learned from all of these writers, and, like most first novels, his book was sometimes imitative. But the imitation was not slavish, not a substitute for original work. It was rather an attempt to use every literary technique he could to help achieve the extraordinarily difficult goal he had set for himself.

For Lockridge, myth was the means by which both past and present are understood. That is, the only true reality is one's personal experience. The multiplication of individual experience, which constitutes life in the aggregate, becomes an understandable approximation of the truth only when its actually fragmentary nature is cast into an arbitrary order through what is agreed upon as history. For example: the Battle of Gettysburg as related in history books and perceived through the plaques on the battle site is myth. Its reality was the multiplicity of shots, sabre strokes, retreats, attacks, barrages, and silences which impinged upon the consciousness of the long-dead soldiers who fought near that town on July 1-3, 1863. Lockridge felt that history, both formal and informal, was a kind of myth quite as much as that in Bulfinch or Frazer. But this latter kind did more to make experience meaningful.

Questioned by his friend and former teacher, "Perfessor" Stiles, Shawnessy says that "A myth is a story that is always true for all men everywhere" (p. 886). From this implied premise that myths represent fundamental patterns in human experience, Lockridge proceeded to his method: the use of as many myths as possible to compress into *Raintree County* as much of human experience as he could. Raintree County is explicitly called a microcosm. Waycross is the crossing of the ways, a crossroads where all things meet. John Wickliff Shawnessy is man, but appropriately he is man as mythic hero. One can identify him in various sections of the novel as Christ, Adam, Aeneas, Apollo, Alexander, Oedipus, Hercules, Actaeon, Siegfried, and Beowulf. He is also William Shakespeare, the Priest of Nemi described by Frazer, and—in the sense of Joyce's H. C. Earwicker—Everyman. But most of all, he is Adam—knowing Paradise, falling, and expiating his sin. He tells the Perfessor and Senator Garwood B. Jones, his boyhood friend and rival, that he has known not several women, but rather "One Eve in several reincarnations" (p. 588). And each of them is marked by a scar or birthmark, which she wears "as a sign of her mortality" (p. 930), a mortality like that of Eve after the fall. Superimposed upon the old myth is that which Shawnessy calls the American myth, "the story of the hero who regains Paradise" (p. 866). This myth is embodied in the experience of the poet-hero, the new Adam who

> learned that Raintree County being but a dream must be upheld by dreamers. So he learned that human life's a myth, but that only myths can be eternal. So he learned the gigantic labor by which the earth is rescued again and again from chaos and old night, by which the land is strewn with names, by which the river of human language is traced from summer to distant summer, by which beauty is plucked forever from the river and clothed in a veil of flesh, by which souls are brought from the Great Swamp into the sunlight of Raintree County and educated to its enduring truths (p. 1021).

Shawnessy's reply to the Perfessor's cynical Darwinian *History of Mankind* is *The Legend of Raintree County,* which he describes as "A little fable with multiple meanings, and a moral for a vestigial tail" (p. 1019). The moral is quoted immediately above; the multiple meanings are found throughout the novel. For example: the Raintree said to grow near Paradise Lake in the heart of the county is a rare Asian species, a planting of Johnny Appleseed, the Tree of Life, the Tree of the Knowledge of Good and Evil, and the familiar tree of genealogy. The myths which relate to each of Johnny's roles are represented by appropriate Raintree County or national events. Each of the major characters is symbolic. Garwood B. Jones is the demagogue; Cassius P. ("Cash") Carney is the financier (turning yellow in maturity he is reminiscent of Midas); Jerusalem Webster Stiles is the cynical intellectual. Nell Gaither (Venus Anadyomene) is called the perfect blend of the spiritual and the erotic. Laura Golden is the spirit of the City in the Gilded Age. Susanna Drake is the ante-bellum South, seen by Johnny as beautiful, guilty, tragic, and tormented. Lockridge invested *Raintree County* with multiple meanings, and he attempted to make them work on many levels: narrative and symbolic, personal and national, particular and universal.

Lockridge's writing sometimes achieves a high degree of technical virtuosity. The book is constructed according to an intricate chronological plan. Events in the morning of the Fourth of July recall incidents in Johnny's childhood and events in the early history of the United States. As the day progresses, these three schedules roughly keep pace with each other. The flashbacks are tied into the day's events by key words which make the transitions. Within episodes, the same sort of junctions are made between the narrative and other material, such as newspaper excerpts, inserted in it. This device was probably used to indicate the continuity of experience and the similarity, in their basic nature, of events separated by time and space.

There is highly effective use of contrast and the contrapuntal method. John's wedding and its consummation go forward with the grim undertone of John Brown's execution. Little Jim Shawnessy is born as Fort Sumter is attacked. Interspersed throughout John's frantic, tragic search for the mad Susanna, who has fled taking the child with her, are fragmentary reports of the confused violence of the colliding armies at Gettysburg. The Great Footrace between Johnny and Flash Perkins has as a foil descrip-

tions of epic competitions between river steamboats, giant loco-
motives, and Sullivan and Corbett. This device can also be used
ironically, as when Johnny first reads Lincoln's Gettysburg
Address in a Chattanooga bordello. Very often Lockridge relates
one event in several ways. Besides the narration and dialogue, a
description may be inserted from one of the local newspapers.
Excerpts from two completely fictitious ones, the *Cosmic Enquirer*
and the *Mythic Examiner,* supply descriptions which are satirical,
humorous, and sometimes ribald. The novel's descriptive passages
come vividly alive, catching the violence of battles and riots, conveying the smoky uproar of conventions, and painting the sweet
beauty of the fertile earth. There are only one or two false notes
in the hundreds of pages of dialogue which catch the soft nuances
of southern speech, the hard nasal tones of the Indiana back-
country drawl, and the clipped accents of city talk. And there
are glowing passages, frequently too purple, but all possessing
beauty in their song of the land and their lament for things that
are lost.

Raintree County presents a panorama of American history,
a chronicle of American literature, and a criticism of American
society during most of the nineteenth century. Excerpts from the
four newspapers mentioned above relate historical events. Many of
the most important ones are seen through Johnny Shawnessy's
eyes, and none of them, not even Lincoln's assassination or the
Pittsburgh strike, seems artificial or contrived to juxtapose the
hero and climactic events in the life of his nation.

There are only brief references to Emerson, Poe, and Thoreau,
but the effect on Johnny and some of his friends of the work of
Whitman, Longfellow, Hawthorne, and Lincoln is shown. One
meets in their passing vogue the Horatio Alger stories, *Uncle Tom's
Cabin*, Civil War memoirs, and the sentimental novels of the middle
and late nineteenth century. The reader sees in all their transience
period pieces such as the illustrated gift book, popular elegiac
verse, and the Tennysonian imitation. Interwoven with the fabric
of the life of which it was a part, this literature gains a special
vividness and relevance.

The national problems which deeply concern Johnny Shawnessy parallel the fall from grace and expiation of sin treated on
the personal level through the myth of Adam. As the national

punishment and atonement for the institution of slavery is the Civil War, so for heedless materialism it is the Gilded Age. The tremendous, onrushing growth of America was to John inevitable, a part of a national destiny. But he felt that the financial titans who flung the iron rails west and reared the smoking factories had done so with ruthless disregard for the human beings who contributed the sweating labor. (The locomotive is presented as the modern equivalent of the Cretan Minotaur.) To John it seemed that the shady manipulation of capital and the exploitation of human and natural resources involved a rejection of the human values implicit in the Declaration of Independence. Equally guilty were the corrupt politicians who swore to represent the people but served only themselves. Communism was anathema to him, but the free-wheeling empire-building of the Gilded Age seemed just as inimical to the spirit of American democracy. Raintree County, and the macrocosm for which it stood, retained archaisms and barbarisms in its moral code. It was a society of Puritan restraints, yet one which said that

> The injured husband may take the life of him who has injured him . . . Terrible as homicide is, this method must, on the whole, be admitted to be the most effectual, the wisest, and the most natural revenge of an outraged husband (p. 216).

Organized religion, as well as that brought by the God-shouting evangelist, is examined closely. The Perfessor attacks the Old Testament Christianity on which it is based as a code springing from the prehistoric past of savage patriarchal Hebrew clans. This is criticism of a culture as well as an institution.

In addition to all its other attributes, *Raintree County* is a comic epic. Jerusalem Webster Stiles is not only an intellectual gadfly and cynical wit; he is also an engaging character in the best picaresque tradition. Like an inverted alter ego, he appears throughout Johnny's life. Living by his wits, goading less agile minds, attempting to run off with the preacher's wife, he is a genuine comic creation of substance and depth. The redoubtable Flash Perkins has a Bunyanesque quality. Ready to outdrink, outrun, or outfight any man in the county, he is fierce and untroubled by intellectual processes, but he is honest and generous. Winning Fourth of July races, capturing Confederate cannon, or joyously challenging a mob in a bawdyhouse, he is an eager spirit living for action and laughter. Garwood B. Jones is successively Johnny's rival for a girl, for journalistic prominence, and for political office. But Johnny knows, and so does Garwood, that he is a charlatan. Completely dominated by self-interest, gifted with spell-binding oratory, he makes his prominent way in the world by cozening the gullible and playing on common wants and fears. And, of course, many of Johnny's amatory adventures are in the comic tradition. There are other touches, such as the medicine show with its phrenologist and seller of guaranteed elixirs. There is the farcical temperance drama climaxed by the burning of the theatre. Accompanying all this is the salty dialogue of farmhands, backwoodsmen, and old soldiers telling outrageous lies about campaigns fought in the long ago.

Why may *Raintree County* be one of the five or six most important novels of this era? Because, despite all its imperfections, it is a sound literary achievement in its technical proficiency, its attempt to interpret a nation and a culture, and its effort to extend this interpretation to life in general. Its faults and virtues are intermixed. The very overcrowding of the book with facts and people and events helps to make it a living panorama of America. Its complex and sometimes cloudy symbolism gives the life of one man and one county relevance to other lives and other places. *Raintree County* is important in yet another way. As Mr. Tindall has suggested, the book has apparently helped to gain popular acceptance for the many-leveled novel.

This novel is also remarkable when it is seen in the perspective of its own time. When other novelists were writing of the desolation of war, of the disillusionment of its aftermath, and of the destruction of old values and orders, Ross Lockridge made an all-consuming effort whose total effect was a reaffirmation of faith in America and the American dream. *Raintree County* is not The Great American Novel, which probably will never be written. But it is a substantial achievement which merits a place in American literature.

THE CASE OF *RAINTREE COUNTY*

LAWRENCE JAY DESSNER

Raintree County, a novel of over a thousand pages, was published, with considerable fanfare, some twenty-five years ago. Its author, an obscure young English teacher from Indiana, who had been supporting his wife and their four children on $2,500 a year, had received, six months prior to publication of his first book, the Metro-Goldwyn-Mayer Novel Award and the $125,000 with which MGM asserted their faith in their judgment. The Book-of-the-Month Club had guaranteed another $25,000, and commercial prospects seemed enhanced by early reviews which spoke of "the Great American Novel," and which referred to the book's possibly offensive sexual explicitness.[1] As if in answer to a press agent's prayer, the Reverend Alfred Barrett of Fordham University denounced the novel as "blasphemous." The editors of *Today's Woman* dispatched a writer to Bloomington, Indiana, to do a human-interest story on the great American success story as exemplified by the author, Ross Lockridge, Jr.[2] And to complete this paradigm of the best-seller's progress in our time, the *New Yorker's* arch and debonair dismissal of the novel, while condescending to discover merit in some aspects of the book, found others to be "swollen," "pretentious," and "absolutely terrible." It was, in sum, "just the sort of plump turkey that they bake to a turn in Hollywood."[3] In its first year, 400,000 copies were sold. By year's end, in the words of America's oracle of popular fashion, *Time Magazine,* it had "floated away in embarrassed silence."[4]

The stage, one might think, is set here for a resurrection, a

213

vindication of this artifact of popular art, and an indictment of those decadent and elitist critics who, blinded by their disdain for the popular, have not judged the novel on its considerable merits. Critical performances of this sort are no longer uncommon, indeed, in some *cul-de-sacs* of the Popular Culture movement, or party, they are the only approved tack. *Raintree County,* however, is not amenable to such treatment. The book's merits, as I have discovered with dismay, and about which I report now with chagrin, are minuscule. Established and establishment critics, for various reasons, about which one may speculate with confidence, have sporadically tried to keep the book alive in this and other cases, with disheartening ease.

The enjoyment of literature, and the study and practice of literary criticism is often, and truly I believe, said to foster the moral virtues of tolerance, sympathy, and compassion. But insofar as the equally moral virtues of clear perception, honest judgment, and painful courage, are concerned, literary criticism may come to seem cruel—although no more cruel than football. We give an E for effort, but no matter how earnest that effort, it is an immaterial factor in our literary evaluation.

In the present case, Ross Lockridge's most earnest effort to write *the* comprehensive American novel is itself at the root of his failure to write one that can be read with pleasure, or even, after a while, with interest. John Shawnessy, and there can be no doubt that this central character of *Raintree County* is another name for Ross Lockridge, wants, furiously, to feel deeply and comprehensively, to ponder the large and capitalized questions of Life, Death, God, Soul, America, and Time. It is a mark of the vastness of his ambition, and of its sublime and self-defeating egotism, that, had *Raintree County* succeeded, it would have been definitive—future novelists and tomorrow's passionate and sensitive young men and women would discover that there was nothing still in need of utterance.

John Shawnessy, for example, contemplates a large rock, older than the civilization that has been built up near it: "The moveless mass of it had been there before the settlers came, had been there when Columbus saw the flowering shores of western islands, had been there when the first man, wandering through the forests of the middle continent discovered a river winding to a lake."[5] The insight, typical of the occasions from which hundreds of such rhapsodies flow, is cerebral and banal. It is not felt. It lacks, precisely, the virtue Coleridge found in Wordsworth, namely "the weight and sanity of thoughts and sentiments, won, not from books, but—from the poet's own meditative observation."[6] Lockridge's thoughts and sentiments, at least the ones he celebrates in *Raintree County,* come from books, and from books poorly written or poorly read. When, or if, the purple prose, extended energetically, succeeds in moving the reader, reaction is sure to follow: the procedure is fraudulent, a manipulation of emotional rhythms and counters which have no basis in experience. It is like a freshman theme on an assigned topic about which the student feels nothing, but over which he knows, or thinks, a bushel of enthusiastic and resounding sentiments should be spread.

The slightest sensation is more deeply felt than the most significant idea, says the English rationalist, and although the dissociation of sensibility his formulation exhibits may, indeed, be undesirable, one does not overcome the liability by an act of will.

It is probable that dinosaurs roamed, in fact that they mated, on the very spot on which I am now standing. John Shawnessy finds notions like this triggers for the expression, in floods and torrents, of his reverence and special sensitivity to the mysteries of existence. It is the defect Coleridge called "mental bombast,"[7] and when it appears, verbal bombast will not be far behind.

Let me return, almost at random, to the text: John Shawnessy "lay a long time thinking of many things. Around him lay the putrid flower of the City of New Orleans, rankly nodding its head above the magnolia swamp. The languid stream of the river, draining all the water of middle America, found its way here through many changing channels to the sea. Mingled with its yellow tide was the water of a little river far away in Raintree County" (p. 452). He is thinking of many things, we are told, but he is expressing, fervidly, a typical banality. And he continues: "It seemed to him then that she lay there couched in mystery like a sphinx, and that her presence and her musical name meant something tragic and mysterious which was at the heart of all human existence. Surely a strange fate had ferried this scarred, lovely creature up the great river to his arms." Such prose, and the moral, linguistic, and philosophic poverty that underlies it is the basic element of *Raintree County*. There is an egotism, and a pomposity, a churning of emotional waters without first getting one's feet wet, that is embarrassing to see wholeheartedly endorsed by Johnny's creator.

"Think I could fall in love with a girl that was afraid to say her soul's her own! I think of her—and dream! I'd wait a million years and never mind it—for her! The trouble with you is, you don't understand what love means. I love tonight. I love the sand, and the trees, and the grass, and the water and the sky and the moon. . . . It's all in me and I'm in it."[8] That is not John Shawnessy but Richard Miller, Eugene O'Neill's gently comic portrait of a sensitive boy of seventeen. Ross Lockridge, in contrast, intones his "Ah Wilderness" with a straight face.

While there is no irony in the presentation of John Shawnessy, there is a potentially complicating factor to be noticed. John's meditations lead to so many revelations that, whatever a critic might say, John has already proclaimed it his own cosmic and wonderful discovery. The market on truth is cornered, criticism preempted. It is a deeply defensive maneuver and one that cannot succeed. John's practice, not his theorizing, defines him, as in this excerpt: "Sometimes it seemed that in some occult way. . . ." Do not we all beg Freshmen to avoid such empty celebration of vagueness? "Sometimes it seemed that in some occult way John Shawnessy was Willie Shakespeare, and that the plays were still waiting to be written and that everyone was somehow Willie Shakespeare and everyone and everything was Johnny Shawnessy."

To quote a bit of Swinburne's teasing of Tennyson:

> One, who is not, we see; but one, whom we see not, is;
> Surely this is not that; but that is assuredly this.
> ***
> God, whom we see not, is; and God, who is not, we see;
> Fiddle, we know, is diddle; and diddle, we take it, is dee.[9]

". . . that life was discovery and not creation—it was permitting oneself to be a great poet and not forcing oneself to be a great poet" (pp. 98-99). Yes, great Art cannot be "forced." Despite the disclaimer, *Raintree County* and Johnny's own work-in-progress are painfully forceful frontal assaults on greatness. This is what follows: "For as he lay on the bank of the Shawmucky, he knew that he too would be a great poet." (Listen to him: "He *knew* that he *too* would be a great poet.") "It seemed to him that he must be a greater poet even than Shakespeare because there was some essence of what he was that Elizabethan England couldn't possibly compose." There is, remarkably, nothing in the text to suggest ironical intent here. Rather, it brings to mind Lockridge's response to a reporter who asked, with not quite a straight face, if he had been influenced by Thomas Wolfe. Lockridge readily acknowledged that influence but added, "I feel that I have a better historical background than Wolfe had."[10] This is the crux of it—the belief, or wish, that Art is made from "historical background," from the reading of many books, and through the exercise of the Will. John Shawnessy entertains the idea that history is myth, a fiction, the product of the collective human sensibility brooding over its condition, that, after all, "feeling comes first." He knows, in fact, all the advanced ideas of his own nineteenth century and of half of ours, and none of them help. There is little perception of feeling in him or in the novel, which is stuffed with the puerilities to which one resorts, in fear and self-defense, from the realities men feel. Human beings can stand very little reality; the Lockridge-Shawnessy amalgam can stand a good deal less than most.

The moral and intellectual and emotional poverty which pervades Lockridge's prose, and which can be demonstrated in short excerpts, also determines the much discussed formal structures of the novel. Its model is the *Ulysses* of James Joyce although there are many other books to which Lockridge's style and structure are obviously indebted. His reading includes, not only primary texts but also modern academic criticism. In turn there has been some academic notice of the complexities of form in *Raintree County*.[11] It is an oddly attractive case, for no matter how far-fetched the analysis gets, *Raintree County*'s text supports it, its allusions and ramifications of imagery and meaning, are printed in red as it were, nuggets of academic gold begging to be discovered. It is as if someone had read Stuart Gilbert's exposition of *Ulysses,* and the files of the *James Joyce Quarterly,* and then

218

confidently set about to write the original novel. But a *Ulysses,* without the richly realized creation of Leopold Bloom, and Molly, and Stephen, and the rest of them, and without the vibrantly keen-eyed and keen-eared verbal presence of Joyce, would be an utterly dead thing.

The last word here I take from the article which most conscientiously discusses "Psychological Symbolism, Archetype, and Myth" in *Raintree County.* Jung, and Freud, and Frazer are brought to bear in a most competent analysis whose last sentence gives the charade away: "Through the use of symbolism, Lockridge gives immense meaning and scope to what would otherwise be a banal historical romance."[12] Despite these words, I cannot but believe that their author knows full well that psychological symbolism is not a substitute for psychology, that there can be no meaning on an unpopulated planet, and that "scope" without individual, particularized human sensibilities, is a mouthwash.

"When you called a thing a name, you gave it form" (p. 803). Shawnessy, who says that, shares, with his creator, this central maxim of the modern profession of English literature. But in his hands the flaw in the precept is revealed. Words can give form to things; they can help us understand, and value, and mitigate what we, I hope not pompously refer to as the human condition. But words can also disguise things, blow mist between ourselves and our perceptions of things. They can be man's best means of leading an examined life, or they can be a means of, in the full light of day, refusing to see things as they really are while appearing, courageously, to be doing just that. *Raintree County* adopts, with remarkable thoroughness, the second of these courses. The disguise, made by words, succeeds. It is a book all about emotion in which no emotion can be discerned. It is *Everyman* with no man in it.

You can't fool all of the people all of the time. The American reading public is to be congratulated for having only temporarily succumbed to the blandishments of press agentry and to the irresponsibilities of critics who should have known better, and who, if they read the novel through, surely did.

JOHN STEINBECK: NO *GRAPES OF WRATH*

JOSEPH WALDMEIR

I met John Steinbeck only once, for a couple of hours out of a couple of days in the Fall of 1963, while I was a Fulbright Professor at the University of Helsinki, and he was passing through the city on his way home from the Soviet Union, where he had toured on a cultural exchange. We talked—I fortunately did more listening than talking—more or less informally, both *tete a tete* and in a small group of students. I cannot quote what he had to say exactly; I didn't have a tape recorder, which was probably all for the best since he hated the formality which a microphone imposed on him. But my memory is vivid enough to enable me to paraphrase very closely the things he had to say; and since what he had to say is of more than passing interest in the context of this essay, with the reader's permission, I'll begin with his remarks, and perhaps, let the remarks color the conclusions which the essay draws.

When, during the course of conversation, I asked Steinbeck which of the younger novelists he liked best, he answered, after only a brief pause for speculation: Jack Kerouac, because he best expresses the speech of the people. He said that the young writer he had toured with also had a fine ear, but he dealt with different people who spoke a different speech, and besides, he wasn't a novelist. He was Edward Albee. A student asked him which of his books he was proudest of, and without hesitation he answered, *The Sea of Cortez*. He was proud of the painstaking, first-hand research that had gone before the book, and he was proud and

219

happy that the research had corroborated and solidified his own non-teleological world view, posited not upon beginnings or endings, but upon a sort of rhythm, an ebb and flow. He said his undergraduate training in the sciences had built a respect for accuracy in him that he had never lost, and had compelled him to research carefully everything he wrote—had sent him not only to the Sea of Cortez but on the long trek with the Okies as well. Still *a propos* of research, he said that a curious, inquiring mind will discover certain things in its adventures which can turn mere inquiry into research, and which can in turn stimulate and perhaps even order the creative impulse. Of particular interest from the point of view of this essay, he gave as a general example his belief that the persistence of popular themes or even stories themselves in a culture—a persistence discoverable through research—justifies a writer's re-use of the theme or rewriting of the story; and as particular examples, he cited his use of Malory's *Morte d'Arthur* as the basis of *Tortilla Flat,* and his retelling of legend in *The Pearl,* and of course, his fictionalized biography of Morgan the pirate in *Cup of Gold.*

He said that he considered himself to be first and foremost a storyteller, and that it is as a teller of stories that he hoped to be remembered. There is no contradiction here. He considered *The Sea of Cortez* and even *Travels With Charlie* to be essentially stories; and his insistence upon accuracy in observation and reporting led him to research the backgrounds of his fiction as assiduously as he did his non-fiction.

It is as a storyteller that I wish to consider him here; but in the narrower conventional sense of fictioneer rather than of travel writer or scientist or journalist. The things he said bear heavily upon this discussion. He had a remarkable ear for the speech of the people; one need only listen to Jim Casy and the Joads and the denizens of Cannery Row to hear it. But it is attested to as well in a negative sense if one listens to the impossibly stilted language of Joseph Wayne in *To A God Unknown,* or to the preposterous cutenesses of Ethan Allen Hawley in *Winter of Our Discontent.* I do not mean however that his ear was fine only when it heard and recorded dialect. Witness the purity, the honesty, of tone and expression in *Pastures of Heaven* and *The Red Pony.* His tendency to research his subject carefully and to use the product of his research in his fiction works beautifully in *Grapes of Wrath* and in the metaphorical marine biology scenes in *Cannery Row* and *Sweet Thursday*. But occasionally, especially when he has researched ideas instead of people, the research takes control of and even subverts character and story. The influence of Jung and Frazer bleeds the life from the characters of *To A God Unknown,* as the intrusive Cain-Abel myth comes close to rendering impotent the power of *East of Eden.* And the credibility of so vital a novel as *In Dubious Battle* is considerably weakened by Mac's set-speech explanations of the strike from the Communist point of view, which read as if they were taken directly from a manual or handbook on revolution. Steinbeck keeps close control of his non-teleological philosophy, though it is certainly there, especially in those works, such as *Of Mice and Men,* and in those episodes, such as the turtle inter-chapter and the scene in which the dike is destroyed in *Grapes of Wrath,* which lend themselves to a Naturalistic interpretation. But he appears at least to back away from enforcing or even insisting upon this potentially harsh philosophical position—largely, I think, because of some things he did not talk about in Helsinki.

Those things are his feeling for people and his feeling for Nature and his feeling for people's feelings about Nature. He did not talk about them, I believe, because nobody asked him about them; but also because they are not the sorts of things one casually introduces into an informal conversation about oneself. But they are there, at the heart of his work, and they, more than anything else, mitigate the harshness of his non-teleological world view. Sometimes they mitigate it too much. Like Hemingway, Steinbeck speaks of the necessity of struggle against the inevitability of loss; but unlike Hemingway, his response frequently has a vaguely soap-opera quality to it. That is to say, sometimes he cares too much, and the inevitability overwhelms him, and his caring pushes his work into and through that sentimentalism with which it has been so often and so justly charged. The breast-feeding of the baby at the beginning of *In Dubious Battle* and of the old man at the end of *Grapes of Wrath* are excellent examples of what I mean. Sometimes the sentimentalism is coupled with anger or indignation, as it is in the *Grapes* interchapter concerned with the sale of the horses whose mares had been beribboned by the little daughter. But most often, and most successfully, it is coupled with humor, as in the portrayals of the good- if not golden-hearted whores and bums of *Tortilla Flat* and *Cannery Row* and *Sweet Thursday*.

His and his characters' feelings for Nature are seldom so sentimentalized. Nature is the epitome if not the proof of the philosophy; in her resides the rhythm, the ebb and flow. Beyond, within her beauty and her majesty rests a force that can be ugly and destructive. But it is an indifferent force; Nature cannot be malevolent, nor benevolent—she simply is. And a man can only come to know her, never to control or even to understand her. The green of the leaf, the warmth of the sun, the softness of the grass, the drought, the flood, the bird and beast of prey are all aspects of a sort of transcendent unity which man can tune in to, but never become a part of. And a man tunes in by observing Nature as she functions and by assisting her to function; by taking a piece of her and gradually making himself a part of that piece. By farming, the highest calling to which a man can aspire. In becoming one with the land, a man is enabled to partake of the essential unity which Nature embodies. And this dignifies and ennobles a man, and fulfills him. It is at this point that Steinbeck is in danger of sentimentalism, with talk of a man's almost primeval desire for a place of his own, with the mystical belief that there can be blood ties between a man and the land, knotted by family graves. But most of all, in his attitude toward the displaced and dispossessed, especially if they have been dis-possessed by Nature. For if Nature is indifferent and capricious, and a man, despite his struggles, can exert no real control over her, then as her "victim," he cannot be tragic, and one's sadness at his victimization may very well be sentimental. But again, the sentimentalism attaches to the man and his fate here, not to his feelings for Nature.

It is possible of course for a novelist to strike a near perfect balance between feeling and fact within incipiently sentimental episodes and between openly sentimental episodes and the novel as a whole. What it takes is absolute honesty on the part of the novelist; a refusal to cheat in his portrayal of character or situation in order to elicit an emotional response in the reader. Steinbeck realizes both possibilities in the two novels I have had most in mind during this discussion: *Of Mice and Men* and *Grapes of Wrath*. The death of Lennie, for example, is loaded with potential sentimentalism which Steinbeck sturdily resists by dwelling on its necessity. And in the process, he elevates the dangerously poignant place-of-our-own day-dreams of George above the sentimental by integrating them, as ironic counterpoint, into the murder itself. And Rose of Sharon's generosity, prompted by Ma Joad's silent entreaty, transcends the sentimental not because of its shock value, but because of the honest conviction of Tom Joad's earlier speech to Ma in which he explains his conversion to a sort of Whitman-like commitment to group man—which conversion is in turn made credible by the still earlier murder of Jim Casy.

Nothing however, not even *The Grapes of Wrath,* as a whole, can rescue the little girl braiding the horses' manes from the depths of sentimentalism, as nothing can rescue Doc's love for the whore, Suzy, in *Sweet Thursday* from it, or the love of the bums and whores for Doc in that novel and in *Cannery Row.* Steinbeck liked the depths; he spent at least a little time there in almost every novel he wrote.

But, to approach finally the subject of this essay, these judgments have been qualitative, of course. Sentimentalism in whole or in part need not hurt the popularity of a novel; indeed, it may enhance it. The reading or play- and movie-going audience, particularly the audience of the 1930's which had been conditioned by the real pathos surrounding their daily lives and the imaginary pathos of the soap opera which entertained them, was hardly to be turned off by the sentimental. In fact, they would be most apt to be turned off by what they would see, perhaps correctly, as the patronizing tone of my intellectual justification of Steinbeck's sentimentalism. They would harumph indignantly at my argument that *Of Mice and Men* and *Grapes of Wrath* are fine works *despite* their sentimentalism; that Steinbeck's honesty rescued them from the very real threat of the maudlin; and that, in effect, that tug at the heartstrings which contributed to their popularity was, fortunately, unable to diminish their quality.

But in a sense, these two novels are straw men, easy to manipulate within the framework of this discussion, primarily because of their topicality. Hence, in order more convincingly to argue that there is no necessary incompatibility between quality and popularity in literature, I would like now to shift away from them toward a work which has not enjoyed their notoriety, though it has certainly achieved a significant measure of popularity in its own right. I refer to the novelette *The Red Pony,* on which the balance of this discussion will focus. If I appear to hedge a bit on the question of its popularity, it is only because it has been for so long required reading in English courses from junior high school through college that one might wonder how genuine its popularity is; and because ordinarily only one part of it, "The Gift," is anthologized;[1] and because a terrible motion picture which successfully made a travesty of the story, may have contributed to its popularity among the non-reading public. However, if I may assume that even those who have been forced to read it or parts of it have found it a compelling experience—and there is supporting evidence for the assumption all the way from my fourteen-year-old through my graduate students--then I believe I can proceed from the further assumption of its popularity.

Furthermore, and most importantly, it is a fine work of art; as good as any that Steinbeck ever achieved. It has no ideological pots to boil, so it lacks the startling built-in dramatics of *Grapes of Wrath* and *In Dubious Battle* and, in a sense, *Of Mice and Men.* It has no overriding mystical-philosophical-theological motif, so it fortunately lacks the pretentiousness of *To A God Unknown,* and to an extent, of *East of Eden* and *Winter of Our Discontent* and *The Pearl.* It goes without saying that, though it has humorous touches in it—after all, Jody is a quite normal growing boy—it lacks the grand comedic quality of *Tortilla Flat* and *Cannery Row* and *Sweet Thursday* and even *The Wayward Bus;* it is not intended to be that kind of story.

It is intended to be, and is, an initiation story, one of the most popular themes in American literature, running from Huckleberry Finn and before through Nick Adams and into Holden Caulfield and beyond. But *The Red Pony* differs from the standard American initiation story in that it is not concerned with the rites of passage from adolescence into manhood, but the passage from the certainties and securities of boyhood into the anguishes and anxieties of adolescence. Jody is a ten- and eleven-year-old boy who discovers life, or who, much as the initiate in the more common situation, has the discovery of life forced upon him, through three experiences with death—the deaths of the pony, Gabilan; of old Gitano who, like Frost's hired man has come home to die; and of the mare, Nellie, who dies throwing the colt which Jody will have to keep alive. What Jody will do with his discovery (it is not yet knowledge) is not a part of the story. All we have at the end, after the death of Nellie, is the portrait of Jody, now suddenly no longer a boy but certainly not yet a man, as he trotted out of the barn:

> He ached from his throat to his stomach. His legs were stiff and heavy. He tried to be glad because of the colt, but the bloody face, and the haunted, tired eyes of Billy Buck hung in the air ahead of him.
>
> (*The Long Valley,* p. 279)

Contrast this final paragraph of the story as a whole with the violence of Jody's reaction to the death of the pony and the desecration of its corpse at the end of "The Gift," and the boy's progress toward discovery, and toward the groping uncertainty of adolescence is manifest.

Manifest in this passage also, as it is in the story as a whole, is Steinbeck's own immense ability to capture the speech of the people. As I said earlier, it is not because the dialogue is in dialect; it really isn't, though the characters in *The Red Pony* certainly talk in the way that people who lived on a ranch in California early in this century probably did—occasionally ungrammatically, with a relatively unsophisticated vocabulary. More than dialogue is involved here. The third person point of view is of course Steinbeck's, but it is filtered through the eyes of the young Jody; and it is with infinite care that Steinbeck describes scene, event, and emotion in a language that, though it might not be precisely a small boy's, is true to the point of view of a small boy. This too, is what he meant, I think, when he spoke of recording the speech of the people; and he does it in this passage and throughout the story without patronizing either the boy or the reader.

Such verisimilitude may result from little more research than Steinbeck's own boyhood memories, but its contribution to the conviction which the story carries is profound. Even more important is the verisimilitude which had to come from more specific research, of the kind that Steinbeck so much respected—the description of the symptoms of strangles in a horse and the homemade, primitive, even brutal cures for it, as well as the description of the Caesarean birth of the dead Nellie's colt—and which contribute immediately to the thematic development of the story. For Steinbeck dramatizes the results of his research here by involving Billy Buck intimately in the story, as he involves Doc, the marine biologist in *Cannery Row* and *Sweet Thursday*. Billy is the man who knows how to do the things which must be done in crucial situations like these, and it is to Billy that the boy must turn when confronted with them. The fact that Billy Buck's knowledge and skill fails in its first test with Gabilan, and is at best a mitigated success in the second with Nellie and her colt, impels Jody's initiation by shaking his boyish confidence that all problems are soluble and that there are infallible places to seek the answers coupled with infallible people to apply them. It is an extremely traumatic experience for Jody, for its focus is on death. Indeed, the major intention of the story is to initiate Jody by confronting him with death. Gabilan dies and Jody kills the buzzard at the end of "The Gift"; the lyrical second section, "The Great Mountain," begins with Jody's slingshot killing of the thrush, and proceeds toward the ritual death of old Gitano and the horse, Easter; and of course, "The Promise" ends as Nellie dies in order that her colt may live. And the intention is reinforced symbolically as Jody identifies the artesian spring with life and the black cypress tree with death immediately after he has beseeched Billy not to let anything happen to Nellie and the colt.

But the colt breeches, and Billy must kill Nellie to save it, and though Billy's feet do not turn completely to clay, still Jody moves beyond his boyish certainties into insecurity and doubt, filled with the sense of dread and guilt so well expressed in that final paragraph of the story quoted above. And this important first step in his growth away from boyhood leads Jody to the threshhold of a Steinbeckean knowledge at first even more disquieting: That Nature is little more than profoundly indifferent force, controllable neither by appeal nor by struggle. Gabilan dies, Nellie's colt breeches, despite the efforts or hopes of Billy or Jody. The best a man can do is recognize and act upon whatever alternatives Nature may provide. She provides none in the case of Gabilan, and so the struggle is useless. She does provide them in the case of Nellie and the colt, however, and Billy makes the choice—life for the colt and death for Nellie. And Nature goes serenely on her Naturalistic way.

But the colt lives. That is the important anti-Naturalistic fact which will eventually lead Jody over the next initiative threshhold into manhood. There may be no teleological design in Nature's cycle, but the cycle exists, and within it, ebb is balanced by flow. Life is as important as death; the flowing spring is as important as the killing tree. All of this is in the story for Jody eventually to learn. This, plus the fact that a man must face life or death as a man, in full awareness of the mortality of all things. Like Billy Buck, who bloodies his hands to make his agonized choice. Or, better, like old Gitano, who cherishes the ancient rapier which is the symbol of his manhood, and carries it proudly before him as he proceeds toward the inevitable completion of Nature's cycle.

Here, as at innumerable points along its course, *The Red Pony* offers opportunities for sentimentalizing. Steinbeck sternly rejects all of them. Instead he holds firmly to the pattern which the story itself dictates, leading the reader into no emotional dead ends or sloughs. And as a consequence, the emotion one feels at its end is honest and earned; for one is convinced that the story has gone exactly where it had to go in the only way possible for it to get there. He has been brought to know Jody, I believe, as intimately as he can ever come to know a fictional eleven-year-old boy. It is a story of which the consummate storyteller that John Steinbeck wished to be remembered as could be justifiably proud.

In the course of our conversations at Helsinki, which have served to guide and organize this discussion generally and the discussion of *The Red Pony* in particular, the name of Ernest Hemingway, then dead barely two years, quite naturally came up; and Steinbeck said one thing that has remained so vividly in my mind that I feel free to use quotation marks around it. "The trouble with Ernest," he said, "was that he wrote with one eye on posterity. No writer should write for posterity."

It was a disturbing statement, both in what it said about Hemingway and in what it at least implied about Steinbeck. About Hemingway, I choose to say nothing here; any comment would rapidly grow into another essay. What disturbed me about Steinbeck was the sort of belligerent sadness which I read into the statement. For of course, all writers write for posterity, and only that writer who feels that his work will not live after him denies that he does. But upon sober reflection, it occurred to me that Steinbeck meant the statement to be taken literally, and by no means as an apology, belligerent or otherwise. He meant, I think, that a writer must write here and now about what he here and now knows; that if he does that well, he will have done the best that he can possibly do. Posterity will make its own judgments regardless; no writer can dictate them, nor should he try. Steinbeck sought with Hemingway "the real thing, the sequence of motion and fact which made the emotion"; but he stopped there, apparently unconcerned that the real thing "would be as valid in a year or in ten years or, with luck and if you stated it purely enough, always. . . ." (*Death in the Afternoon*, p. 2). That would take care of itself.

I say apparently unconcerned; I still can't believe that he didn't at least hope that his work would live into posterity. I do believe that he did write of and for his own time, and that it is this as much as anything else that has made so much of his work so popular. But I also believe that this popularity, if honestly earned by growing out of a concern for as real a thing as possible, is not incompatible with quality. And that such a work as this describes—such a work as *The Red Pony* or *Grapes of Wrath*—will the author or nil he, must endure.

BALLYHOO, GARGOYLES, & FIRECRACKERS: BEN HECHT'S AESTHETIC CALLIOPE

ABE C. RAVITZ

Immediately after World War I and during the early 1920's, when American Best and Better Seller lists advertised Harold Bell Wright and Rafael Sabatini, Gertrude Atherton and Edna Ferber, Zane Grey and Emerson Hough, the devil's darling of literary gadflies was Mr. Ben Hecht, erstwhile Chicago foreign correspondent, columnist, and dabbler in letters whose critical eruptions, delivered in a form of Middlewestern Menckenese, regularly caricatured the pretensions of the contemporary American intellectual Establishment. Courting notoriety as a cynical post-war demon, Hecht assumed a guise of popular negation similar to that effete, careless, *fin-de-siècle* diabolism of Edgar Saltus and James G. Huneker—two of his creative idols—and became to one segment of the nation's literati pure, distilled anathema; to others, an incendiary iconoclast, endeavoring honestly to rout the mawkish forces of popular, nectareous romance, to put to rest the likes of a Peter B. Kyne, who in 1923 could dedicate his novel *Never the Twain Shall Meet:* "To a little girl—who believed that when the fairies married, one might, by lying very quietly in the grass, hear the bluebells ringing." As early as 1918 James Branch Cabell had derisively referred to Hecht as a mere "jongleur";[1] and by 1922 Vernon L. Parrington had dismissed him as "a burnt-out rocket."[2] Sherwood Anderson called him a "smarty" whose glibness and cleverness would probably destroy whatever creative talent there actually was;[3] and Kenneth Rexroth corroborated this sentiment

Reprinted by permission from the *Journal of Popular Culture,* Bowling Green State University, Volume I:1, pp. 37-51.

when he observed that Hecht could have been a good writer but had been corrupted by his experience as "police-court reporter."[4] Yet it was Ezra Pound who soundly asserted: "Why should I come back to the God-forsaken desert [America]? There is only one intelligent man in the whole United States to talk to—Ben Hecht."[5] It is clear that this literary showman had made a considerable reputation for himself, for he had come to represent an antidote to popular literary cults, to the American Booboisie, to national Comstockery, to genteel humorists, and to panty-waist journalists. His critical bombshells, though momentarily popular, were moulded into a literary warhead created by an intellectual comedian—a dark one.

Ben Hecht had vaulted directly from headlines of the Chicago *News* to those nearly sacred pages of the famous *Smart Set,* edited by America's two wicked cosmopolites, H. L. Mencken and George Jean Nathan. At a time when the *Smart Set* was in financial difficulties Hecht was impressed into contributing as many as eight stories to a single issue, of course under such imaginative, Mencken-ascribed pseudonymns as John Henslowe Saltonstall, Ethan Allan Lowell, and the Reverend Dr. Peter Cabot-Cabot.[6] For the Chicago *News* the flamboyant Hecht would attempt to destroy the then considerable and ever-burgeoning fame of novelist James Branch Cabell, whose greatness had been enthusiastically advanced by numerous reputable critics of the day, notably Burton Rascoe and Carl Van Doren. Thundered the passionate critical assassin:

> Mr. Cabell's style of writing bristles with the maudlin and lachrymose romantics such as fascinate the shop-girls in the pages of George Barr McCutcheon. And then too has Mr. Cabell's irony a way of losing itself in the burbles of profound and academic inanities. Also he is lacking in the courage of his disillusion, and . . . because of this lack of courage does his irony become a sort of meandering wistfulness like the whine of a little old man suffering from false teeth. Finally Mr. Cabell is lacking as a poet. He is unable to create those illusions so necessary for the reality of fiction. . . . So Cabell remains the sardonic professor mouthing in the boring rhetoric of the classroom.[7]

But Hecht was not merely the hatchet-wielding, pedestrian journalist; he emerged from the well-cultivated press rooms of perhaps the nation's most enlightened newspaper group: for the earlier Chicago literary journalists—B.L.T. (Bert Liston Taylor), Eugene Field, and George Ade—had been followed by men of comparable talent and performance—Vincent Starrett, Harry Hansen, and Henry Justin Smith.[8] So the apprenticeship of Ben Hecht was part practical journalism and part intellectual saturation in letters: Arthur Machen, J. K. Huysmans, Remy de Gourmont, Anatole France.[9] Thus, while the young man was lampooning the literati and twirling off glib screeds for Nathan and Mencken, he also became a regular contributor to Margaret Anderson's *Little Review,* the leading avant-garde periodical in the esoteric world.[10]

And then came the novels from Hecht's freely-flowing and well-lubricated pen. *Erik Dorn* (1921), a dreary tale of a cynical journalist; in 1924 he rewrote this book as *Humpty Dumpty,* a dreary tale of a precious, cynical novelist. *Gargoyles* (1922), vaguely modeled after Robert Herrick's *Memoirs of an American Citizen* and Dreiser's *Financier,* quickly disintegrated into a facile tale of "four-flushers" and "chippie chasers" as the shadowy career of a sardonic political opportunist was chronicled from bawdy house to Congress. One of the varied publishing adventures of the day included the privately-printed, privately-circulated, blatantly overpriced suggestive novel, one that would tease the censors, inflame the prudes, and challenge the general tenor of Comstockery: Hecht appeared on this scene too, bringing out *Fantazius Mallare,* subtitled A Mysterious Oath—a novel (2,000 copies were printed to be sold at $12.50 per) clearly derivative of Huysmans and Oscar Wilde; a medley of bizarre sensations and extravagant debauchs was vaguely perpetrated by a decadent dandy. In 1924, two years after publication of the tale, Hecht and Wallace Smith, his illustrator, (Rascoe had asserted that the illustrations were not phallic symbols; merely phallic) were fined $1,000 each after entering pleas of *nolle contendere* to the charge of sending obscene literature through the mails.[11] With *1001 Afternoons in Chicago* Hecht came upon a literary vehicle that finally enabled him to unify journalism and fiction; his sketches of the city, inspired no doubt by George Ade's earlier tintypes of Windy City life, treated themes of poverty and loneliness, the statics of slum and tenement that Carl Sandburg, his contemporary and friend, was then moulding into verses exploring all devious byways in the "city with the big shoulders."

At this moment in time, too, Ben Hecht had come face to face with an artist who, for a number of years, would be his alter ego: the eccentric and even then legendary Maxwell Bodenheim. A wild-looking Lothario who was relentlessly pursued by women (one committed suicide when he criticized her poetry as "sentimental slush"), Bodenheim is recalled, unfortunately, only as the unkempt radical drifting about Greenwich Village lanes offering poems for sale. But this man was not merely the itinerant, haphazard minstrel literary history has come to judge; actually, before the publication of Eliot's *Wasteland* in 1920, Maxwell Bodenheim was regarded by many as the leading poet in America, and, in addition, as a vigorous, foremost critical intelligence. Indeed, on September 28, 1917, the youthful Hart Crane, who had just moved to New York, wrote to his mother back home in Ohio:

> Maxwell Bodenheim called the other evening, complimented my poetry excessively, and has taken several pieces to the editor of *The Seven Arts,* a personal friend of his. Bodenheim is at the top of American poetry today . . . [he] is a first-class critic . . . and I am proud to have his admiration and encouragement.[12]

Poetry magazine, the *New Republic,* the *Dial,* the *Nation, Harper's, Bookman,* the *Yale Review* happily opened their pages to Bodenheim, this reputable, talented poet and insightful commentator.[13] As totally insulated against the newspapers as Ben Hecht was involved in them, Bodenheim had been in Chicago as a marginal member of the literary army of Liberation that had come to characterize the vibrant Renaissance;[14] there, his temperament made him a natural acquisition for Ben Hecht and his bookshop coterie of *cognoscenti.* Bodenheim, too, had plans for an underground novel like *Fantazius Mallare: Seven Sneers,* he had tentatively entitled the projected collection of tales, fortunately only dreamed but never written.[15] And Bodenheim, like Hecht, was outside the Establishment of writers: he had even told Hart Crane that he, Bodenheim, "after four years of absolute obscurity . . . is succeeding in getting published only through the adverse channels of flattery, friendships, and 'pull.' " He warned the young Ohioan that "Editors are generally disappointed writers who stifle any genius or originality as soon as it is found. . . ."[16]

Maxwell Bodenheim was forever dreaming of financial security. He was a seriously dedicated artist; but even minimal financial reward forever eluded him. By the time he and Hecht had become fast friends, "Bogie" would consider any means to survive with his pen, for, like Hecht, he enjoyed the rhetorical process of writing—juggling words, fabricating metaphors, carelessly playing with phrases. And Ben Hecht in mid-1923, during the last gasps of Renaissance literary explosion, had a proposition. He would begin a revolutionary, intellectual newspaper, the Chicago *Literary Times*. Bodenheim, as associate editor at thirty dollars per week, would be the New York correspondent. The poet eagerly accepted. Perhaps as a salaried contributor a multiplicity of his drives and ambitions could be achieved. He would be economically secure. His pen and his works would be frequently advertised. He could bait and scathe his literary enemies who, safely protected in the Establishment, were keeping him outside the fringe of recognition. He could, maybe, become a celebrity as well as a recognized poet.

So on March 1, 1923, Volume I, Number 1 of the Chicago *Literary Times* was published. The price was ten cents for a tabloid-sized, garishly colored newssheet that eventually came to offer a number of categorical guarantees:

> The Times takes the Blues out of Art
> The Times will put firecrackers in your head
> The Times is a sandbag for Bunk
> The Times is the only Aesthetic Calliope on the street.[17]

The character and personality of this cerebral blast became ineffaceably moulded at the outset. Vincent Starrett tells that "Hecht's original intention was to launch this extraordinary journal with a street parade. There were to be brass bands, perhaps a calliope, and a half a mile of floats showing the writers and critics of Chicago in action, each identified by a banner. . . ."[18] This circus, however, never came to State Street. But the ballyhoo went on: "The Times is as irresponsible as a bride. The Times is as Noisy as a Pond full of Frogs. The Times is as gay as a champagne bottle. The Times Boos, hisses, mocks, and chuckles at the buncombe of its day—Take the Times as a Tonic."[19] Until June 1, 1924, then, this literary comic strip, which achieved circulations of 15,000 and 17,000, and which was financed by Pascal Covici, who mistakenly regarded it as a house organ for his bookstore and publishing firm,[20] regaled, alienated, and antagonized; entertained, challenged, and spoofed as it tried to incite a Pianissimo Revolt emanating from the shadows of Bughouse Square. The Hecht-Bodenheim sheet had scarcely been in circulation three months when the editorial pages of the New York *Times* noted that the blasts whirling from the shores of Lake Michigan were reaching Gotham:

Startling the Radicals

Shocking the bourgeois has become too stale and tame a sport for Chicago. The game of advanced radicals in that city is now to horrify the radicals of the East. It is played with great zest in the last number of the Chicago Literary Times, a periodical edited by Mr. Ben Hecht, with Maxwell Bodenheim as his associate. They set themselves up as the real Goths and Vandals of the liberal movement, and have no patience with those "radical journals" of New York that keep up "an unceasing caterwauling for justice, heroism, sanity, and beauty of soul."[21]

The "rough and irreverent spokesmen," as Hecht and Bodenheim were called, now settled down in earnest to turn out what their mast announced as a bi-monthly "Modern Sardonic Journal."

The stance of Hecht and Bodenheim continued as the free-wheeling negation so amenable to village seers and crossroads atheists of the late 19th century in Middlewestern America: Henry Fitch Ware, the "Ironquill" poet of Topeka whose newspaper verses advocated Ingersoll's ethical postures, and Francis Ellingwood Abbott, the Darwinist nay-sayer of Toledo, had represented this ethos of frontier skepticism in an earlier time.[22] The targets of the Chicago *Literary Times,* though, were the popular, established writers and critics whose very careers came to be symbolized for Hecht and Bodenheim by what they called the corrosive New York literary scene, or more precisely "The National Cemetery of Arts and Letters." There are "Six Critics" who must be grouped together, Hecht and Bodenheim asserted:

1. Critics whose feeble minds tire under the impact of ideas and leave them whimpering desperately for "real books."

2. Critics who belabor the degeneracy and un-Americanism of all that fails to gratify their imbecile illusions.

3. Critics who hate books, whose impotent brains burn with wrath at the sight of everything that illuminates their inferiority.

4. Critics struggling to convince themselves and their wives of their purity by railing against the indecency of mirrors.

5. Critics who elevate their eyebrows, blush, stick out their little fingers, and pick their teeth behind a napkin in the mad hope of being mistaken for gentlemen by the bridge-tender's wife who subscribes for the paper.

6. New York critics.[23]

Being pointedly personal, the *Times* took great glee in singling out for private treatment those eminently respectable authors who had made New York their base of operations: thus, a *dramatis personae* for the uninitiate:

> Christopher Morely: Sliding Billy Watson in Cap and Gown
> Brander Matthews: A full-length picture of God by Rube Goldberg
> Burton Rascoe: A yesterday's orchid in the Broadway buttonhole[24]

An editorial note charted the literary course of a current Manhattan favorite:

> The painstaking mediocrity of Stephen Vincent Benet has already established him as the literary hero of the Christian Scientists and the Seventh Day Dialecticians. He is still a bit too ripe for the Baptists but pessimism is premature. The lad has a future.[25]

And snarling Bodenheim noted from the "Literary Suburbs" of Manhattan that

> We are troubled a little at present by the light skit and parody epidemic. Mr. Louis Untermyer, Mr. Robert Benchley, and Mr. Christopher Morely are all skipping in pursuit of the easy laugh, although said laugh has the bad

habit of becoming coy. . . .[26]

Franklin Pierce Adams, the well-known FPA of the "Conning Tower" newspaper column in the New York *World* and *Tribune* had the misfortune in 1923 to publish a volume called, even more unfortunately, *So There;* the *Times,* lying in ambush, blasted the "inane, girlish title" as well as the "vapid, giggling, emaciated puns and frothy jovialities. . . ."[27] In this continued assault on the New York group, young E. E. Cummings simply became "The *Dial*'s Darling";[28] Gilbert Seldes, Edmund Wilson, and Malcolm Cowley were lumped together as a "gang" doting on critical hyperbole and absurd reduction.[29] Henry Seidel Canby was a sincere conservative, therefore not to be trusted.[30] Only John Macy was grudgingly admitted to "stand apart from the yelping cliques of his day. . . ."[31] Maxwell Bodenheim issued a heartfelt blast against the Manhattan Establishment when the Pulitzer Prize for poetry in 1922 went to Edna St. Vincent Millay, unjustly he felt, over candidates Conrad Aiken, E. A. Robinson, and William Carlos Williams; wrote discouraged Bodenheim in a sad fury:

> In my present mood the Eastern literary situation suggests a mundane swamp, coerced by lanterns, filled with an undulating game of malevolence, and obsessed by the conviction that it represents a plateau that governs American thought and culture. . . .[32]

Obviously much impressed by the achievement of Williams, aroused Bodenheim observed that "The East of America is too busily engaged in worshipping flimsy cleverness to notice him."[33] At length it was what Hecht and Bodenheim came to regard as the essential corruption of the Gotham sophisticated, clever dabbler that incited the capering editors to issue a manifesto enforcing the position of their radical newspaper:

> We have no particular indignation for New York. The comic supplement blaa blaa of its literary hecklers and book scratchers is a bit too obvious for comment. . . . The thing that vaguely depresses us about New York is its long ears. The magazines devoted to the Higher Culture—the *Nation,* the *Dial,* the *Freeman,* the *New Republic,* the *Broom,* and alas, the *Little Review* stand on the racks of

our favorite bookstore and, occasionally, we read them. They depress us. They have long ears. They have long noses. They seem to be suffering from the lack of a good drink or a good physic. They are continually talking about Art as if it were their dead grandmother. They are continually discussing literature as if it were a Leading Citizen. We always picture editors walking around in high hats and white gloves like amateur pall bearers.[34]

The New York critical men-about-town, who have neither "energy" nor "appetites" are hollow minds revelling in little but phony "dignity"; these Literary Gentlemen move inevitably and "stubbornly toward the casual anti-climax of their death."

The vendetta with New York, however, was only a portion of the creative mission doggedly pursued by Hecht and Bodenheim. Leading literary lights of past and present had to be dragged before their bar of buncombe for scrutiny and evaluation. Thus Lloyd Lewis, a sometime contributor to the *Times,* exposed Longfellow's character Evangeline as a sex obsession victim, for she was "a beautiful rustic moron, silent, docile but filled with a sullen determination to mate."[35] The deadly collaborators, now zealous debunkers of literary myth and legend, called the roll of "Impossible People":

Thackeray — The green grocer's Dostoevsky
Whittier — Psychoneurosis Hysteria-Americana
Milton — The inventor of the wall paper heaven
Zola — The love of stinking
Whitman — Flypaper in a high wind
Kipling — A literary corpse shrieking for the embalmer
Pater — A stained-glass window overlooking the dictionary
H. G. Wells — The keg of lemonade at the Socialist picnic[36]

Bodenheim's contributions included "Poets, Poets Everywhere / And Hardly a line to read," a succinct series of judgments on contemporary singers, freely bundling together jinglemen and artists:

Edgar Guest: A piece of homemade candy wrapped up in a $1,000 bill.
Robert Frost: The New England States bubbling about their brooks and boulders with the occasional intrusion of a melodramatic farmhand.

Edna Millay: Feminine sophistication not too subtle for
the simple-minded or too simple for those
who prefer emotional caviar.[37]

And into the sights of the capricious critics lumbered the imposing figure of Gertrude Stein, discoverer of what the editor identified as "platitudes" of "radicalism." The *Times* offered a domestic drama, "Gittin' Gertie's Goat": The scene, Farmer Brown's home; a quarrel is in progress:

Mr. Brown: Shut upset yourself.
Mrs. Brown: Brown, you're a clown, a big brown clown,
a Brown round town, a clown done brown,
a Brown run down. Shut yourself upset![38]

From these arabesque salvos, the Chicago *Literary Times* went on to develop an astonishing shock treatment by which to publicize works and alleged aberrations of currently successful authors. Thus, the newspaper headline as a tool of literary criticism:

PUEBLO INDIANS DENY COMPLEX
D. H. LAWRENCE PLUMBS REDMAN'S SOUL
"SAVAGE SEX LIFE VULGAR" SAYS BRITISH LOVE
     EXPERT
"TRIBAL PASSION LACKS ART"
ABORIGINES PROTEST PSYCHOANALYSIS INQUIRY
     BOARD[39]

Sherwood Anderson, whose *Winesburg, Ohio,* had, evidently, made him one of the Establishment but whose latest novel Hecht had once called the "wistful idealization of the masculine menopause" came in for a banner of his own:

SHERWOOD ANDERSON STARTS SOUL CANVASS
"HOW'S YOUR PLUMBING" ASKS BUSINESSMAN-
AUTHOR IN NEW NOVEL. "IS YOUR HOUSE IN
ORDER?" MANY MARRIAGES WINS SILK-LINED
DERBY IN ALL-JUVENILE SWEEPSTAKES[40]

Nor could the *Times* refrain from sniping at the academic novelist, who was characterized as a "blue-law" Puritan prude:

PROF. IN RIGOR MORTIS FLAYS HIS ACTIVE YOUTH
ROBERT HERRICK, IN HIGH HAT, ATTACKS SEX
PROBLEM. ALARMS OLD MAIDS. "HOMELY LILIA"
BANNED BY ANTI-CIGARETTE LEAGUE[41]

And an excoriation of the popular author ("hack author" would
be the epithet of Hecht) came by the same glaring formula:

HUGH WALPOLE, SECRETARY ANGLO-AMERICAN
POT-BOILERS UNION, CHARGES ART IN DANGER.
BRITISH AUTHOR ANNOUNCES WORLD TOUR IN
CRUSADE ON EGO MENACE. "I WILL TOUR THE
WORLD UNTIL LITERATURE IS SAFE" PROMISES
POT-BOILER CHIEF.[42]

The *Times* could even fabricate a comment on style through this
technique of yellow journalese:

DREISER, GAY DOG, WEEPS ON WITNESS STAND:
TELLS ALL.[43]

The ultimate in this literary caricature was Hecht's vision as a
derby-hatted, cane-waving barker at a side-show carnival endeavoring
to lure parading customers into the big tent to see the scribbling
freaks, each of whom was cartooned:

The Hairless Ape, Gene O'Neill
The Greatest Living Skeleton Mind, Hugh Walpole
Lefty Lee, The India Rubber Ego, Edgar Lee Masters
Swatty the Mystic, Sherwood Anderson: He talks in his
    sleep and bewilders the most astute; come upon the
    inside and listen to this great somnambulist.[44]

So concluded the pitchman at the Wrangling Brothers circus.
    The intellectual charade continued despite the zany format
and atmosphere deliberately established by Hecht and Bodenheim;
the Chicago *Literary Times* was a true vehicle for their honest
opinions of the contemporary literary scenes, not merely a gross
collection of verbal somersaults. Both authors had an acute sense
of showmanship, an appreciation of the bizarre, and a feeling for
the ridiculous; a strong current of seriousness underlies most of
their critical evaluations, although encased in soaring metaphor.
They would expose the seemingly magical creation of literary

fetishes on the instant as a muckraker would cry out against patent medicine fraud. The major sin of the editors was to assume confidently that each current literary fashion was a transient one, destined to pass very rapidly across an ever-shifting intellectual horizon. Thus:

> The Waste Land by T. S. Eliot [was] a poem of a jazzy intellectualism, an epic of abstruse nonsense, destined to become the Bible of all poets who to be great think it essential to be misunderstood.[45]

Eliot's influential manifesto in verse became a creative poison to the critical cohorts of West Washington Street; it was to be regarded as an ephemeral fad like Dr. Coué, the "latest Jesus," an exercise in effete obscurantism, popular only for its being intellectually fashionable. It was "in." And a review of The Vegetable, the drama by F. Scott Fitzgerald, revealed further the antagonism Hecht and Bodenheim nurtured for those most popular writers and celebrities of the moment:

> This play was written by a ringleader among a class of flippant garrulously obvious writers who are at present busily engaged in scratching and playfully slapping the face of society without cutting beneath the rouged skin. In this way they may pose as devilish, fearless investigators of shams and follies without endangering their popularity. . . . Mr. F. Scott Fitzgerald is one of the prosperous, boisterous members of this band and he accomplishes the old trick of swatting hypocrisies and fondling them at the same time. . . .[46]

Bodenheim, depressed by his own lack of popular success, blindly saw no hope for American poetry:

> Sandburg with his slang, fatalistic excitements and nursery fables; Lindsay with his jazz drivels and revival meeting frenzies; Masters with his solemn ornate narratives; Frost with his emaciated psychological searches; Untermyer with his Freudian shrieking explorations—they will all fade away in a more sophisticated future age. . . .[47]

Hecht, however, in a rare burst of affirmative statement, identified Ulysses as charting the only feasible course for experimental novelists to follow. There is a future for fiction; the anti-novel had yet to appear:

> *Ulysses* by James Joyce [is] The first Herculean effort to disorganize the Wells, Walpole, Thackeray, Galsworthy, Hall Caine school of hammock fictioneers. A book which operates on the presumption that there is room for intelligence in the novel art form.[48]

But D. H. Lawrence was not so fortunate; his *Women in Love* was to Hecht "An amateur blueprint of sexual impulses poorly remembered by the author."[49]

Materials for such a tabloid as the *Literary Times,* however, quickly became limited. The vendettas suggested and encouraged were generally ignored. New York circles of aesthetes were being infiltrated by refugees from the diminishing Chicago Renaissance. Ben Hecht even began to lose interest in his energetic adventure; tired repetition became too apparent on the formerly sparkling pages. Savage but impotent Bodenheim continued to issue jeremiads against fellow contemporary poets. Soon the paper became less concerned with literary personalities and more involved in social debates and notorious fallacies of the 'Twenties.' There began to appear monotonous and lengthy debates on religion, a favorite pastime of vaudeville; there came a "continued" tale called "Cutie, A Warm Hearted Mama,"[50] an abandoned piece of suggestive salaciousness and pointless humor; even installments of Bodenheim's unexpurgated, however tame, autobiography were run. Ultimately only huge scare headlines (WAR!) could apparently keep the enterprise going. Hecht tried to maintain enthusiasm by running in each issue new tales of his proven successful *1001 Afternoons in Chicago;* at last, however, his final story, "My Last Park Bench," wryly observed that its author now has better things to do than merely sit and collect cinders under his collar. Ben Hecht too joined the Literary Gentlemen of New York. Editor Henry Justin Smith wrote in the Chicago *News* that flags must fly at half mast, for Hecht had truly left the town.[51] His Chicago *Literary Times* was closed down; it faded instantly into the evanescent shadows of literary history. It had been, actually, a final gasp of Liberation. By 1926 Samuel Putnam was writing in the *American Mercury,* "Chicago: An Obituary."[52]

Ben Hecht later tempered the charges he had directed at the gargoyles of his day. No longer did he "explode epithets under the Old Ladies' Home." With his sense of the theatrical and his business eye, Hollywood, eventually, was a natural move for him. There he scripted some of the most popular and successful movies of the 1930's: *Gunga Din, Viva Villa, Scarface;* he wrote for Broadway; late in his career he even acquired a television show. Maxwell Bodenheim, travelling a downward path to notoriety, became the lower New York roustabout, the Village King of Bohemia until he and his wife were murdered. The brief collaboration of 1923-1924, however, must remain a prominent commentary on a unique state of mind characterizing the Chicago Renaissance in twilight. After the Liberation came the excess, the *Times.* Without the cynical, diabolic humor behind the fundamentally serious editors, their publication might be described by the current term, Camp. Their failure was not in lack of serious intent, but in irresponsibly and strenuously maintaining the narrow, insular views they attributed to their enemies, in trying to spawn witless literary warfare, in sponsoring their own peculiar brand of literary cliquesmanship. During the days of its brief, frenzied mission, then, this journalese cathartic, its colorful pages, its colored papers, reduced literature to sport and painted sanctimonious, pietistic phrase-makers as personal buffoons. Twice a month, the Chicago *Literary Times,* Ben Hecht's aesthetic calliope, would come, in motley, to town, replete in fuchsia, yellow, or green pages to shock and startle. The heavy firepower of the major Renaissance army had already left the scene; only stray bits and pieces of literary shrapnel remained to be whizzed through the air. It was a noteworthy show, not at all eclipsed by other gaucheries of a wild day. The Hecht word-machine was perhaps most substantially, though by accident, chronicled by Vachel Lindsay, himself a dynamic participant in the Chicago literary aspiration, in his syncopated, jazzy "The Kallyope Yell":

> Circus day's tremendous cry:
> I am the Kallyope, Kallyope, Kallyope!
> Hoot toot, hoot toot, hoot toot, hoot toot
> Willy willy willy wah hoo!
> Sizz fizz. . . .

I will blow the proud folk down,
    (Listen to the lion roar!)
I am the Kallyope, Kallyope, Kallyope
Tooting hope, tooting hope, tooting hope, tooting hope,
Willy willy willy wah hoo!

Hoot toot, hoot toot, hoot toot, hoot toot
Whoop whoop, Whoop whoop,
Whoop whoop, Whoop whoop,
Willy willy willy willy wah Hoo!
    Sizz. . . .
    Fizz. . . .[53]

NOTES

Louis Filler: *Introduction: A Question of Quality*

[1]Trent essentially maintained this position in his *History of American Literature, 1607-1865* (1908), when he was an esteemed professor of literature at Columbia University, though by then impressed by an edition of four of Melville's novels put out in 1892. He now saw Melville as a "romancer" who had won the "warm commendation of Robert Louis Stevenson," and *Moby Dick* as an "on the whole genuine . . . work of genius . . . were [it] not for its . . . frequently inartistic heaping up of details, and its obvious imitation of Carlylean tricks" (pp. 390-391). A succeeding member of the Columbia University staff, Raymond M. Weaver, opened the subject wide with his *Herman Melville, Mariner and Mystic* (1921); but Columbia Ph.D. Charles Roberts Anderson's 1939 *Melville in the South Seas* retrospectively endorsed Trent by reaffirming his status as a romancer: "The figure of Herman Melville that emerges from the ensuing pages is a simpler and more convincing one than the conventional dramatization. His South Sea experiences, stripped of their romantic trappings, are still bright with high-hearted adventure. . . . The portrait contains slight touch of foreboding gloom or impending tragedy, small hint of the 'mystic' or the philosopher, no trace of the beard which later muffled the lamentations of America's mid-Victorian Jeremiah" (p. 7). In a new introduction to his book (1966 ed.), Anderson shelved his earlier preface and introduction as "hav[ing] no relevance today."

[2]James Woodress, ed., *American Literary Scholarship, an Annual/1966* (Durham, 1968), 158.

Charles S. Holmes: *Ring Lardner: Reluctant Artist*

[1]H. L. Mencken, *The American Language*, 2nd ed. (New York: Knopf, 1921), pp. 274-7 and 404-5; Carl Van Doren, "Beyond Grammar: Ring W. Lardner: Philologist among the Low-brows," *Century*, CVI (July, 1923), 471-5.

[2]Sherwood Anderson, "Four American Impressions," *The New Republic*, XXXII (October 11, 1922), 171-3; Edmund Wilson, "Mr. Lardner's American Characters," *Dial*, LXXVII (July, 1924), 69-72.

[3]Virginia Woolf, "American Fiction," *The Moment and Other Essays* (London: Hogarth Press, 1947), pp. 94-104.

[4]Harry Salpeter, "The Boswell of New York," *The Bookman*, LXXXL (July, 1930), 384.

[5] Clifford M. Caruthers (ed.), *Ring Around Max: the Correspondence of Ring Lardner and Maxwell Perkins* (De Kalb, Ill.: Northern Illinois University Press, 1973), p. xiii.

[6] *Dial*, LXXVII (July, 1924), 69-72.

[7] F. Scott Fitzgerald, "Ring," *The New Republic*, LXXVI (October 11, 1933), 254-5.

[8] "What Is the American Language?" *Bookman*, LIII (March, 1921), 81-2.

[9] Howard Webb, "The Development of a Style: the Lardner Idiom," *American Quarterly*, XII (Winter, 1960), 482-92.

[10] Walton Patrick, *Ring Lardner* (New York: Twayne Publishers, 1963), p. 39.

[11] "Comedians of the Diamond," *Outing*, LVI (May, 1910), 213-20.

[12] "Mr. Dooley, Meet Mr. Lardner," *The 7 Lively Arts* (New York: Sagamore Press, 1957), p. 114.

[13] "Introduction," *The Ring Lardner Reader* (New York: Charles Scribner's Sons, 1963), p. xvii.

[14] Otto Friedrich, *Ring Lardner* (University of Minnesota Pamphlets on American Writers, No. 49, Minneapolis: University of Minnesota Press, 1965), p. 12.

[15] Reprinted in Gilbert Seldes (ed.), *The Portable Ring Lardner* (New York: Viking Press, 1946), p. 571.

[16] Gilbert Seldes, "Introduction," *The Portable Ring Lardner*, p. 49.

[17] Walton Patrick makes this point in his *Ring Lardner*, p. 49.

[18] *Ring Lardner: A Biography* (Garden City: Doubleday, 1956), p. 159.

[19] Clifton Fadiman, "Ring Lardner and the Triangle of Hate," *Nation*, CXXXVI (March 22, 1933), 315-17.

[20] Seldes, "Introduction," *The Portable Ring Lardner*, p. 18; also Caruthers, "Foreword," *Ring Around Max*, pp. xiii-xiv.

[21] Reprinted in *The Portable Ring Lardner*, p. 598.

Jay Martin: *Erskine Caldwell's Singular Devotions*

[1] *The Nation*, 120 (February 11, 1925), 333.

[2] Caldwell, *Writing in America* (New York: Phaedra Publishers, 1967), p. 119.

[3] For an account of this series see Caldwell, *Call It Experience: The Years of Learning How to Write* (New York: Duell, Sloan and Pearce, 1951), pp. 185-6.

[4] *Writing in America*, p. 119

[5] *Call It Experience*, pp. 42, 60.

[6] *Call It Experience*, pp. 70-71.

[7] *Call It Experience*, p. 103.

[8] Caldwell and Margaret Bourke-White, *You Have Seen Their Faces* (New York: Modern Age Books, Inc., 1937), n.p. (Photos follow p. 48 of text.)

[9] *You Have Seen Their Faces,* n.p. (Photo follows half-title page.)

[10] My observation is derived from Archibald MacLeish's description of his own photo-text book, *Land of the Free—U.S.A.* (1938). It is, he says, "the opposite of a book of poems illustrated by photographs. It is a book of photographs illustrated by a poem." Quoted in James Korges, *Erskine Caldwell* (Minneapolis: University of Minnesota Press, 1969), p. 14.

[11] For the important action of "imprisoning" the image, which should be further explored elsewhere, see Margaret Bourke-White's comments on the use of lenses and flash equipment in *You Have Seen Their Faces,* p. 51.

[12] Caldwell, *The Bastard* (New York: The Heron Press, 1929), pp. 13-14.

[13] "Caldwell: Maker of Grotesques," *The Philosophy of Literary Form,* 2nd ed. Baton Rouge: Louisiana State University Press, 1967.

[14] Caldwell, *The Sacrilege of Alan Kent* (Portland, Maine: Falmouth Book House, 1936 [©1931]), pp. 18, 28, 28-9, 29-30, 33.

[15] *You Have Seen Their Faces,* p. 19.

[16] Caldwell and Margaret Bourke-White, *North of the Danube* (New York: The Viking Press, 1939), p. 16.

[17] Caldwell, *In Search of Bisco* (New York: Farrar, Straus and Giroux, 1965), p. 7.

[18] Caldwell and Margaret Bourke-White, *Say, Is This the U.S.A.* (New York: Duell, Sloan and Pearce, 1941), p. 176.

[19] Quoted in John Berryman, *Stephen Crane* (New York: William Sloan, 1950), p. 6.

[20] cf. Robert W. Stallman, ed., *Stephen Crane: An Omnibus* (New York, 1961), p. 191.

[21] *The Bastard,* pp. 193-4. Ellipses are Caldwell's.

[22] *Call It Experience,* p. 132.

[23] *Call It Experience,* p. 235.

[24] Caldwell, *Jackpot: The Short Stories of Erskine Caldwell* (Garden City, N. Y.: The Sun Dial Press, 1943), pp. 29, 112, 253, 491.

[25] *Writing in America,* p. 75.

[26] *Call It Experience,* p. 108.

[27] *Jackpot,* p. 271.

[28] "In Defense of Myself," Portland, Maine, n.d. [1929].

[29] *Faulkner at Nagano;* quoted in Korges, *Erskine Caldwell,* p. 6.

[30] *Call It Experience,* p. 222.

[31] Information taken from most recent editions of paperback copies; Signet Books of New American Library, Inc.

[32] Caldwell, *Tobacco Road* (New York: A Signet Book, 1959 [1932]), p. 84.

[33] Caldwell, *God's Little Acre* (New York: A Signet Book, 1961 [1933]), p. 158.

[34] *Call It Experience,* p. 134.

Ronald Lora: By Love Possessed: *The Cozzens-Macdonald Affair*

[1] Henry James, *Theory of Fiction,* ed. by James E. Miller, Jr. (Lincoln, Nebraska: University of Nebraska Press, 1972), 297.
[2] Malcolm Cowley, *New York Times Book Review* (August 25, 1957), pp. 1, 18.
[3] *New York Times,* November 15, 1928; May 30, 1929; July 6, 1929.
[4] John T. Frederick, "Love By Adverse Possession: The Case of Mr. Cozzens," *College English* 19 (April, 1958), p. 315.
[5] James, *Theory of Fiction,* p. 273.
[6] Alfred Kazin, *Bright Book of Life: American Novelists and Storytellers from Hemingway to Mailer* (Boston: Little, Brown and Co., 1973).

Edgar M. Branch: *James T. Farrell: Four Decades After* Studs Lonigan

[1] Conversation with Edgar M. Branch, December 24, 1962.
[2] "The World Is Today," *Thought,* 25, No. 37 (1973), 17.
[3] "Reflections at Fifty," *Reflections at Fifty and Other Essays* (New York: Vanguard Press, 1954), p. 65.
[4] From a photograph of the column "Athenaeum" in the *Maroon,* 1, No. 7 (Summer, 1929).
[5] "Reflections at Fifty," p. 65.
[6] "Some Observations on Naturalism, So Called, in Fiction," *Reflections at Fifty,* p. 150.
[7] *Ibid.,* p. 148.
[8] *Boarding House Blues* (New York: Paperback Library, 1961), pp. 150-51, 211.
[9] *Ibid.,* p. 151.
[10] Alfred Kazin, "Continuing the Saga of Danny O'Neill," New York *Herald Tribune Books,* September 18, 1938, p. 9.
[11] "Technique as Discovery," *Forms of Modern Fiction,* ed. William Van O'Connor (Minneapolis, 1948), p. 29.
[12] "Naturalism and Ritual Slaughter," *New Leader,* 31 (December 18, 1948), p. 10.
[13] "C'est Droll," *American Book Collector,* 11 (June, 1961), p. 33.
[14] As expressed by Miss Gelfant in a talk at the Glassboro Symposium honoring Farrell, December 5, 1973.
[15] "Consciousness and Social Order: The Theme of Transcendence in the Leatherstocking Tales," *Western American Literature,* 5 (1970), 190.
[16] Quoted by Farrell in "On the Function of the Novel," *Reflections*

at Fifty, p. 21.

[17] Letter from Farrell to Sherwood Kohn, December 10, 1960.

[18] *Human Nature and Conduct* (New York: Henry Holt and Company, 1922), p. 170.

Ray B. Browne: *Irving Wallace: Independent Drummer*

[1] *Journal of Popular Culture,* IX:3, pp. 513-14; 521.

David Sanders: *John Dos Passos as Conservative*

[1] *The Big Money* (New York, 1936), 462. Subsequent page references will be incorporated in the text of this essay.

[2] In his Introduction to the Modern Library edition of *The 42nd Parallel* (New York, 1934).

[3] "Dos Passos and the Social Revolution," *New Republic,* LVIII:256 (April 17, 1929).

Peter Viereck: *Vachel Lindsay: The Dante of the Fundamentalists*

[1] Burke-Simon quotes are from New York *Times,* March 20, 1960, p. 43, and Paris *Herald-Tribune,* ed. p., April 2, 1960.

[2] For a parallel analysis of Crane's machine symbolism see P. Viereck, "The Poet of the Machine Age," essay in the *Journal of the History of Ideas,* N. Y., January 1949; also reprinted as appendix of Viereck, *Strike Through the Mask,* N. Y., Scribner, 1950.

[3] In 1964, when the Western plebeian-rightist Goldwater defeated the *eastern* aristocratic-liberal Rockefeller for the Republican nomination, this pseudo-conservative neo-populism was a case of smashing Plymouth Rockefeller.

[4] Lindsay's reputed dying words, after swallowing a bottle of searing Lysol: "They tried to get me; I got them first." cf. Hart Crane's comparable *cri de coeur:* "I could not pick the arrows from my side,"—with his similar frustrated optimism (so much more tragic than Eliotine pessimism) about the mechanized "American dream."

[5] For full documentation (no space here) of this admittedly debatable hypothesis, see the section "Direct Democracy: From Populist Left to Nationalist Right," pp. 129-223, in P. Viereck, *The Unadjusted Man,* Boston, Beacon Press, 1956.

Louis Filler: *Meyer Levin's* Compulsion

[1] What kind of analysis? Caveat.
[2] Meyer Levin, *The Old Bunch* (New York, 1937), "Author's Note."
[3] Aesthetics vs. social. Caveat.
[4] Mr. Levin comments: "This is not a proper statement. I used some of the reporter activities of Goldstein in the activities of Sid Silver but surely never felt an identity with Goldstein. Indeed, in that sense, I hardly knew him!" (Goldstein and James Mulroy worked as a team.)
[5] Does this make it a better novel than we had supposed? Caveat.
[6] Levin, *Compulsion* (New York, 1956), 88.
[7] So why was *this* book popular? Sensationally basically. Caveat.
[8] Really? Rescue by social value. Caveat.
[9] What kind of understanding? Caveat.
[10] Mr. Levin thinks Leopold only pretended to be devoutly religious so as to get pardoned. He judges Leopold's "learning" to have been "merely flashy," otherwise he would have done more in prison.
[11] Value by association. Caveat.
[12] The style is flat, pseudo-literary hack. Caveat.
[13] Trite. Caveat.
[14] Declarative sentence. Caveat.
[15] Shallow. Caveat. The passage is from *Compulsion*, 143-45.
[16] Filler agrees. Show how. Caveat.
[17] Unproven. Caveat.
[18] Leopold, *Life Plus 99 Years* (New York, 1958), 370.
[19] *Ibid.*, 58.
[20] What's your point? Caveat.
[21] Does Levin show this kind of thing? Caveat.
[22] J. Anthony Lukas (New York, 1971).
[23] Of what? Caveat.
[24] Drugstore cheap psychoanalysis. Caveat.
[25] Levin, *Compulsion*, 300-1.

Robert Olafson: *B. Traven and* The Death Ship *as High Culture*

[1] Walter M. Langford, *The Mexican Novel Comes of Age* (Notre Dame: University of Notre Dame Press, 1971), p. 58. On Traven's identity:
Through the gracious cooperation of Rosa Elena Lujan [Traven's widow] we now know that Berick Torsvan, Ret Marut, B. Traven and Hal Croves were all the same person. Born in Chicago in 1890, Traven was quite young when he moved with his parents to England and later to Germany. Here he became an actor for a time. Subsequently, he founded *Der Zeigelbrenner* and was deeply involved in the Bavarian Socialist Republic. On escaping his death sentence [as Ret Marut], he wandered across several

European countries, without papers, until he finally signed on as a crewman of a "death ship" out of Spain. As already stated, he reached Mexico in 1922. The publication in Berlin in 1925 of *The Cotton Pickers* [published as short stories and sketches about work in the daily newspaper *Vorwartz* in 1925 and as the novel *Der Wobbly* in 1926, following the publication of *The Death Ship* earlier that same year] launched his amazing and significant literary career.

[2] The name Gerard Gales appears in *The Cotton Pickers*. We infer, however, that this is the same character.

[3] Traven sees Conrad and O'Neill as being too romantic; this is his *bias* and does not do complete justice to each author.

[4] *Government, The Carreta, The March to the Monteriá, The Troza, The Rebellion of The Hanged* and *The General from the Jungle*.

See: Robert B. Olafson, "B. Traven: Two Novels on *The Underdogs in Mexico*," *Mexican Life*, June, 1971, p. 16 ff. The essay studies the development of Traven's authentic "Mexican" voice by examining *The Treasure of the Sierra Madre* and *The Rebellion of The Hanged*. The former was published in 1927, the latter in 1936; although Traven's observations on Mexico are good in *The Treasure*, they are vastly improved in *The Rebellion*, published nine years later.

Dianne F. Sadoff: *Norman Mailer to Posterity*

[1] "Norman Mailer: The Embattled Vision," in *Doings and Undoings* (New York, 1964), p. 179.

[2] "A Quest for Peril: Norman Mailer," in *A World More Attractive* (New York, 1963), p. 123.

[3] *Norman Mailer* (New York, 1972), p. 3.

[4] *Contemporaries* (Boston, 1962), p. 250.

[5] "The Radical Moralism of Norman Mailer," in *Norman Mailer: A Collection of Critical Essays*, ed. Leo Braudy (Englewood Cliffs, N.J., 1972), p. 43.

[6] *The Performing Self* (New York, 1971), p. 50.

[7] Steven Marcus, "An Interview with Norman Mailer," in Braudy, pp. 38, 39.

[8] Howe, *Contemporaries*, pp. 124-28.

[9] Leo Bersani, "Interpretation of Dreams," in Braudy, p. 120, quoting Hardwick: Philip Rahv, "Crime Without Punishment," in *The Myth and the Powerhouse* (New York, 1965), pp. 234-43; Stanley Edgar Hyman, "Norman Mailer's Yummy Rump," in Braudy, pp. 104-08.

[10] "Interpretation of Dreams," p. 120.

[11] Norman Mailer, *An American Dream* (New York, 1970), p. 34. All references in my text are to this Dell Edition.

[12] *The Performing Self*, p. 52.

[13] *Sexual Politics* (New York, 1969), p. 328.

Joseph Blotner: Raintree County *Revisited*

[1] Charles Lee, *New York Times Book Review,* January 4, 1948, p. 21.
[2] Orville Prescott, *Yale Review,* XXXVII (March, 1948), 574.
[3] William York Tindall, "Many-leveled Fiction: Virginia Woolf to Ross Lockridge," *College English,* X (November, 1948), 65-71.
[4] *Time,* LII (December 20, 1948), 101.
[5] James Hilton, *New York Herald Tribune Book Review,* January 4, 1948, p. 2.
[6] Elizabeth Johnson, *The Commonweal,* XLVII (February 13, 1948), 450.
[7] Ross Lockridge, Jr., *Raintree County* (Boston: Houghton Mifflin Co., 1948), p. 788. The pages from which further quotations are drawn will be indicated in the text.
[8] In this role as in others Johnny is a symbol for a whole group. This is made clear in one dream-fantasy in which he is a Roman centurion.

Lawrence Jay Dessner: *The Case of* Raintree County

[1] Review of *Raintree County,* Howard Mumford Jones, *Saturday Review,* Jan. 3, 1948; Charles Lee, "Encompassing the American Spirit," *New York Times Book Review,* Jan. 4, 1948; and see *Book Review Digest* (1948). My data derives from these reviews and from the obituary notice, *New York Times,* March 8, 1948, pp. 1, 15.
[2] Nanette Kutner, "Ross Lockridge, Jr.—Escape from Main Street," *Saturday Review,* June 12, 1948, pp. 6, 7, 31.
[3] Hamilton Basso, Jan. 10, 1948, pp. 72-73.
[4] Dec. 20, 1948, p. 101.
[5] *Raintree County* (Boston: Houghton Mifflin, 1948), p. 297. Subsequent page numbers, in the text, refer to this edition.
[6] *Biographia Literaria,* ch. 22.
[7] *Ibid.*
[8] Eugene O'Neill, *Ah, Wilderness* (New York: Random House, 1933), conflated from pp. 127, 129, 132.
[9] "The Higher Pantheism in a Nutshell," 1880, first and last couplets.
[10] Kutner, p. 6.
[11] William York Tindall, "Many-leveled Fiction: Virginia Woolf to Ross Lockridge," *College English,* 10 (Nov. 1948), 65-71; Joseph L. Blotner, "*Raintree County* Revisited," *Western Humanities Review,* 10 (Winter, 1955-1956), 57-64; Boyd Litzinger, "Mythmaking in America: 'The Great Stone

252

Face' and *Raintree County,*" *Tennessee Studies in Literature,* 8 (1963), 81-84.
    [12]Delia Clarke, "*Raintree County*: Psychological Symbolism, Archetype, and Myth," *Thoth,* Fall, 1970, 31-39.

Joseph Waldmeir: *John Steinbeck: No* Grapes of Wrath

    [1]Along with Peter Lisca, *The Wide World of John Steinbeck* (1958), I do not consider "The Leader of the People" to be a part of *The Red Pony,* though it is ordinarily included as Part IV in editions subsequent to *The Long Valley* (1938). In the first place, it is not Jody's story, but Grandfather's; and in the second place, it contributes little or nothing to what Jody learns through the triply traumatic experience with death in *The Red Pony.*

Abe C. Ravitz: *Ballyhoo, Gargoyles, & Firecrackers: Ben Hecht's Aesthetic Calliope*

    [1]Padraic Colum and Margaret Freeman Cabell (Editors), *Between Friends: Letters of James Branch Cabell and Others* (New York, 1962), p. 38. Letter from JBC to Burton Rascoe, April 18, 1918.
    [2]"The Beginnings of Critical Realism in America," *Main Currents in American Thought* (New York, 1958), p. 386. Parrington damned Fitzgerald and Hecht at the same time and with similar enthusiastic abandon.
    [3]Howard Mumford Jones and Walter B. Rideout (Editors), *Letters of Sherwood Anderson* (Boston, 1953), p. 119. SA to Roger Sergel some time after December 25, 1923: "The smartiness will perhaps defeat Ben. It may have already."
    [4]*An Autobiographical Novel* (New York, 1966), p. 181. "Sob-sister journalese was the distinguishing characteristic of the Chicago Renaissance."
    [5]Colum and Cabel (Editors), p. 79. Rascoe in a letter to Cabell dated August 17, 1918, quoted Pound's alleged reply "to a Chicago poet who asked why he didn't return to America. . . ."
    [6]William Manchester, *The Sage of Baltimore: The Life and Times of H. L. Mencken* (New York, 1952), p. 96.
    [7]Cabell rather courageously reprints this fusillade along with other attacks upon his literary competence in an appendix to *Beyond Life* (New York, The Modern Library, 1919); the section is entitled "Some Other Books by Mr. Cabell (With Tributes of the Press)."
    [8]For treatment of the earlier group of newspapermen see Bernard Duffey, *The Chicago Renaissance in American Letters* (Michigan State University Press, 1956), pp. 10-26. The later journalists are sketched thoroughly in Book Four of Ben Hecht's autobiography, *A Child of the Century* (New

York, 1954).

[9] Vincent Starrett, *Born in a Bookshop* (University of Oklhaoma Press, 1965), pp. 126-127. Arthur Symons and George Moore were other writers included in the newspapermen's reading "syllabus."

[10] The *Little Review*, edited by Margaret Anderson with Ezra Pound as its foreign correspondent, printed experimental literary contributions by Joyce, Eliot, Jean Cocteau, Ford Madox Ford, Wyndham Lewis, and other controversial authors of the moment. See Frederick J. Hoffman, Charles Allen, and Carolyn F. Ulrich, *The Little Magazine* (Princeton, 1947), pp. 52-67. Several tales Hecht later included in his collection called *Broken Necks* originally appeared in the *Little Review*: "Decay," "Fragments," "Life," "Nocturne," "Broken Necks," "Black Umbrellas," and "The Yellow Goat."

[11] New York *Times,* February 5, 1921, p. 21.

[12] Brom Weber (Editor), *The Letters of Hart Crane* (New York, 1952), p. 9.

[13] Bodenheim published poetry in nearly all of the prestigious journals of his day. The *Nation*, in addition, published two of his major statements on literature and the creative process: "Psychoanalysis and American Fiction" (June 7, 1922) and "Truth and Realism in Literature" (October 8, 1924).

[14] "The community of Liberation" is Duffey's fortuitous label pinned very properly on the vibrant, passionate, intense intellectual, artistic, and Bohemian yearnings symbolized by the Renaissance spirit.

[15] Jack B. Moore, "Maxwell Bodenheim's Unwritten Masterpiece," *Bulletin of the New York Public Library* (September, 1966), 471-475.

[16] Weber (Editor), p. 9.   [17] February 15, 1924.

[18] Starrett, pp. 194-195.   [19] February 1, 1924.

[20] *A Child of the Century,* pp. 338-339.

[21] New York *Times*, July 29, 1923, II, p. 4.

[22] Eugene Fitch Ware (1841-1911), popular newspaper poet, had brought out eleven editions of *Rhymes by Ironquill* by 1902; F. E. Abbott, Journalist and freethinker, between 1870 and 1886 published a sheet called *The Index* in which he pilloried the orthodoxies of the age.

[23] March 1, 1923.   [24] *Ibid.*
[25] *Ibid.*   [26] April 1, 1923.
[27] June 15, 1923.   [28] July 1, 1923.
[29] *Ibid.*   [30] *Ibid.*
[31] *Ibid.*   [32] June 15, 1923.
[33] July 1, 1923.   [34] March 1, 1923.
[35] April 1, 1923.   [36] March 1, 1923; March 15, 1923.
[37] September 1, 1923.   [38] September 15, 1923.
[39] March 1, 1923.   [40] *Ibid.*
[41] *Ibid.*   [42] *Ibid.*
[43] March 15, 1923.   [44] April 1, 1923.
[45] March 1, 1923.   [46] May 15, 1923.

[47] August 1, 1923. [48] April 1, 1923.

[49] *Ibid.* [50] April 15, 1924.

[51] *A Child of the Century,* p. 355. Ashton Stevens of the Chicago *Herald-Examiner* authored the piece on the front page.

[52] August, 1926, 417-425.

[53] *Collected Poems* (New York, 1964), p. 122.

INDEX

Cup of Gold (Steinbeck, J.), 236
Cummings, E. E., 9, 40, 236

D
Dahlberg, Edward, 51
Dante, Alighieri, 124 *et seq.*, 164
Darrow, Clarence, 153, 157
David Graham Phillips (Ravitz, A. C.), 2
Davis, Angela, 151
"Day with Conrad Green, A" (Lardner, R.), 31
Dead Lecturer, The (Jones, LeRoi), 175
Dean, James, 122
Dean, General William, 122
Death in the Afternoon (Hemingway, E.), 228
"Death in the Country, A" (Benét, Stephen V.), 172, 178
Death Ship, The (Traven, B.), 160
Deep South (Caldwell, E.), 41, 53
Defoe, Daniel, 170
Des Imagistes (Pound, E., ed.), 44
"Devil and Daniel Webster, The" (Benét, S. V.), 172, 173, 177
Dewey, John, 85, 87, 88
Diaz, Porfirio, 169
Dickens, Charles, 3, 8 *et seq.*, 167
Dickinson, Emily, 179, 193
District of Columbia, The (Dos Passos, J.), 117
Divine Comedy, The (Dante, A.), 136
Donne, John, 202
Don't Shoot, We Are Your Children (Lukas, J. A.), 157
Doolittle, Hilda, 40, 44, 194
Dos Passos, John, 6, 7, 27, 40, 93, 115 ff., 150, 151
Dostoevski, Fyodor M., 100
Drayton, Michael, 196
de la Mare, Walter, 196
Dreiser, Theodore, 150, 156, 162, 231, 239
Dunne, Finley Peter, 31

E
Earnshaw Neighborhood, The (Caldwell, E.), 53
East of Eden (Steinbeck, J.), 221, 224
Education of Henry Adams, The (Adams, H.), 1
Einstein, Albert, 95
Eisenhower, Dwight D., 122
Elder, Donald, 37
Eliot, George, 19, 20
Eliot, T. S., 40, 135, 151, 170, 175, 195, 196, 201
Elkin, Stanley, 49
Ellman, Richard, 172
Emerson, Ralph Waldo, 42, 130, 132, 133, 134, 135, 210
Engle, Paul, 174
Erik Dorn (Hecht, B.), 231
Explication, 150, 151

F
Fabulous Originals, The (Wallace, I.), 92
Fadiman, Clifton, 38
Fan Club, The (Wallace, I.), 102 ff.
Fantazius Mallare (Hecht, B.), 231, 232
Farrell, James T., 7, 27, 80 ff., 150
Faulkner, William, 27, 42, 52, 74-75, 98, 132, 205
Federalist Papers, 132
Ferber, Edna, 1, 229
Few Figs from Thistles, A (Millay, Edna St. V.), 194
Fiedler, Leslie, 20, 86, 163
Field, Eugene, 231
Fielding, Henry, 207
50 Modern American and English Poets (Untermeyer, L.), 172
Financier, The (Dreiser, T.), 231
Fischer, John, 57
Fitzgerald, F. Scott, 2, 27, 28, 29, 38, 40, 42, 240
Follett, Wilson, 46
Ford, Ford Madox, 43